The Politics of Authoritarian Rule

What drives politics in dictatorships? Milan W. Svolik argues that all authoritarian regimes must resolve two fundamental conflicts. First, dictators face threats from the masses over which they rule – this is the *problem of authoritarian control*. A second, separate, challenge arises from the elites with whom dictators rule – this is the *problem of authoritarian power-sharing*. Crucially, whether and how dictators resolve these two problems are shaped by the dismal environment in which authoritarian politics takes place: in a dictatorship, no independent authority has the power to enforce agreements among key actors and violence is the ultimate arbiter of conflicts. Using the tools of game theory, Svolik explains why some dictators, like Saddam Hussein, establish personal autocracy and stay in power for decades; why leadership changes elsewhere are regular and institutionalized, as in contemporary China; why some authoritarian regimes are ruled by soldiers, as Uganda was under Idi Amin; why many dictatorships, like PRI-era Mexico, maintain regime-sanctioned political parties; and why a country's authoritarian past casts a long shadow over its prospects for democracy, as the unfolding events of the Arab Spring reveal. When assessing his arguments, Svolik complements these and other historical case studies with the statistical analysis of comprehensive original data on institutions, leaders, and ruling coalitions across all dictatorships from 1946 to 2008.

Milan W. Svolik is Assistant Professor of Political Science at the University of Illinois at Urbana-Champaign. He received his Ph.D. in Political Science from the University of Chicago. Svolik's articles on authoritarian politics, transitions to democracy, and democratic consolidation have appeared in leading political science journals, including the *American Political Science Review* and the *American Journal of Political Science*. His research interests include comparative politics, political economy, and formal political theory.

Cambridge Studies in Comparative Politics

General Editor
Margaret Levi   *University of Washington, Seattle*

Assistant General Editors
Kathleen Thelen   *Massachusetts Institute of Technology*
Erik Wibbels   *Duke University*

Associate Editors
Robert H. Bates   *Harvard University*
Stephen Hanson   *The College of William and Mary*
Torben Iversen   *Harvard University*
Stathis Kalyvas   *Yale University*
Peter Lange   *Duke University*
Helen Milner   *Princeton University*
Frances Rosenbluth   *Yale University*
Susan Stokes   *Yale University*

Other Books in the Series

Series list continues following the Index.

The Politics of Authoritarian Rule

MILAN W. SVOLIK

University of Illinois, Urbana-Champaign

CAMBRIDGE
UNIVERSITY PRESS

CAMBRIDGE UNIVERSITY PRESS
Cambridge, New York, Melbourne, Madrid, Cape Town,
Singapore, São Paulo, Delhi, Mexico City

Cambridge University Press
32 Avenue of the Americas, New York, NY 10013-2473, USA

www.cambridge.org
Information on this title: www.cambridge.org/9781107607453

First published 2012

Printed in the United States of America

A catalog record for this publication is available from the British Library.

Library of Congress Cataloging in Publication data

Svolik, Milan W., 1977–
The politics of authoritarian rule / Milan W. Svolik, University of Illinois,
Urbana-Champaign.
    pages cm. – (Cambridge studies in comparative politics)
Includes bibliographical references and index.
ISBN 978-1-107-02479-3 (hardback) – ISBN 978-1-107-60745-3 (paperback)
1. Authoritarianism.   2. Authoritarianism – Case studies.   I. Title.
JC480.S87   2012
320.53–dc23   2012012615

ISBN 978-1-107-02479-3 Hardback
ISBN 978-1-107-60745-3 Paperback

Mojím rodičom, Daniele Švolíkovej a Milanovi Švolíkovi.

Contents

Figures

Tables

Acknowledgments

I have been thinking about the ideas in this book at least since I was a graduate student at the University of Chicago. I have been long fascinated by both the politics of dictatorships and the analytical challenges involved in its study. Compared to authoritarian politics, democratic politics is orderly. The "rules of the game" can be counted on. Candidates campaign, sometimes they squabble, but then – voters vote. In dictatorships, the presumed "rules of the game" are routinely broken and backstabbing is far from metaphorical.

For teaching me how to tackle such conceptual problems with the rigor of modern social science, I owe an immense intellectual debt to my advisors Duncan Snidal, Carles Boix, and Roger Myerson. I have had the privilege to discuss the inner workings of Stalin's dictatorship with Ron Suny; our conversations have been a source of lasting inspiration for me. At Chicago, I have also been fortunate to have interacted with an incredibly sharp cohort of fellow graduate students. That intellectual adventure has shaped my approach to political science ever since.

Many friends and colleagues read and discussed with me portions of this book. For this, I am grateful to Julia Bader, Robert Bates, Mark Beissinger, Allyson Benton, Carles Boix, Bruce Bueno de Mesquita, Paul Cantor, José Cheibub, Rafaela Dancygier, Alexandre Debs, Georgy Egorov, Abel Escribà-Folch, Jennifer Gandhi, Barbara Geddes, Scott Gehlbach, Hein Goemans, Anna Grzymala-Busse, Sergei Guriev, Petra Hendrickson, Burak Kadercan, Patrick Kuhn, Xiaoting Li, Peter Lorentzen, Beatriz Magaloni, Eddie Malesky, Stephen Morris, Roger Myerson, Monika Nalepa, Bob Powell, Adam Przeworski, Rachel Riedl, Tyson Roberts, Neil Robinson, Mehdi Shadmehr, Victor Shih, Daniel Slater, Duncan Snidal, Konstantin Sonin, Ron Suny, Jay Ulfelder, Andrea Vindigni, and Jessica Weeks. I would also like to thank participants at seminars at the University of California at Berkeley, the University of Chicago, the University of Illinois, the University of Michigan, Princeton University, the University of Rochester, Yale University, and numerous conferences. Parts of this book were written while I was visiting at the

Center for the Study of Democratic Politics at Princeton University and stationed at the Cline Center for Democracy at the University of Illinois. I would like to thank Larry Bartels and Pete Nardulli for their support during these periods.

I have benefited greatly from the generosity and insights of my colleagues at the University of Illinois. Jake Bowers, Xinyuan Dai, Paul Diehl, Tiberiu Dragu, Zach Elkins, Sam Frost, Brian Gaines, Jude Hays, Jim Kuklinski, Bob Pahre, Gisela Sin, Bonnie Weir, and Matt Winters have offered comments and criticisms at various stages of this book. My thanks go especially to José Cheibub, whose encouragement and guidance make this project seem so easy in retrospect.

I was fortunate to receive excellent and detailed comments on the entire manuscript from Giacomo Chiozza, Lucan Way, and several anonymous referees. Carles Boix, José Cheibub, Jennifer Gandhi, Monika Nalepa, Pete Nardulli, and Duncan Snidal offered invaluable guidance on the book's publication. I am also grateful to Hein Goemans, whose data were incredibly helpful at the early stages of this project. Seden Akcinaroglu, Svitlana Chernykh, Aya Kachi, Donksuk Kim, Dan Koev, Alex Sapone, Tatiana Švolíková, and Nini Zhang all provided valuable research assistance at various stages of this project. I am especially indebted to Michael Martin for his outstanding help with data collection, editing, and indexing. Students in my 2010–2012 undergraduate and graduate classes on the politics of dictatorships suffered through the early drafts of several chapters – their feedback was instrumental in helping me frame the book's overarching argument.

I would also like to thank my editor at Cambridge University Press, Lew Bateman, for his interest in the project and his consideration of the professional pressures faced by a junior political scientist, as well as Margaret Levi for including the manuscript in the Cambridge Studies in Comparative Politics series.

Finally, I thank my family and friends for their support along the way. My wife Bonnie has been a source of endless love and energy at every stage of the writing process. She patiently read and reread, edited and re-edited the entire manuscript. Exactly when it counted, she has been my toughest critic and my greatest supporter.

This book is dedicated to my parents, to whom I owe the most.

Portions of this book rely on research that has been published or draws on collaborative work. Parts of Chapter 3 have appeared as "Power-Sharing and Leadership Dynamics in Authoritarian Regimes" in the *American Journal of Political Science* (2009). More importantly, I have had the good fortune to collaborate with and learn from Carles Boix; parts of Chapter 4 draw on our joint paper "The Foundations of Limited Authoritarian Government: Institutions and Power-Sharing in Dictatorships."

1

Introduction

The Anatomy of Dictatorship

Still democracy appears to be safer and less liable to revolution than oligarchy. For in oligarchies there is the double danger of the oligarchs falling out among themselves and also with the people . . .

Aristotle, *The Politics*, Book 5

[W]herein men live without other security, than what their own strength, and their own invention shall furnish them . . . , the life of man [is] solitary, poor, nasty, brutish, and short.

Thomas Hobbes, *Leviathan*

Bashar al-Asad was not meant to be a dictator. Although he was the son of Syria's long-serving president, Hafez al-Asad, Bashar's education and career were nonpolitical. In 1988, at the age of twenty-three, he received a degree in ophthalmology from the University of Damascus and moved to London four years later to continue his medical residency. Hafez al-Asad had instead groomed Bashar's older brother, Basil, as his successor. Yet Bashar's seclusion from politics ended in 1994 when Basil died in an automobile accident. Bashar was recalled from London, entered a military academy, and quickly advanced through the ranks, while his father spent the last years of his life eliminating potential challengers to Bashar's succession.[1]

Consider Bashar al-Asad's delicate position on July 17, 2000, when he became the Syrian president. Given his unexpected path to power, how does he best ensure his survival in office? What threats should he expect and how will he deal with them?

Alas, the contemporary political scientist is not well equipped to become the new Machiavelli. If Bashar al-Asad were concerned about politically succeeding in a democracy, students of politics might offer him suggestions ranging from how to best target voters in campaigns to the implications of electoral systems

---

[1] See Hinnebusch (2002), Leverett (2005), and Perthes (2006).

1

for partisan competition.[2] But of course, if Bashar al-Asad lived in a democracy, he would not have been in a position to inherit a presidency.

Although growing at a fast pace, contemporary scholarship on dictatorships has so far generated only a fragmented understanding of authoritarian politics. Extant research increasingly studies authoritarian parties, legislatures, bureaucracies, and elections, as well as repression, leadership change, and regime stability across dictatorships.[3] Yet in most cases, these facets of authoritarianism are examined individually, in isolation. In turn, we lack a unified theoretical framework that would help us to identify key actors in dictatorships; locate the sources of political conflict among them; and thereby explain the enormous variation in institutions, leaders, and policies across dictatorships.[4] At both the empirical and theoretical level, we are without a general conceptual heuristic that would facilitate comparisons across polities as diverse as Mexico under the Institutional Revolutionary Party (PRI), Saddam Hussein's Iraq, and contemporary China. This book attempts to fill that void.

I argue that two conflicts fundamentally shape authoritarian politics. The first is between those who rule and those who are ruled. All dictators face threats from the masses, and I call the political problem of balancing against the majority excluded from power *the problem of authoritarian control*. Yet dictators rarely control enough resources to preclude such challenges on their own – they therefore typically rule with a number of allies, whether they be traditional elites, prominent party members, or generals in charge of repression. A second, separate political conflict arises when dictators counter challenges from those with whom they share power. This is *the problem of authoritarian power-sharing*. To paraphrase Aristotle's warning in this chapter's epigraph, authoritarian elites may fall out both with the people and among themselves.

Crucially, whether and how dictators resolve the problems of power-sharing and control is shaped by two distinctively dismal features of authoritarian politics. First, dictatorships inherently lack an independent authority with the power to enforce agreements among key political actors, especially the dictator, his allies, and their repressive agents. Second, violence is an ever-present and ultimate arbiter of conflicts in authoritarian politics. These two intrinsic features uniquely shape the conduct of politics in dictatorships. They limit the role that political institutions can plausibly play in resolving the problems of power-sharing and control, and they explain the gruesome manner in which so many dictators and dictatorships fall. Authoritarian politics takes place in the shadow of betrayal and violence.

In brief, the central claim of this book is this: Key features of authoritarianism – including institutions, policies, as well as the survival of leaders and regimes – are shaped by the twin problems of power-sharing and control against

---

[2] See, e.g., Green and Gerber (2004) and Cox (1997), respectively.
[3] See subsequent chapters for a detailed discussion of this literature.
[4] Bueno de Mesquita et al. (2003) and Wintrobe (1998) are two notable exceptions to the tendency for fragmentary explanations of authoritarian politics.

the backdrop of the dismal conditions under which authoritarian politics takes place. They explain why some dictators, like Saddam Hussein, establish personal autocracy and stay in power for decades; why leadership changes elsewhere are regular and institutionalized, as in contemporary China; why some authoritarian regimes are ruled by soldiers, as Uganda was under Idi Amin; why many dictatorships, like PRI-era Mexico, maintain regime-sanctioned political parties; and why a country's authoritarian past casts a long shadow over its prospects for democracy.

In the chapters that follow, I develop theoretical arguments that elaborate on and qualify this claim, and I present empirical evidence that supports it.

1.1 THE TWO PROBLEMS OF AUTHORITARIAN RULE

A typical journalistic account of authoritarian politics invokes the image of a spontaneously assembled crowd in the central square of a country's capital; throngs of people chant "Down with the dictator!" as the leader engages in a desperate attempt to appease or disperse the assembled masses. Some of these accounts end with the dictator's downfall, potentially opening the way for a democratic future.

Recall the Romanian dictator Nicolae Ceauşescu, whose brutal and erratic rule ended in 1989 after a government-sanctioned rally swelled into a successful popular uprising. Following nearly a decade of severe shortages of essential goods under a draconian austerity program, riots erupted in the town of Timişoara in December 1989. When the government called for a rally in the capital of Bucharest – during which Ceauşescu intended to condemn the riots – the crowd of roughly 100,000 people grew unruly and demanded that Ceauşescu step down. Ceauşescu first attempted to quell the protesters with promises of higher salaries but, when unsuccessful, he ordered the security forces to disperse the crowd. After protests abruptly spread across the country, however, the army refused to continue to use force against the population. Within three days, Ceauşescu was arrested and, after a summary military trial, he was executed along with his wife.[5]

The confrontation between Ceauşescu's regime and the Romanian masses epitomizes the first of the two fundamental problems of authoritarian rule that I identify – *the problem of authoritarian control*. Most academic studies of authoritarian politics frame the central political conflict in dictatorships in these terms alone, that is, as one between a small authoritarian elite and the much larger population over which it rules. The now-classic literature on totalitarianism (Arendt 1951; Friedrich and Brzezinski 1965) examined the instruments with which authoritarian elites dominate the masses, like ideology and secret police. More recently, Gandhi and Przeworski (2006) and Gandhi (2008) argued that the threat of popular opposition compels dictators to share rents and establish certain political institutions (e.g. legislatures) that lend

---

[5] For an account and analysis of these events, see, e.g., Siani-Davies (2007).

credibility to such concessions. And while Acemoglu and Robinson (2001) and Boix (2003) focus on transitions to democracy, they also identify the possibility of a mass uprising as the chief threat to a dictator's hold on power, and they emphasize the role of repression in precluding a regime change.[6]

Yet the view of authoritarian politics as primarily one of a struggle between the elites in power and the masses excluded from power is severely incomplete. If the problem of authoritarian control were indeed the paramount political conflict in dictatorships, then we would expect dictators to fall after a defeat in a confrontation with the masses, as Ceauşescu did in 1989. Simply stated, conventional wisdom dictates that if and when things go wrong for dictators, it will be because of a successful popular uprising.

Comprehensive data on leadership changes in dictatorships sharply contradict this conventional understanding. Figure 1.1 summarizes the various nonconstitutional ways by which dictators lose office. It includes all 316 authoritarian leaders who held office for at least one day between 1946 and 2008 and lost power by nonconstitutional means.[7] Such means include any type of exit from office that did *not* follow a natural death or a constitutionally mandated process, such as an election, a vote by a ruling body, or a hereditary succession. Among the 303 leaders for whom the manner by which they lost power could be ascertained unambiguously, only thirty-two were removed by a popular uprising and another thirty stepped down under public pressure to democratize – this accounts for only about one-fifth of nonconstitutional exits from office. Twenty more leaders were assassinated and sixteen were removed by foreign intervention.

Yet as Figure 1.1 strikingly reveals, the remaining 205 dictators – more than two-thirds – were removed by regime insiders: individuals from the dictator's inner circle, the government, or the repressive apparatus. In my data, I refer to this type of leader exit from office as a *coup d'état*.[8] This is how Leonid Brezhnev replaced Nikita Khrushchev in 1964, how a group of military officers ousted the Ghanian President Kwame Nkhruma in 1966, and how the recently deposed Tunisian President Zine El Abidine Ben Ali got rid of his predecessor in 1987. Coups overshadow the remaining forms of exit from office even after we set aside those dictators who stayed in office for less than a year – these

---

[6] Even in O'Donnell and Schmitter's (1986) and Przeworski's (1991, chap. 2) classic work, where elite defections by "soft-liners" lead to a democratic transition, the initial impetus for elite defection often comes from mass pressures for democratization.

[7] I focus on nonconstitutional leadership changes because, in these instances, a leadership change most plausibly occurred nonconsensually – against the will of the incumbent leader. (It might not be surprising that an authoritarian incumbent would be replaced by a political or institutional insider when a leadership change is consensual, as during a hereditary succession for instance.) I describe these data in detail in Chapter 2; see also the codebook on my Web site.

[8] Here, the term *coup d'état* refers to a forced removal of an authoritarian leader by *any* regime insider, not necessarily the military. (The latter is often implied in popular usage of the term.) For a discussion of the various terms associated with a couplike removal of governments, see Luttwak (1968, Chap. 1).

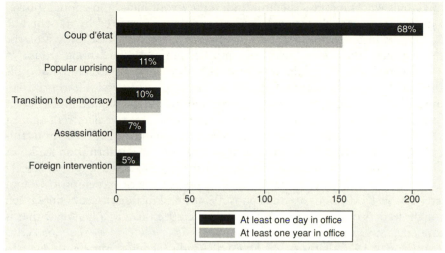

FIGURE 1.1. Nonconstitutional exits from office of authoritarian leaders, 1946–2008. *Note:* Percentages refer to a category's share of all nonconstitutional exists. Exits of interim leaders are not included. Unambiguous determination of exit was not possible for thirteen leaders.

short-lived leaders may have been more vulnerable because of their inexperience in office or a weaker hold on power.[9]

Thus as far as authoritarian leadership dynamics are concerned, an overwhelming majority of dictators lose power to those inside the gates of the presidential palace rather than to the masses outside. The predominant political conflict in dictatorships appears to be not between the ruling elite and the masses but rather one *among* regime insiders. This is the second of the two problems of authoritarian rule that I identify: the problem of authoritarian power-sharing. The evidence I just reviewed suggests that to understand the politics of dictatorships, we must examine why and how a conflict among authoritarian elites undermines their ability to govern.[10] I undertake this task in Part I of this book.

1.1.1 The Problem of Authoritarian Power-Sharing

When he assumed office, Bashar al-Asad – like most dictators – did not personally control enough resources to govern alone. Toward the end of his life, Bashar's father Hafez al-Asad assembled a coalition of old comrades-in-arms, business elites, and Baath Party officials who would support his son's succession to the Syrian presidency.[11] This is what I call a *ruling coalition* – a set of

---

[9] I elaborate on the latter rationale in Chapter 3.
[10] Various aspects of such conflicts among authoritarian elites have been studied by Ramsayer and Rosenbluth (1995), Geddes (1999a), Bueno de Mesquita et al. (2003), Brownlee (2007a), Gehlbach and Keefer (2008), Magaloni (2008), Myerson (2008), and Guriev and Sonin (2009).
[11] See Leverett (2005) and Perthes (2006).

individuals who support a dictator and, jointly with him, hold enough power to guarantee a regime's survival. This terminology is inspired by its semantic counterpart in Soviet politics: Stalin's inner circle came to be known as the "select group," the "close circle," or – most commonly – the "ruling group."[12]

Chapters 3 and 4 explain why power-sharing between a dictator and his ruling coalition so frequently fails. A key obstacle to successful authoritarian power-sharing is the dictator's desire and opportunity to acquire more power at the expense of his allies. In dictatorships, the only effective deterrent against such opportunism is the allies' threat to replace the dictator. Throughout this book, I refer to such elite-driven attempts to remove an authoritarian leader as *allies' rebellions*, mirroring the language of the right to a "baronial rebellion" recognized by the Magna Carta of 1215. Of course, the closest empirical counterpart of such rebellions are the coups d'état that I just discussed. Quite often though, leaders of successful rebellions characterize them in a language that is more suggestive of their righteous motives – as in the case of the Corrective Revolution of 1970 that brought Hafez al-Asad's faction of the Baath Party to power in Syria.

Chapter 3 examines the most blatant failure of authoritarian power-sharing: the emergence of personal autocracy. I explain why a power trajectory along which an authoritarian leader, like Joseph Stalin, assumes office as the "first among equals" but succeeds over time in accumulating enough power to become an invincible autocrat is both possible and unlikely. The possibility of such "upward mobility" is intimately tied to the distinctively toxic conditions under which authoritarian elites must operate. When they cannot rely on an independent authority to compel the dictator to share power as agreed and when violence looms in the background, a small dose of uncertainty about a rebellion's success will limit the allies' ability to credibly deter the dictator from attempting to usurp power at their expense. If he succeeds in several such attempts, the dictator may accumulate enough power to entirely undermine the allies' capacity to stop him. Hence the emergence of personal autocracy should be a rare but nevertheless systematic phenomenon across dictatorships.

This logic implies that the interaction between a dictator and his allies generally takes only two politically distinct forms. Under the first, which I call *contested autocracy*, politics is one of balancing between the dictator and the allies – the allies are capable of using the threat of a rebellion to check the dictator's opportunism, albeit imperfectly. By contrast, *established autocrats* have acquired so much power that they can no longer be credibly threatened by their allies – they have effectively monopolized power. In fact, many accounts by classical philosophers and historians identify precisely this analytical distinction: Machiavelli distinguishes between the King of France, who cannot take away the privileges of his barons "without endangering himself," and the Turk, whose ministers are his "slaves." Meanwhile, historians of the Soviet Union distinguish between the pre–Purges and the post–Purges Stalin that achieved

---

[12] The corresponding Russian terms are *uzkii sostav, blizhnii krug,* and *rukovodiashchaia grupa,* respectively. See Gorlizki and Khlevniuk (2004, 47).

"limitless power over the fate of every Soviet official"; and historians of China distinguish between the pre–1958 Mao, who "listened to interests within the system," and the "later Mao," who simply overrode them.[13] Hence the transition from contested to established autocracy represents the degeneration of authoritarian power-sharing into personal autocracy.

Chapter 3 thus explains the emergence of a prominent class of dictatorships that have been alternatively referred to as *personalist, neopatrimonial, or sultanistic*.[14] In these regimes, leaders have managed to wrestle power away from the individuals and institutions that originally brought them to power – whether they be parties, militaries, or dynastic families. My arguments clarify why such dictators – like Fidel Castro, who ruled Cuba for a half-century until his retirement in 2008 – emerge across all kinds of dictatorships, develop personality cults, and enjoy long tenures: They have effectively eliminated any threats from their ruling coalition. This last point helps us understand not only the variation in the length of dictators' tenures but also the manner by which they lose office. When established autocrats ultimately leave office, it is most likely by a process that is unrelated to the interaction with their allies. Accordingly, Saddam Hussein was brought down by a foreign occupier, Muammar Qaddafi by a popular uprising, and Joseph Stalin by a stroke – none of them at the hands of their inner circle.

My emphasis shifts from the failure of authoritarian power-sharing to its potential success in Chapter 4. One factor that exacerbates the gruesome character of dictatorships is the secrecy that typically pervades interactions among authoritarian elites. Yet unlike the potential for violence or the lack of an independent authority that would enforce agreements among the dictator and his allies, the lack of transparency among authoritarian elites might be curtailed, if not eliminated, by adopting appropriate political institutions. These most often take the form of high-level, deliberative, and decision-making bodies – committees, politburos, or ruling councils – and are usually embedded within authoritarian parties and legislatures.[15]

Formal political institutions alleviate monitoring problems in authoritarian power-sharing in two distinct ways. Institutions like the Politburo Standing Committee of the Communist Party of China (1949–present), the Chilean Junta Militar de Gobierno under Pinochet (1973–1990), and the Consultative Council of Saudi Arabia (1993–present) typically establish formal rules concerning membership, jurisdiction, protocol, and decision making that both facilitate the exchange of information among the ruling elites and provide for an easy assessment of compliance with those rules.[16] Thus regular, institutionalized

---

[13] See Machiavelli (2005[1513], 16–17), Khlevniuk (2009, 247), and Teiwes (2001, 79).

[14] On these concepts, see Zolberg (1966), Roth (1968), Jackson and Rosberg (1982), Snyder (1992), Bratton and Van de Walle (1997), Linz and Chehabi (1998), Geddes (1999a), and Brownlee (2002).

[15] On authoritarian parties, see Brownlee (2007a), Geddes (2008), Gehlbach and Keefer (2008), Greene (2007), Magaloni (2006), and Smith (2005); on legislatures, see Gandhi and Przeworski (2007), Gandhi (2008), Malesky (2009), Ramseyer and Rosenbluth (1995), and Wright (2008a).

[16] See Barros (2002), MacFarquhar (1997a), and Herb (1999) on these institutions in Chile, China, and Saudi Arabia, respectively.

interaction between the dictator and his allies results in greater transparency among them and, by virtue of their formal structure, institutions provide a publicly observable signal of the dictator's commitment to power-sharing. The first mechanism prevents misperceptions among the allies about the dictator's actions from escalating into unnecessary, regime-destabilizing confrontations; the second mechanism reassures the allies that the dictator's potential attempts to usurp power will be readily and publicly detected.

As we shall see in Chapter 4, the above functions have been notably performed by the political machinery that has governed Chinese leadership politics since Jiang Zemin. After Deng Xiaoping's reforms in the 1980s, key decision-making bodies within the Chinese Government and the Communist Party began meeting regularly, following formal rules of consultation, division of labor, and consensual decision making. At the same time, tenure in key government posts – including the presidency and premiership – was limited to no more than two five-year terms, and informal rules about similar term limits as well as retirement age provisions were established for those within leading party bodies.[17] Formal political institutions in dictatorships thus alleviate monitoring problems in authoritarian power-sharing and, as we shall see after examining data from all dictatorships throughout the period 1946–2008, they indeed enhance the stability of authoritarian ruling coalitions.

Crucially, Chapter 4 clarifies not only the benefits but also the limits to the contribution of institutions to authoritarian power-sharing. While institutions have the potential to alleviate monitoring problems in authoritarian power-sharing, the dictator's opportunism must not only be detected but also punished. As in Chapter 3, the credibility of any threat by the ruling coalition to sanction the dictator ultimately depends on the allies' ability to remove him from office. Chapter 4 clarifies how the balance of power between the two relates to the intensity of the allies' collective action problem in replacing the dictator and, hence, to the credibility of that threat. We will see that the dictator's compliance with institutional constraints will be self-enforcing only under a permissive balance of power within the ruling coalition. Institutions will be ineffective or break down when not backed by a credible threat of force.

This is why, in China, formal institutions of "collective leadership" successfully governed the tenures of Jiang Zemin and Hu Jintao but failed to constrain Mao Zedong and Deng Xiaoping. Jiang and Hu were "first among equals" within two evenly balanced political coalitions. By contrast, Mao and Deng commanded a following and charisma that eclipsed any of their contemporaries. Chapter 4 thus answers a major conceptual and empirical question that has preoccupied research on authoritarian politics: When and why do some dictatorships establish and maintain institutions that effectively constrain their leaders?

---

[17] See Baum (1997), Huang (2008), Li (2010), Manion (1992), Miller (2008), Nathan (2003), and Teiwes (2001).

1.1.2 The Problem of Authoritarian Control

In March 2011, the Arab Spring came to Syria. Protests against Bashar al-Asad's regime broke out in the southern city of Dera'a on March 18 and, by the end of the month, mass protests erupted across the entire country. This is when Bashar al-Asad found himself facing the second of the two fundamental problems of authoritarian rule examined in this book: the problem of authoritarian control. Recall that this problem concerns the conflict between the authoritarian elites in power and the masses that are excluded from power.

Asad's first response to the protests was to offer restive Syrians some proverbial "carrots." In fact, even before the actual protests began, the regime had already frozen rising electricity prices, increased heating-oil subsidies, and raised salaries for public workers – anticipating that the wave of uprisings emerging across the Middle East may spread to Syria. A few weeks later came the "sticks": By late April, the government was stepping up arrests, imprisoning activists, and firing live rounds on demonstrators across the country.[18]

Bashar al-Asad's response to the Arab Spring exemplifies two principal ways in which dictators resolve the problem of authoritarian control: *repression* and *co-optation*. I study these two instruments of authoritarian control in Part II of this book.

At least since Machiavelli, political thinkers have offered varied advice about whether it is better to be loved than feared. Machiavelli favored the latter because "a wise prince should establish himself on that which is in his own control and not in that of others."[19] More recently, Wintrobe (1998) explicitly contrasted repression and co-optation, treated the two as substitutes, and attributed the variation in their use across dictatorships to the preferences of individual dictators. Others have addressed repression and co-optation in isolation. The classic literature on totalitarianism and bureaucratic authoritarianism in Latin America focuses primarily on repression, as does more recent research.[20] Meanwhile, in the literature on elections, legislatures, and parties in dictatorships, the key mechanism is almost exclusively co-optation.[21]

---

[18] See "Hard Choices for the Government," *The Economist*, 22 January 2011; "E.U. Bans Syrian Oil as Protests Continue," *The New York Times*, 3 September 2011; "A Cycle of Violence May Take Hold," *The Economist*, 9 April 2011; and "More Stick Than Carrot," *The Economist*, 12 May 2011.

[19] Chap. XVII, "Concerning Cruelty And Clemency, And Whether It Is Better To Be Loved Than Feared" in Machiavelli (2005 [1513]).

[20] On totalitarianism, see Friedrich and Brzezinski (1965) and Arendt (1951); on bureaucratic authoritarianism, see O'Donnell (1973) and Stepan (1974, 1988); for more recent research on repression, see Davenport (2007), Gregory et al. (2006), Gregory (2009), Lorentzen (2009), and Robertson (2011). In a related line of research, Egorov et al., (2009) and Lorentzen (2008) examine the role of censorship in dictatorships.

[21] On elections, see Blaydes (2007) and Lust-Okar and Jamal (2002); on legislatures, see Gandhi and Przeworski (2006), Gandhi (2008), and Malesky (2009); on parties, see Brownlee (2007a), Gehlbach and Keefer (2008), and Magaloni (2006, 2008).

At first glance, the difference between repression and co-optation may seem to be simply one between negative and positive incentives for compliance with the regime – "sticks and carrots" in popular parlance. Repression, however, is much more than co-optation's evil twin. When we examine the two in isolation or treat them as substitutes, we may overlook that differences in their use have far-reaching consequences for the political organization and vulnerabilities of dictatorships.

Heavy reliance on repression – typically by the military – entails a fundamental moral hazard: The very resources that enable a regime's repressive agents to suppress its opposition also empower it to act against the regime itself. Hence once soldiers become indispensable for a regime's survival, they acquire political leverage that they can exploit. Militaries frequently do so by demanding privileges, perks, and policy concessions that go beyond what is necessary for suppressing the regime's opposition – they claim a seat at the table when the spoils of their complicity are divided. As Machiavelli warns in *The Prince*, those emperors who come to power by "corrupting the soldiers" become hostages of "him who granted them the state."[22] This is why the former Tunisian President Zine El Abidine Ben Ali kept his military small and underequipped; why the Iraqi Baath regime disposed of its uniformed accomplices immediately after it came to power in 1968; and why Mao Zedong insisted that the Party must always command the gun.

Nevertheless, no dictatorship can do away with repression. The lack of popular consent – inherent in any political system where a few govern over the many – is the "original sin" of dictatorships. In fact, many dictators do not have much leeway when deciding how much to rely on soldiers for repression. In regimes that face mass, organized, and potentially violent opposition, the military is the only force capable of defeating such threats. For dictators in these circumstances, political dependence on soldiers may be insurmountable.

Meanwhile, other dictators simply inherit politically entrenched militaries when they come to power. These regimes, in turn, must concede to soldiers greater resources, institutional autonomy, and influence over policy. This is why the Egyptian military presides over a complex of commercial enterprises (Cook 2007, 19); why the Honduran military won complete autonomy over its budget and leadership positions after it brought President Ramón Villeda Morales to power in 1954 (Bowman 2002, Chap. 5); and why, in 1973, the Uruguayan military had its political influence institutionalized in a National Security Council that assisted several docile presidents in "carrying out national objectives" (Rouquié 1987, 251).

Chapter 5 explains why bargaining over such concessions between a government and politically entrenched militaries takes a peculiar form: Each side consciously manipulates the risk of actual military intervention, even though both would prefer to avoid it. Military dictatorships emerge when, in the process

---

[22] Chap. VII, "Concerning New Principalities Which Are Acquired Either by the Arms of Others or by Good Fortune," in Machiavelli (2005[1513]).

of such brinkmanship, either the military or the government "rocks the boat" too much.[23] Authoritarian reliance on repression is thus a double-edged sword: It sows the seeds of future military interventions.

The analysis in Chapter 5 in turn clarifies why so many dictators wear a military uniform. Political control over militaries – in both dictatorship and democracies – is a political problem before it is a cultural or institutional one. When deciding how much to rely on repression, dictators make a trade-off between their exposure to external threats from the masses and their vulnerability to internal threats from their repressive agents. In dictatorships where a few in power control a disproportionate share of wealth, repression is simply more attractive than co-optation. In these regimes, it is cheaper for the regime to pay its repressive agents to suppress any opposition than to assuage it by co-optation – even after accounting for the Faustian bargain that such reliance on repression entails. In turn, we should see more sticks than carrots in countries where a few wealthy landowners control the economy, where command of the government amounts to ownership of the country's natural resources, and where a minority excludes a majority from power on ethnic or sectarian grounds. Such polity-wide, structural factors explain why some dictators maintain perfect political control over their militaries, why others are under effective military tutelage, and why military interventions threaten many new democracies.

My focus shifts attention shifts from sticks to carrots in Chapter 6, which examines why some dictatorships establish and maintain a regime-sanctioned political party. Many authoritarian regimes favor one or several political parties, but only some – like PRI–era Mexico, Saddam Hussein's Iraq, and contemporary China – establish a party structure that effectively maintains a loyal, popular base for the regime. Chapter 6 identifies three core institutional features that turn authoritarian parties into effective instruments of authoritarian control: (1) hierarchical assignment of service and benefits, (2) political control over appointments, and (3) selective recruitment and repression. Briefly, the first feature entails assigning costly, politically valuable party service – often in the form of ideological proselytizing, intelligence gathering, and mobilization for regime-sanctioned events – early in a party member's career while delaying the benefits of party membership – which typically entail better employment and promotion prospects or privileged access to education and social services – to

---

[23] Existing research shows that military dictatorships are systematically associated with a range of outcomes. Geddes (1999b) and Hadenius and Teorell (2007) show that when compared to single-party and personalist dictatorships, military dictatorships are the most common form of authoritarian government prior to the 1990s, yet they also have the shortest lifespan (Geddes 1999b; Brownlee 2009); leaders of military dictatorships are less likely to survive in office than leaders of nonmilitary dictatorships (Geddes 1999b; Gandhi 2008) and they tend to be deposed by further coups (Nordlinger 1977; Debs 2009); and military regimes are also more resilient than personalist regimes or monarchies to international sanctions (Escribà-Folch and Wright 2008) and they also are more likely than single-party regimes to initiate military disputes (Lai and Slater 2006).

a later point. As a result, by the time party members reap the benefits of seniority, their costly service becomes "sunk investment": Once expended, it cannot be recovered or transferred across political coalitions.

These organizational features of authoritarian parties therefore accomplish more than simply distribute rewards in exchange for party members' loyalty to the regime, as the extant literature frequently concludes. That could be accomplished without the institution of a party. After all, dictators frequently assuage popular discontent by redistributing land, subsidizing basic goods, or even distributing cash – as the Bahraini king did in the wake of the Arab Spring when he promised each family the equivalent of more than two thousand U.S. dollars.[24] Rather, these features of internal party organization effectively exploit natural career aspirations among the population in order to foster an enduring stake in the perpetuation of the regime among its most productive and ideologically agreeable segments. As Bratton and Van de Walle (1997, 86) put it in their study of African transitions to democracy, members of such parties have little option but "to sink or swim" with the regime.

Chapter 6 thus clarifies why authoritarian parties are best thought of as incentive structures that encourage sunk political investment by their members; why they serve to marginalize opposition rather than to co-opt it; and why party dictatorships with these organizational features survive under less favorable circumstances than dictatorships without them, even if the latter expand the same resources on co-optation. I also explain why dictatorships need the actual institution of the party; why some dictatorships find co-optation via parties less attractive than the alternatives of repression or co-optation by social spending alone; and why former authoritarian party elites so frequently continue to hold a firm grip over the politics of nascent democracies.

This discussion outlines the first step in the overarching theoretical argument that I develop in this book: In dictatorships, political battle lines emerge as often among those in power as they do between the elite and the masses. I identify these two distinct conflicts as the problems of authoritarian power-sharing and control. When I previously presented the two conflicts separately, it was primarily for analytical clarity and the heuristic value of such expositional separation. As my discussion of repression and co-optation implies, the two problems are often interconnected: When indispensable in repression, soldiers transform from obedient agents into political rivals who demand a cut from the spoils of their complicity. Meanwhile, in order to co-opt effectively, authoritarian parties promise upward mobility that over time begets a new political elite. Repression and co-optation thus each empower different actors and institutions. Dictators' response to the problem of authoritarian control therefore shapes the likely contours of the conflict over power-sharing.

Jointly, the two problems clarify why many nominally democratic institutions – especially legislatures, parties, and even some elections – serve distinctively authoritarian ends: They help dictators resolve the problems of power-sharing and control. Whereas legislatures serve to represent the diversity

---

[24] See "Bahrain's King Gives out Cash Ahead of Protests," *Reuters*, 12 February 2011.

of political interests in democracies (see, e.g., Manin 1997), their role in dictatorships is to enhance the stability of authoritarian power-sharing by alleviating commitment and monitoring problems among authoritarian elites. Whereas parties in democracies coordinate the political activities of like-minded citizens (see, e.g., Aldrich 1995), regime parties under dictatorship serve to co-opt the most capable and opportunistic among the masses in order to strengthen the regime. These arguments contrast sharply with the tone of existing research, in which discussions of authoritarian institutions are all too often cast in a mold borrowed from the study of democratic politics – as if authoritarian institutions were just less-perfect versions of their democratic counterparts. The conclusions in this book differ: Under dictatorship, nominally democratic institutions serve quintessentially authoritarian ends.

The theoretical framework in this book contributes to our understanding of a range of empirical outcomes in dictatorships. The analysis of the problem of power-sharing in Chapters 3 and 4 explains the variation in the duration of dictators' tenures and the stability of authoritarian ruling coalitions. It also clarifies why the manner by which dictators enter and leave office is linked to the length of their rule and the institutions that they employ. I support each of these arguments by examining comprehensive data on leadership change and ruling-coalition stability across dictatorships. Meanwhile, when I address the problem of authoritarian control in Chapters 5 and 6, I account for the recurrence of military dictatorships in some countries and the maintenance of regime-sanctioned political parties in others. Consistently with my arguments, we will see that military interventions recur in economically unequal societies and dominant, not necessarily single, authoritarian parties indeed contribute to the longevity of dictatorships.

As the discussion so far suggests, however, the potential for and limits to resolving the problems of authoritarian power-sharing and control are fundamentally shaped by the distinctively grim circumstances under which authoritarian politics takes place. The second conceptual step in this book's overarching argument involves appropriately accounting for those conditions in the study of authoritarian politics.

1.2 THE AUTHORITARIAN SETTING

Authoritarian politics has always been a ruthless and treacherous business. For most dictators, merely dying in bed is a significant accomplishment. Consider again Bashar al-Asad: In spite of his father's thirty-year rule, Bashar al-Asad did not have many reasons to feel secure when he assumed the presidency upon his father's death in 2000. Hafez al-Asad acceded to power in 1970 amid a bloody internal struggle over the direction of the Syrian Baath Party that left the defeated faction purged and its leaders jailed for life.[25] Meanwhile, the period between Syria's independence in 1946 and the Baath takeover in 1963 witnessed so much political turmoil – including at least seven military coups

[25] See Van Dam (1979, Chap. 5); see also Seale (1990) and Zisser (2001).

d'état – that one observer labeled Syria during this period "the world's most unstable country."[26]

Although journalistic accounts of the brutality or eccentricities of dictators make for a thrilling read, their shock value may eclipse an important conceptual point: This gruesomeness stems from two distinctive features of authoritarian politics. First, dictatorships inherently lack an independent authority with the power to enforce agreements among key political actors. Second, violence is an ever-present and the ultimate arbiter of political conflicts in dictatorships. These two distinctively dismal features have far-reaching consequences for the conduct of authoritarian politics – and hence for its study.

The absence of an independent authority that would enforce agreements among key political players is the essence of dictatorship. After all, the presence of an actor with such authority would imply a check on the very powers that dictators and their allies want to command. As a result, promises made at one point by the dictator, his allies, or the regime's repressive agents may be broken later, when they become inconvenient.[27] This facet of authoritarianism decidedly limits the role that political institutions can plausibly play in resolving the problems of authoritarian power-sharing and control – as well as the assumptions that political scientists can reasonably make about them.

Therefore why Xi Jinping – the presumptive heir to Hu Jintao as the "paramount" leader of China – is expected to be bound by the same institutionalized rules of "collective leadership" that have governed the last two generations of Chinese leadership is a question that must be answered rather than a point to be assumed. After all, the apparatus of contemporary Chinese collective leadership is not far from that to which the Chilean junta that came to power in the coup of 1973 aspired. The junta was initially supposed to govern by unanimous consent and its presidency was to rotate among its four members. Soon, however, Pinochet came to dominate: In 1974, he compelled other members of the junta to appoint him president, replaced unanimous decision making by a majority rule, and foreclosed any further considerations of rotation of the presidency. In 1978, Pinochet expelled from the junta Gustavo Leigh, the air-force representative and Pinochet's most vocal opponent. From that moment on, according to Arriagada (1988, 37), Pinochet began to act as "the de facto, if not the de jure, Generalissimo of the Armed Forces."[28]

---

[26] See Rubin (2008, Chap. 2).

[27] Beginning with North and Weingast (1989), several such commitment problems were identified and studied in authoritarian politics: the credibility of a dictator's promises to redistribute wealth (Acemoglu and Robinson 2001, 2005; Boix 2003), to reward current or future allies (North and Weingast 1989; Bueno de Mesquita et al. 2003; Acemoglu et al. 2008a; Myerson 2008; Guriev and Sonin 2009; Albertus and Menaldo, forthcoming), to moderate in the punishment of misperforming subordinates (Egorov and Sonin, forthcoming), and to refrain from interfering in politics once out of office (Debs 2009).

[28] For an account of Pinochet's consolidation of power within the junta, see also Constable and Valenzuela (1993, Chap. 3) and Spooner (1999, Chap. 4). Barros (2002) examines interactions within the junta and documents the opposition to Pinochet within the junta before and after Leigh's ouster. In his account, Pinochet never attained the absolute dominance commonly attributed to him.

A related concern emerges in the context of authoritarian control. Dictators are wary about relying on their militaries for repression with good reason. When indispensable for a regime's survival, repressive forces metamorphosize from an obedient servant into a potential political rival – regardless of any formal constraints on their prerogatives. This is what General Idi Amin Dada did in Uganda after he became indispensable in Milton Obote's suppression of opposition to his eventual consolidation of dictatorial powers. Beginning in 1965, Obote used Amin's loyal following within the armed forces to eliminate opposition, first in the parliament, then from the country's ceremonial president, and ultimately from within his own party. By the time Obote established a full-fledged dictatorship, he needed Amin and his army more than Amin needed Obote (Mutibwa 1992, 64). In 1971, Idi Amin deposed Obote in a military coup d'état and established what would become one of the most brutal dictatorships of the twentieth century.

In authoritarian politics, therefore, no independent third party can be realistically expected to enforce commitments among key actors – whether it be the dictator's promise to share power with his allies, the repressive agents' pledge to obediently serve their masters, or the dictator's allies' agreement to collectively replace him in a rebellion if he attempts to usurp power.

This concern is compounded by the looming possibility of resolving political conflicts with violence. In authoritarian politics, the option of violence is never off the table: Political conflicts may be, and indeed frequently are, resolved by brute force. For every peaceful, negotiated, or institutional resolution of a political conflict, there is a crude alternative in which brute force plays a decisive role. The expulsion of the air force representative and Pinochet's chief critic Gustavo Leigh from the Chilean junta in 1978 proceeded by a show of force: the occupation of air force headquarters and installations by the army, in violation of the decree laws that were supposed to regulate decision making within the junta.[29]

Under dictatorship, therefore, institutionalized "rules of the game" cannot be taken at face value. But this does not amount to saying that institutions are epiphenomenal – that they merely mirror the power relations among the dictator, his allies, the regime's repressive agents, and the masses excluded from power. Institutions do have the capacity to prevent unnecessary, regime-destabilizing conflicts in authoritarian politics, but only when institutionalized "rules of the game" rest on mutual advantage and respect the power of key participants. Put in the jargon of modern political science, authoritarian institutions must be self-enforcing.[30]

Although settings in which actors cannot take their agreements to be binding and may resolve conflicts violently can, in principle, be analyzed in natural

---

[29] These were Decree Laws 527 and 991; see Barros (2002, Chap. 2).

[30] Of course, the requirement that political outcomes be self-enforcing underlies most modern explanations of institutional choices in any political regime as well as transitions between regimes, as in the literature on "self-enforcing democracy" (Przeworski 1991, 2011; Boix 2003; Acemoglu and Robinson 2005; Fearon 2008). But unlike in the study of authoritarian politics, concerns about defection from key constitutional provisions can be safely assumed away in the study of democratic politics.

language, the conceptual issues involved in their analysis have been prominently articulated and rigorously examined in social-scientific applications of game theory.[31] Accordingly, I draw on these techniques and develop new formal models of authoritarian power-sharing, institutional choice, repression, and co-optation in Chapters 3 through 6. While technical exposition tends to seem inviting to "authorized personnel only," I hope this downside is outweighed by what I see as a commitment to the dictum "Trust but verify." By formalizing my arguments, I can be more explicit about my assumptions, more transparent in my reasoning, and more specific about the empirical implications of my arguments than if I developed and presented them only verbally.[32]

The two distinctive aspects of authoritarian politics – the absence of an independent authority that would enforce mutual agreements and the ever-present potential for violence – also highlight why the nature of politics fundamentally differs between dictatorships and democracies. By definition, we consider a country to be democratic only if it resolves political conflicts nonviolently, typically by elections, legislative votes, and cabinet decisions. Furthermore, a country ceases to be a democracy the moment a few key mechanisms – especially electoral rules and the respect of certain liberties – are circumvented, even if nonviolently. Thus when Cox (1997) examines how electoral rules shape voters' behavior or when Laver and Schofield (1990) study the politics of coalition governments, they can safely assume away any concerns about whether governments, parties, or voters will actually comply with constitutional provisions or the outcomes of elections. By definition, a failure to do so would turn a democracy into a dictatorship.

Students of authoritarian politics cannot make such convenient assumptions.[33] While frequent, backstabbing is only metaphorical in democracies. In dictatorships, it is literal: According to the data described earlier, about one-third of leadership changes in dictatorships involve overt violence and about two-thirds of them are nonconstitutional – they depart from official procedures or established conventions. While not all dictatorships resolve political conflicts violently all of the time, and formal rules appear to constrain some dictators at least some of the time, this may be precisely because the option of violence looms in the background, thereby precluding the need to carry it out and enforce compliance with institutional rules. To paraphrase Thomas Hobbes's famous line in this chapter's epigraph: Because authoritarian elites live without other security than their own strength, their life is nasty, brutish, and often short.

---

[31] For an introduction to game theory and formal political theory, see, e.g., McCarty and Meirowitz (2007), Morrow (1994), Myerson (1991), and Osborne (2004).

[32] For a discussion of the value and limits of game-theoretic analysis in the social sciences, see Aumann (1985), Bates et al. (1998), Geddes (2003, Chap. 5), Kreps (1990), Morton (1999), Myerson (1992, 1999), Powell (1999, Chap. 1), Rubinstein (1991), and Tsebelis (1990, Chap. 2).

[33] A similar point applies to the study of regime change; see Acemoglu and Robinson (2001, 2005), Boix (2003), and Przeworski (1991, 2005, 2011).

This sharp conceptual dichotomy between authoritarian and democratic politics guides how I collect and organize data on dictatorships. Chapter 2 defines a dictatorship to be a country that fails to elect its legislature and executive in free and competitive elections. Empirically, then, I follow Alvarez et al. (1996) and think about the differences between dictatorships and democracies as first of all in kind and only then in degree.[34] Meanwhile, the questionable relevance of political institutions under dictatorship leads me to complement data on formal institutions by other, more credible measures of their binding power. I therefore use original, detailed data on the timing and manner of entry into and exit from office for all authoritarian leaders throughout the period 1946–2008.

Chapter 2 outlines how I organize the extraordinary diversity in institutions and leadership transitions observed across dictatorships. This diversity obtains partly because dictatorship is a residual category that contains all countries that do not meet established criteria for democracy and partly because of dictatorship's richer and longer pedigree. I also argue that in our attempts to organize authoritarian politics, we should abandon the prevailing practice of classifying dictatorships into a few ideal types or according to their prominent descriptive features. That approach is flawed for several reasons: It collapses multiple and distinct conceptual dimensions of authoritarian politics into a single typology; it results in categories that are neither mutually exclusive nor collectively exhaustive; and it requires difficult classification judgments that weigh incommensurable aspects of authoritarian politics. These flaws compromise the validity and reliability of empirical inferences based on such data. I propose an alternative approach, one that explicitly identifies the conceptual dimensions of authoritarian politics being measured and then develops appropriate scales for each dimension.

1.3 PLAN OF THE BOOK

The remainder of this book begins with Chapter 2, in which I define what I mean by *dictatorship* and organize the extraordinary heterogeneity in institutions and leaders in authoritarian politics. I clarify why I essentially follow Alvarez et al.'s (1996) procedural and minimalist approach to the classification of regime types, and I illustrate the flaws of existing approaches to the classification of dictatorships with a discussion of Geddes's (1999b) typology of dictatorships.

I also present the data used throughout this book, which cover the period 1946–2008 and are situated at three levels of observation: the country level, the ruling-coalition level, and the leader level. At the country level, I measure four dimensions of the political organization of dictatorships: military involvement in politics, restrictions on political parties, legislative selection, and executive selection. I also introduce a new measure of authoritarian stability, which I

---

[34] I am paraphrasing Elkins's (2000, 293) restatement of the position of Alvarez et al. (1996).

TABLE 1.1. *An Outline of the Outcomes Explained in This Book*

Political Conflict	Outcomes Explained		Book Chapter
	Political Institutions	Leadership Change	
Authoritarian power-sharing	Personality cults, personnel rotation	Tenure duration, coups d'état versus natural exits from office	Chapter 3
	High-level deliberative and decision-making bodies within parties and legislatures, elections	Ruling-coalition survival, constitutional versus nonconstitutional leadership transitions	Chapter 4
Authoritarian control	Political control over militaries	Military intervention and government	Chapter 5
	Internal organization of regime-sanctioned parties	Ruling-coalition survival	Chapter 6

call a *ruling-coalition spell*. Finally, I describe my data on leadership changes across dictatorships, which record the timing and manner of dictators' entry into and exit from office, their institutional origin and political affiliation prior to assuming office, as well as the use of violence and the participation of the military in these events.

The core of this book consists of Chapters 3 through 6. Table 1.1 summarizes the conceptual organization as well as the empirical evidence presented. As the discussion throughout this introductory chapter indicates, each chapter addresses a different facet of authoritarian politics: the emergence of personal autocracy, the role of institutions and collective-action problems in authoritarian power-sharing, the origins of military dictatorships, and the contribution of regime parties to authoritarian stability. Each is, therefore, sufficiently theoretically and empirically self-contained to be read à la carte; however, doing so may miss the interconnectedness between the problems of authoritarian power-sharing and control that this introductory chapter highlights.

Chapter 7 discusses, the implications of my arguments for several prominent policy questions. I begin by explaining why so many dictators preside over policy disasters. I next clarify why so few dictatorships depersonalize political authority, solve succession crises, and maintain viable institutions of collective leadership. I conclude by discussing why the Middle East's authoritarian past casts a long shadow over its prospects for democracy after the so-called Arab Spring.

2

The World of Authoritarian Politics

[We] have next to consider how many forms of government there are, and what they are.... Tyranny is a kind of monarchy which has in view the interest of the monarch only; oligarchy has in view the interest of the wealthy; democracy of the needy. None of them the common good of all.

Aristotle, *Politics*, Book 3

Happy families are all alike; each unhappy family is unhappy in its own way.

Tolstoy, *Anna Karenina*

The President lives here [at the Chapultepec Castle], but the man who gives orders lives across the street.

A wisecrack during the Maximato (1928–1934)[1]

Dictatorships come in many shapes and sizes. For seventy years, Mexican leaders came from only one party, the Institutional Revolutionary Party (PRI), but nevertheless left office every six years after regular, albeit flawed, elections. Meanwhile, in Argentina, a junta of generals designed elaborate rules about how to share power, only to abandon them after they took office in 1976, governing for the next seven years in quick succession and by crude repression. And in North Korea, a dynasty of fathers and sons has ruled for decades, each dying on the throne after maintaining a personality cult reminiscent of premodern despotism.[2] In short, dictatorships come with a variety of institutions, leaders, and outcomes: They may have legislatures, parties, and even elections; they exist in some of the poorest but also some of the wealthiest countries around the world; and their leaders may wear a crown or a military uniform and stay in office for days or decades.

This chapter organizes this extraordinary political diversity across dictatorships. How to do so is far from obvious for at least two reasons. First,

---

[1] See Krauze (1997, 430).
[2] On Mexico, see Krauze (1997) and Magaloni (2006); on Argentina, see Rock (1987) and Remmer (1989); and on North Korea, see Demick (2009) and Oh and Hassig (2000).

19

dictatorship is a residual category that contains all countries that do not meet established criteria for democracy. At a minimum, such criteria require that free, fair, and competitive elections determine the composition of the legislature and – often indirectly – the executive. More demanding criteria may require that governments respect certain civil liberties – such as the freedom of religion (Schmitter and Karl 1991; Zakaria 1997) – or that the incumbent government and the opposition alternate in power at least once after the first seemingly free election (Huntington 1993; Przeworski et al. 2000; Cheibub et al. 2010). Failure to satisfy any of these criteria may brand a country as a dictatorship.

The understandable result is an exceptionally diverse set of polities, unified perhaps only by the failure to meet one or more criteria for democracy. To paraphrase Tolstoy, whereas democracies are all alike, each dictatorship may be undemocratic in its own way.[3]

The second challenge in organizing the world of authoritarian politics stems from the questionable relevance of formal institutions under dictatorship. As discussed in Chapter 1, authoritarian politics takes place under distinctively dismal conditions. Authoritarian elites cannot rely on an independent authority to enforce their agreements, and violence is the ultimate arbiter of political conflicts. Hence *whether* and *which* institutions actually matter for the conduct of authoritarian politics is far from apparent and neither is *who* matters. As the epigraph at the beginning of this chapter about Plutarco Calles's continuing influence after he resigned from the Mexican presidency highlights, under dictatorship, the man who gives orders may not reside in the presidential palace but rather across the street from it.[4]

Before moving forward with the substantive arguments in this book, therefore, it is essential to precisely define what I mean by dictatorship and to organize the extraordinary heterogeneity in institutions and leaders across dictatorships. As I clarify in this chapter, I essentially follow Alvarez et al.'s (1996) procedural and minimalist approach to the classification of regime types. After excluding any periods of foreign occupation, the collapse of state authority, or civil war, I say that a country is a dictatorship if it fails to elect its legislature and executive in free and competitive elections. This definition implies a sharp dichotomy between authoritarian and democratic politics. The arguments in this chapter clarify why the difference between dictatorship and democracy is best thought of first as one of kind and only then as one of degree.

The data used throughout this book are situated at three levels of observation: the country level, the ruling-coalition level, and the leader level. In devising

---

[3] Collier and Levitsky (1997) discuss how the creation of diminished subtypes of democracy provides better differentiation among the various ways in which a polity may fail to satisfy the criteria for democracy. Przeworski et al. (2000) and Cheibub et al. (2010) defend the minimalist conception of democracy adopted herein.

[4] Plutarco Elías Calles stepped down from the Mexican presidency in 1928 but nevertheless overshadowed his three successors; see Krauze (1997, 430).

the categories that organize these data, I attempt to overcome several important limitations of existing approaches to classifying dictatorships. Most existing typologies fail to recognize that they implicitly collapse multiple, distinct conceptual dimensions of authoritarian politics into a single typology. This is a direct consequence of the prevailing practice of classifying dictatorships into a few ideal types, as in the case of a "totalitarian" dictatorship, or according to their prominent descriptive features, as in the case of a "bureaucratic authoritarian" regime. The resulting categories are typically neither mutually exclusive nor collectively exhaustive, and they require difficult classification judgments that weigh incommensurable aspects of authoritarian politics, thereby compromising the validity and reliability of empirical inferences based on them. The prevailing usage of Geddes's typology of personalist, military, and single-party dictatorships, which I discuss in this chapter, illustrates these shortcomings.

Rather than classifying dictatorships into ideal types or according to their prominent descriptive features, we should instead explicitly identify the conceptual dimensions of authoritarian politics that we want to measure and then develop appropriate scales or typologies for each one. At the country level, I use four such dimensions: military involvement in politics, restrictions on political parties, legislative selection, and executive selection. Their choice is guided by the theoretical arguments developed throughout this book. As we shall see in this chapter, their joint distribution provides a more representative summary of the immense institutional heterogeneity across dictatorships than a typology based on a few ideal types or prominent descriptive features.

Another major challenge in organizing authoritarian politics is the questionable relevance of formal institutions in dictatorships. Because dictatorships lack an independent authority that would enforce compliance with institutionalized "rules of the game," the political significance of institutions that ostensibly govern authoritarian politics cannot be taken at face value. This is why I collected detailed data on leadership change across dictatorships. How dictators actually assume and lose power speaks louder than the rules that presumably regulate it.

As in the case of authoritarian political institutions, the conceptual organization of my data on authoritarian leadership change is guided by the empirical implications of theoretical arguments in subsequent chapters. For all dictators who held power for at least one day between 1946 and 2008, I record the timing and manner of their entry into and exit from office, as well as the use of violence and the participation of the military in these events.

Finally, I introduce a new measure of authoritarian stability, which I refer to as a *ruling-coalition spell*. It consists of an uninterrupted succession in office of politically affiliated authoritarian leaders – typically from the same government, party, family, or military junta – and is based on my data on the institutional origin of authoritarian leaders and their political affiliation prior to assuming office. Some of my claims about the effect of institutions on the stability and longevity of authoritarian rule, as well as many claims in the existing literature, are evaluated most appropriately at this level of observation. Thus my claim in Chapter 6 that regime-sanctioned political parties serve as effective tools of authoritarian co-optation does not pertain to the durability of dictatorship as a regime type or to the survival of individual dictators but rather to the continuity in power of leaders from the same political coalition – as in the case of Mexico under the PRI. By using data on ruling-coalition spells, I avoid confounding these distinct levels of analysis.

All data codebooks and estimation code used throughout this book are available at a dedicated page on my Web site.[5]

2.1 WHAT COUNTS AS A DICTATORSHIP?

Although far from extinct, dictatorships have been declining both in number and as a proportion of all regimes since the early 1970s. As we will soon see, transitions to democracy have in spite of a few hiccups outnumbered democratic breakdowns during the last three decades.[6] Especially since the end of the Cold War, surviving dictatorships have at least nominally come to resemble democracies in terms of their formal institutions (Diamond 2002; Levitsky and Way 2002; Schedler 2006). The few that defy this trend, especially the likes of North Korea or Saudi Arabia, appear to be stuck in an atavistic state, anachronistic and at odds with the rest of the world.

In short, few contemporary dictatorships admit that they are just that. If we were to trust dictators' declarations about their regimes, most of them would be democracies. According to President Aleksandr Lukashenko, present-day Belarus has had "so much so-called democracy that it has made [Belorussians] nauseated."[7] Even more often, contemporary dictatorships would be an improvement on democracy: Muammar Qaddafi's Libyan Jamahiriya was a committee-governed "direct democracy," solving the contradictions inherent in capitalism and communism (Mattes 2008, 59); Vladimir Putin's Russia is a "sovereign democracy," ensuring that the country is governed not by Western meddlers but rather by the Russian nation; and even China professes to be "the people's *democratic* dictatorship."[8]

It is therefore essential to explicitly state how we recognize a dictatorship when we see it. I follow Przeworski et al. (2000), Boix (2003), and Cheibub et al. (2010) in defining a *dictatorship* as an independent country that fails to satisfy at least one of the following two criteria for democracy: (1) free and competitive legislative elections and (2) an executive that is elected either directly in free and competitive presidential elections or indirectly by a legislature in parliamentary systems. Throughout the book, I use the terms *dictatorship* and *authoritarian*

---

[5] See https://netfiles.uiuc.edu/msvolik/www/.

[6] See also Merkel (2010); Diamond (2008) and Puddington (2008) have a more pessimistic view about the future of democracy.

[7] On Lukashenko's statement, see "Belarus Leader Blames Excess of Democracy for Bombing," *The New York Times*, 21 April 2011.

[8] On "sovereign democracy," see Masha Lipman, "Putin's 'Sovereign Democracy'," *The Washington Post*, 15 July 2006.

regime interchangeably and refer to the heads of these regimes' governments as simply *dictators* or *authoritarian leaders*, regardless of their formal title.[9]

By identifying the allocation of executive and legislative powers by competitive elections as the principal difference between dictatorships and democracies, I am following Schumpeter's (1950) and Dahl's (1971) procedural approach to the classification of regime types and its minimalist operationalization by Alvarez et al. (1996) and Boix (2003).[10] A notable – and controversial – feature of the latter is the sharp dichotomy that it draws between dictatorship and democracy. Before anything else, regimes are either democracies or dictatorships. By contrast, a large literature argues that rather than being a dichotomy, differences between dictatorships and democracies are better thought of as falling along a continuum or a larger number of discrete categories. The Polity Scale (Marshall and Jaggers 2008) is an example of the former; the proliferating categories of "authoritarianism with adjectives," such as competitive (Levitsky and Way 2002, 2010), electoral (Schedler 2006), or semi-authoritarianism (Ottaway 2003), exemplify the latter (see also Diamond 2002).

The arguments in Chapter 1 highlight how the conduct of politics fundamentally differs between dictatorships and democracies. The two distinctive features of authoritarian politics introduced in the preceding chapter – that is, the absence of an independent authority that would enforce mutual agreements and the ever-present potential for violence – imply a sharp divergence between authoritarian and democratic politics. Once free and competitive elections no longer decide who holds power, repression and violence substitute for platforms and electoral rules. Even in dictatorships with elections, therefore, genuine competition for power takes place elsewhere, with brute force rather than electoral rules deciding who gets to hold power. In Vladimir Putin's Russia, for instance, the real struggle for power seems to be taking place among competing factions of *siloviki* – former KGB officers within the government – with selective prosecutions of leading government officials serving as bargaining chips.[11] Thus although an incumbent's eventual margin of victory may be the subject of intense debates in many dictatorships with elections, *who* is going to win is a forgone conclusion.

Hence, however descriptively accurate, any emphasis on the competitive or electoral features of many dictatorships should not lead us to think of these regimes as diminished, less perfect forms of democracy. Doing so amounts to treating a pregnancy as just a few extra inches of waistline. Throughout this

[9] See Gandhi (2008, Chap. 1) for an excellent discussion of the historical and contemporary usage of the term *dictatorship*; see also Bobbio (1989).

[10] A procedural view of democracy classifies regime types according to how they operate; by contrast, a substantive view also considers the outcomes that regimes produce (Dahl 1971). A minimalist approach emphasizes the advantages of a few transparent criteria in the measurement of regime type (Alvarez et al. 1996).

[11] See, e.g., Robert Amsterdam, "The Real Power Struggle," *The New York Times*, 2 December 2008.

book, the difference between dictatorship and democracy is decidedly one of kind before it is one of degree.[12]

My empirical strategy for identifying dictatorships and democracies therefore also conceives of the differences between the two regime types as a dichotomy. Nevertheless, I depart from Przeworski et al. (2000), Boix (2003), and Cheibub et al. (2010) in two ways. First, I do not require that the incumbent and the opposition alternate in power before a country is considered democratic. Przeworski et al. (2000, 23–30) adopt such an alternation criterion because they suspect that in some of the countries that hold seemingly free and fair elections, the government would not step down if the opposition actually won. The latter, however, is a quality that is fundamentally unknowable about any government that has been reelected, even if the same or another incumbent already gave up power after losing an election in the past. All that we learn from any single democratic alternation is that a particular government was willing to step down after it lost a particular election.[13] Hugo Chávez, for instance, managed to turn Venezuela into a dictatorship by suppressing the press, intimidating opposition, and manipulating electoral laws – even though he was preceded in office by no fewer than eight democratically elected presidents.[14] Therefore, I focus on whether any single legislative or executive election was free and competitive when adjudicating whether a country is a dictatorship or a democracy.[15]

---

[12] I am borrowing Elkins's (2000, 293) sharp restatement of Alvarez et al.'s (1996) position. The empirical dichotomy between dictatorship and democracy is matched by how the discipline theorizes about regime change: Transitions to democracy as well as reversals to dictatorship are conceived of as fundamental political transformations rather than gradual shifts along a dictatorship-democracy continuum.

[13] Furthermore, Przeworski et al. (2000) apply the alternation criterion retroactively – once alternation occurred, they consider a country democratic even during the period that preceded alternation in power, as long as it appears to have held free and fair elections. This contradicts the stated purpose of the alternation criterion – to use an *observable* indicator to ascertain whether a government is in fact willing to step down if it loses an election. However, a government's willingness to step down after a lost election in year t is not an observable indicator of its willingness to step down in year $t - 1$ or in year $t + 1$. For instance, with the exception of an eleven-month period between 1993 and 1994, the Liberal Democratic Party (and its premerger predecessors) ruled Japan from its first post–World War II election in 1946 until its defeat in the 2009 election. A retroactive application of the alternation criterion would then consider Japan to be democratic starting in 1946, even though recent findings raise questions about the fairness of Japanese elections during the early post–World War II period (see, e.g., Tim Weiner, "C.I.A. Spent Millions to Support Japanese Right in 50's and 60's," *The New York Times*, 9 October 1994). The approach in this book ultimately relies on a judgment call about which of the twenty-three elections that preceded the Liberal Democratic Party's electoral defeat in 2009 were free and competitive. On the alternation criterion, see also Cheibub et al. (2010).

[14] See, e.g., "A Coup against the Constitution," *The Economist*, 1 January 2011.

[15] See the codebook for further details. The effective differences between my data and those coded by Przeworski et al. (2000), Boix (2003), and Cheibub et al. (2010) are minimal. However, according to my coding, for instance, Botswana has been a democracy since its independence in 1966.

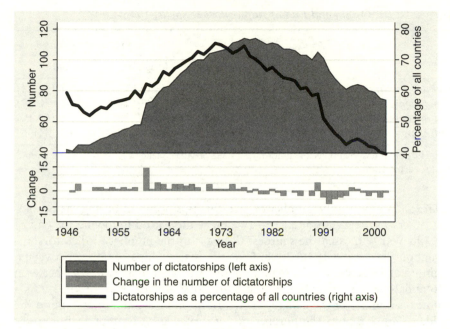

FIGURE 2.1. The number and change in the number of dictatorships, 1946–2008.

In a second departure from Przeworski et al. (2000), Boix (2003), and Cheibub et al. (2010), I exclude from my data on dictatorships any periods of foreign occupation, the collapse of state authority, or a major civil war. Although such periods trivially fail to satisfy the criteria for democracy, polities in such circumstances cannot be meaningfully considered to be authoritarian. Bosnia between 1992 and 1995 was neither a democracy nor a dictatorship – it was at civil war. Periods like this one are best characterized by the lack of *any* sovereign political authority.[16] I identify them using the Polity IV data (Marshall and Jaggers 2008), the Correlates of War (Sarkees 2000), and the UCDP/PRIO Armed Conflict Dataset (Gleditsch et al. 2002; Themnér and Wallensteen 2011).[17]

The resulting data cover the period 1946–2008 and contain 4,696 authoritarian country-years. As shown in Figure 2.1, between 41 and 114 dictatorships exist in any given year during this period.[18] The number of dictatorships generally grew from 1946 to the late 1970s and declined thereafter. In proportional terms, however, the share of dictatorships among all countries already began to decline at the beginning of the 1970s. As the lower part of Figure 2.1 illustrates,

[16] Previous large-N research on dictatorships has ignored such periods. This risks conflating the instability that typically accompanies foreign occupations, the collapse of state authority, or civil wars with authoritarian politics.

[17] This parallels the category of anarchy in Magaloni and Kricheli (2010). See the codebook for further details.

[18] These numbers correspond to 1947 and 1977/1979, respectively.

TABLE 2.1. *The Origin and End of Authoritarian Spells, 1946–2008*

	Frequency (%)	
	Origin	End
Breakdown of/transition to democracy	58 (29.15)	97 (48.74)
Independence	72 (36.18)	11 (0.50)
Lack of sovereign authority	34 (17.09)	38 (19.10)
Continuance from before 1946 to after 2008	35 (17.58)	63 (31.66)

Note: The unit of observation is an authoritarian spell. See the codebook for details about coding rules for each category.

the largest increase in the number of dictatorships occurred during the decolonization era of the 1950s and 1960s, whereas the period following the end of the Cold War witnessed the sharpest decrease in the number of dictatorships throughout the period 1946–2008. Overall, dictatorships comprise between a minimum of 39 percent and a maximum of 75 percent of all countries between 1946 and 2008, corresponding to the years 2008 and 1972, respectively. As a graphical summary of the geographic distribution of dictatorships around the world, Figure 2.2 plots the number of authoritarian years that each country contributes to the data throughout the period 1946–2008.

I refer to an uninterrupted period of dictatorship in a particular country as an *authoritarian spell*. The countries in the data have experienced between one and four authoritarian spells throughout the period 1946–2008. As summarized in Table 2.1, most authoritarian spells originate in newly independent countries (i.e., 36 percent) and after democratic breakdowns (i.e., 29 percent); this was the case of Cambodia in 1953 and Chile in 1973, respectively. The remaining 33 percent of authoritarian spells either began prior to 1946 (e.g., the Soviet Union) or emerged after a period of foreign occupation, collapse of state authority, or civil war (e.g., Mao's China in 1949).

On the other hand, the largest number of authoritarian spells – about one half – end in a transition to democracy. A further 19 percent end as a result of foreign occupation, the collapse of state authority, or civil war; a negligible number end after a country ceases to exist. As of 2008, there were 63 (i.e., 32 percent) surviving authoritarian spells. Brazil in 1985, Afghanistan in 2001, Yugoslavia in 1991, and Cuba in 2008 are respective examples of these categories. The origin and end of all 199 authoritarian spells in the data are listed in the appendix at the end of this chapter.

2.2 MAKING SENSE OF INSTITUTIONAL HETEROGENEITY UNDER DICTATORSHIP

As is apparent in Figure 2.2, any attempt to explain authoritarian politics must confront its extraordinary scope and diversity. A major source of this diversity is that dictatorship is a residual or negative category defined in the

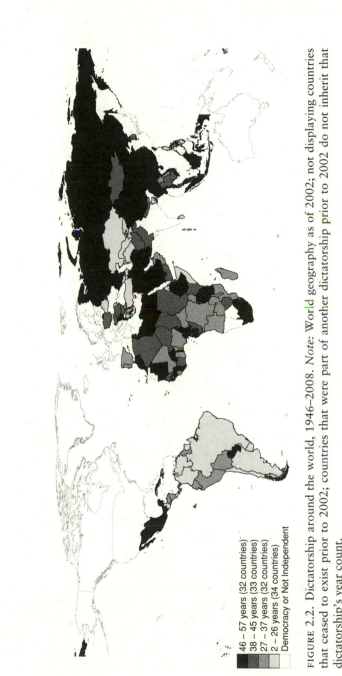

FIGURE 2.2. Dictatorship around the world, 1946–2008. *Note:* World geography as of 2002; not displaying countries that ceased to exist prior to 2002; countries that were part of another dictatorship prior to 2002 do not inherit that dictatorship's year count.

46 – 57 years (32 countries)
38 – 45 years (33 countries)
27 – 37 years (32 countries)
2 – 26 years (34 countries)
Democracy or Not Independent

first place by what democracy is not. This book, as well as virtually all research on authoritarian politics, first establishes a set of criteria that defines what a democracy *is* and then considers any country that fails to satisfy those criteria to be a dictatorship.

This practice places essentially no limit on the institutional heterogeneity among dictatorships. Dictatorships thus occur in countries whose institutions at least nominally mirror standard democratic institutions – and, as we just saw, many dictatorships in fact do emerge after democratic breakdowns – as well as in countries with a highly idiosyncratic or traditional institutional makeup. Iran, with its Council of Guardians and Assembly of Experts, is an example of the former; Saudi Arabia, with its quasifeudal system of overlapping dynastic and religious authorities, is an example of the latter.[19] As Barbara Geddes concluded, "different kinds of authoritarianism differ from each other as much as they differ from democracy" (1999b, 121).

Typologies that attempt to impose order on this heterogeneity have a long pedigree in political science. When restricted to dictatorships, Aristotle distinguished between the government of one and a few, Montesquieu between despotic and monarchical regimes, and Machiavelli between absolute and limited princes – all of which actually parallel the power-sharing equilibria of established and contested autocracy that I develop in Chapter 3.

In contemporary political science, the heterogeneity of authoritarian politics – as well as prevailing global trends – have been matched by a correspondingly diverse and evolving set of typologies. Dictatorships used to be totalitarian (Arendt 1951; Friedrich and Brzezinski 1965), authoritarian (Linz 1975), and bureaucratic authoritarian (O'Donnell 1973); one-party (Huntington 1970) and military (Nordlinger 1977; Perlmutter 1977); as well as sultanistic (Linz and Chehabi 1998), patrimonial (Weber 1964), and neopatrimonial (Jackson and Rosberg 1982; Snyder 1992; Bratton and Van de Walle 1997) – all with further variations and subcategories.[20] The proliferation of elections after the end of the Cold War has since shifted the discipline's attention to competitive (Levitsky and Way 2002, 2010), electoral (Diamond 2002; Schedler 2006), and semi-authoritarian regimes (Ottaway 2003). Most recently and comprehensively, Geddes (1999b) distinguishes among personalist, military, and single-party dictatorships; Gandhi (2008) among civilian, military, and monarchical dictatorships; and Magaloni and Kricheli (2010) among military, monarchic, single-party, and dominant-party authoritarian regimes.

Building on this scholarship, I devise and collect my own data on the political organization of dictatorships. In doing so, I attempt to overcome several important limitations of existing typologies.

A major flaw of most existing typologies is the practice of classifying dictatorships into ideal types or according to several prominent, descriptive features. This approach typically collapses *multiple, conceptually distinct* dimensions of

---

[19] See Buchta (2000) on Iran and Herb (1999) on Saudi Arabia.
[20] See Chaps. 1 and 2 in Brooker (2000) for a review of these concepts.

authoritarian politics onto a single typology. The "types" of dictatorship that emerge, in turn, (1) *are neither mutually exclusive nor collectively exhaustive* and (2) *require difficult classification judgments that weigh incommensurable aspects of authoritarian politics*. These consequences compromise the validity and reliability of these typologies, limiting their appropriateness as general-purpose typologies of dictatorships.

As an illustration of these limitations, consider Geddes's (1999b) classification of dictatorships into personalist, military, and single-party types – arguably the most frequently used typology in empirical research on authoritarian politics.[21] In a seminal article, Geddes (1999b) examined the disparate incentives that elites in the three pure types of dictatorship face when confronted with the possibility of a regime breakdown, examined the different means by which those regimes transition to democracy, and made her data publicly available.[22] The wave of new scholarship on authoritarian politics that builds on Geddes's arguments and data collection is evidence of the catalyzing effect that the availability of comprehensive, cross-sectional time-series data can have on comparative political research.[23]

Unfortunately, the prevailing usage of Geddes's typology has largely disregarded her warning against using the categories of personalist, military, and single-party dictatorships as descriptive of formal institutional characteristics; overlooked the substantial overlap among these categories; and ignored the rich set of indicators that Geddes employed when classifying dictatorships into the three pure types and their hybrids (see Geddes 2003, chap. 2). The resulting practice belies the immense institutional heterogeneity across dictatorships and fails to recognize that the categories of personalist, military, and single-party dictatorship refer to multiple, conceptually distinct dimensions of authoritarian politics.

Consider the difference between military and single-party dictatorships: The main feature of the former is that it is run by professional soldiers; a key characteristic of the latter is that it establishes and governs through a single political party (Geddes 1999b, 121). Yet these two pure types reflect different conceptual dimensions of the political organization of dictatorships. The first is an extreme degree of *military involvement in politics*; the second is a specific form of a *restriction on political parties*. Hence the former conceptual dimension may range from a purely civilian government (e.g., Czechoslovakia under Communist rule, 1948–1989) to indirect and direct military involvement in politics (e.g., Panama under Noriega, 1983–1989, and Argentina under the Junta, 1976–1983, respectively). Meanwhile, restrictions on party organization

---

[21] As of December 2011, Geddes's original 1999 conference paper had been cited almost 500 times according to Google Scholar. Her related papers and book chapters have several additional hundreds of citations.

[22] See also Geddes (1999a) and Chap. 2 in Geddes (2003).

[23] See, for instance, Brownlee (2009), Escribà-Folch and Wright (2008), Frantz (2007), Frantz and Ezrow (2009, 2011), Lai and Slater (2006), Ulfelder (2005), Weeks (2008), and Wright (2008a, 2008b).

can range from a complete ban on political parties (e.g., Chile under Augusto Pinochet's military dictatorship, 1973–1987) to a single government-sanctioned party (typical for communist countries) to only minor restrictions on party organization (e.g., Mexico under the PRI, especially 1946–2000).

The category of personalist dictatorship reflects high values of at least two other distinct conceptual dimensions of the political organization of dictatorships. The first is the *concentration of power* in the hands of the dictator. Although it is rare, power in some dictatorships may be dispersed across individuals, institutions, and levels of government, as it was in Mexico toward the end of the PRI's rule. On the other hand, Joseph Stalin's and Mao Zedong's despotic rule exemplifies the upper limits on the power that a single individual can acquire. Thus they correspond to the other extreme of this conceptual dimension.

Yet in other cases, the category of personalist dictatorship also appears to reflect a high level of another conceptual dimension: the *personalization of political interactions*.[24] This facet of personalism is sometimes characterized as neopatrimonial rule (Jackson and Rosberg 1982; Snyder 1992; Bratton and Van de Walle 1997; Brownlee 2002) or sultanism (Linz and Chehabi 1998). When Jackson and Rosberg (1982), Bratton and Van de Walle (1997), and Linz and Chehabi (1998) write of personalism, they refer to polities in which key political interactions are based on personal ties and traditional authority rather than formal institutions and rules. Whereas a high concentration of power in the hands of a dictator allows him to supersede many formal rules and institutions, the understanding of personalism as a high degree of concentration of power is distinct from one that emphasizes the personal nature of political interactions. Although both Stalin and Mao acquired immense amounts of power, they relied heavily on impersonal, formal rules, parties, and the bureaucracy in order to govern.[25]

As a consequence of this conceptual inconsistency, the categories of personalist, military, and single-party dictatorship are neither mutually exclusive nor collectively exhaustive. As an example of this difficulty, consider the case of Syria: During Hafez al-Asad's thirty-year rule, the Syrian regime ruled via a single party, the Baath Party.[26] Yet at the same time, key posts in the government and security apparatus were held by military officers who supported Asad's takeover of the Baath Party in 1970. Hence the Syrian regime between 1970 and 2000 was ruled by military officers and maintained a single ruling party as well. Meanwhile, by the time of his death in 2000, Hafez al-Asad was an undisputed leader of the Syrian government, military, and Baath Party

[24] See Geddes (1999b, 121–2).

[25] On the operation of Stalin's ruling circle, see Khlevniuk (2009) and Gorlizki and Khlevniuk (2004); on Mao, see MacFarquhar (1997a) and MacFarquhar and Schoenhals (2006).

[26] Nominally, Syria has allowed for parties other than the Baath Party, but they must participate in the National Progressive Front, which is dominated by the Baath Party; see, e.g., Hinnebusch (2002, Chap. 4). I code as a "single-party" any dictatorship that nominally allows for multiple parties but requires that these operate under the leadership of a single party or as a single front.

(Hinnebusch 2002, Chap. 4) and built up a personality cult inspired in its aesthetic by the Soviet Union under Stalin (Wedeen 1999). As this case illustrates, the simultaneous establishment of a single-party, military involvement in politics and a high concentration of power in a dictator's hands are neither logically nor empirically exclusive.[27]

Meanwhile, some dictatorships do not fit any of the three categories and are missing from Geddes's original data. This is especially the case for monarchies (e.g., Saudi Arabia) or regimes that simply do not experience military interventions, do not have a single party, and are not governed by a leader who managed to monopolize power (e.g., contemporary Iran). Geddes's typology thus fails to be collectively exhaustive.

Another difficulty that arises in Geddes's typology is that classification judgments must weigh conceptually incommensurable aspects of authoritarian politics. This is evident in the difficult judgments that must be made in classifying regimes that share the features of several of the three pure types (see, e.g., Geddes 1999a, 20–3). It is especially pronounced in judging whether a regime is personalist: Personalist leaders emerge in dictatorships governed by the military (e.g., Augusto Pinochet in Chile, 1973–1990), by a single party (e.g., Joseph Stalin in the Soviet Union, 1924–1953), and sometimes by both (e.g., Hafez al-Asad in Syria, 1970–2000). Because personalist dictators rarely banish their military or party from government after they consolidate power, it is particularly difficult to objectively ascertain the occurrence and timing of a transition from a military or single-party dictatorship to a personalist one – primarily because each of the three types measures a different aspect of authoritarian politics.[28]

These difficulties – the lack of exclusiveness or exhaustiveness across categories and the use of categories that weigh conceptually incommensurable aspects of authoritarian politics – limit the validity and reliability of data based on Geddes's typology as well as the type of inferences that can be drawn from it. If, for instance, we are interested in the role of single parties in dictatorships, the relevant comparison groups are not military or personalist dictatorships but rather those dictatorships that do not restrict partisan organization to a single party. That group is best ordered by differentiating between regimes that ban parties entirely and those that allow for multiple parties. The two subsets may function very differently and therefore compare to single-party regimes in different, possibly opposing, ways. We entirely miss such differences when we instead use military and personalist dictatorships as a comparison

---

[27] Geddes (1999a) recognizes this difficulty when she creates hybrid regime types (see also Hadenius and Teorell 2007), which comprise 25 percent of her data. Nevertheless, in empirical work that relies on Geddes's typology, these hybrids have often been subsumed under one of the pure types, treated as a separate hybrid category, or ignored.

[28] Slater (2003) discusses such transitions within parties and militaries. He uses the terms *machine* and *junta* to describe an oligarchic balance of power within the two institutions and the terms *bossism* and *strongman* to describe personalization of power within parties and militaries, respectively.

TABLE 2.2. *Restrictions on Political Parties and Military Involvement in Authoritarian Politics, 1946–2008*

Military Involvement in Politics	Restrictions on Political Parties
None	Parties banned
Indirect	Single party
Personal	Multiple parties
Corporate	

Note: See the codebook for details about coding rules for each category.

group. Therefore, the use of categories that weigh conceptually incommensurable aspects of authoritarian politics results in poorly formed comparison groups and potentially flawed inferences.

These limitations are not confined to Geddes's typology – I used it only as an illustrative example. Most typologies that classify dictatorships into a few ideal types or according to prominent descriptive features collapse multiple, conceptually distinct dimensions of authoritarian politics onto a single typology. They are, in turn, neither mutually exclusive nor collectively exhaustive and often ask for difficult classification judgments that weigh incommensurable aspects of authoritarian politics. The resulting categories have limited validity, reliability, and use as conceptually appropriate comparison groups.

2.3   THIS BOOK'S APPROACH TO POLITICAL ORGANIZATION OF DICTATORSHIPS

As a foundation for the empirical work in this book, I devised and collected data on the political organization of dictatorships that attempt to overcome the limitations of existing typologies. Rather than classifying dictatorships into ideal types or according to their prominent descriptive features, I first identified the conceptual dimensions of authoritarian politics that I want to measure and then developed an appropriate scale for each dimension. The choice of dimensions is guided by the key aspects of the political organization of dictatorships that I explain throughout this book.

At the country level, I measure four conceptual dimensions: *military involvement in politics*, *restrictions on political parties*, *legislative selection*, and *executive selection*. Tables 2.2 and 2.3 summarize the categories used in their measurement.

When measuring military involvement in authoritarian politics, I distinguish among *none*, *indirect*, *personal*, and *corporate* military involvement. As outlined in the discussion of Geddes's typology, some dictatorships experience no military involvement in politics (or a purely civilian government), whereas, in others, the military indirectly affects politics, even if the formal head of the government is a civilian. I consider military involvement in authoritarian

TABLE 2.3. *Legislative and Executive Selection in Dictatorships, 1946–2008*

Concentration of Power	
Legislative	Executive
None	Unelected
Unelected or appointed legislature	One party or candidate
One party or candidate per seat	Selected by a small, unelected body
Largest party controls more than 75% of seats	Elected by more than 75% of the vote
Largest party controls less than 75% of seats	Elected by less than 75% of the vote
Nonpartisan legislature	

Note: See the codebook for details about coding rules for each category.

politics to be direct when the head of the government is a professional soldier who entered office in a coup d'état with overt military involvement, after a civil war, or was elected as the candidate of a military junta.[29]

I further distinguish between two forms of direct military involvement: corporate and personal. Military involvement is corporate if the political influence of the military within the government has been institutionalized by establishing a decision-making body or enacting a policy that formally incorporates the military into customarily civilian areas of the government (such as education or the management of the economy); otherwise, military involvement is personal. The corporate and personal forms of direct military involvement distinguish between instances in which the military participates in the government as an institution and those in which a single or a few individuals who happen to be professional soldiers gain political preeminence. The Chilean Junta Militar de Gobierno under Pinochet (1973–1990) is an example of the former; the latter occurred in the case of Franco's tenure in office in Spain (1939–1975).[30]

When measuring restrictions on political parties, I distinguish among authoritarian regimes that allow for *none, single,* and *multiple* parties.[31] Examples of each category were provided in the discussion of Geddes's typology of dictatorships.

Figures 2.3 and 2.4 summarize the pattern of military involvement and restrictions on political parties in dictatorships throughout the period 1946–2008. The two vertical axes display the cumulative proportion across individual categories by year; the right vertical axis displays the cumulative proportion across the categories of each dimension in the opposite direction. Figure 2.3 shows that, in 1970, about 65 percent of all dictatorships were governed by

[29] Thus, the election of a professional soldier into office (e.g., Juan Perón's third term, 1973–1974) does not alone constitute direct military involvement. However, the election of Julio Rivera, who was the president of El Salvador between 1962 and 1967 does because he was the uncontested candidate of the military junta in the presidential election.

[30] See Barros (2002) on the operation of the Chilean junta and Payne (1987) on Franco's government.

[31] Gandhi (2008) and Cheibub et al. (2010) use a similar measure of restrictions on political parties.

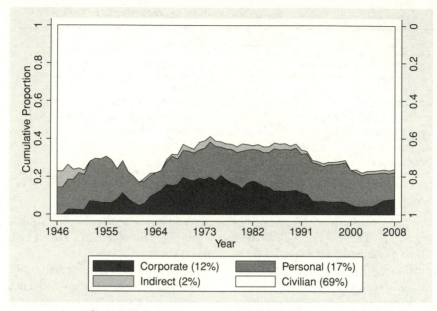

FIGURE 2.3. Military involvement in authoritarian politics, 1946–2008. *Note:* Overall
distribution of individual categories in parentheses.

civilians; the military governed indirectly through civilian figureheads in 2 percent of all dictatorships; and the remaining 33 percent were governed directly
by the military. Among the latter, the military's involvement was roughly split
between personal and corporate involvement. Figure 2.4 shows that in the same
year, about 18 percent of all dictatorships banned political parties, 43 percent
maintained a single political party, and the remaining 39 percent allowed multiple parties to exist.

The joint distribution of restrictions on political parties and military involvement in authoritarian politics in Figure 2.5 highlights that military and single-
party rule are far from mutually exclusive or collectively exhaustive.[32] In fact,
direct military rule with a ban on political parties and civilian rule with a single
party – two combinations of military involvement in authoritarian politics and
restrictions on political parties that most closely correspond to Geddes's pure
military and single-party dictatorships – jointly account for only about 5 and
27 percent of all observations, respectively. The joint distribution of these
distinct conceptual dimensions – rather than their classification into ideal
types – thus provides a more representative summary of the institutional heterogeneity in the political organization of dictatorships.

When I measure the dimensions of legislative and executive selection, I build
on the categories in Beck et al.'s (2001) indices of legislative and executive competitiveness. I revised and extended Beck et al.'s data, which span the period

[32] To simplify the presentation, I exclude the category of indirect military involvement, which
accounts for only 2 percent of observations.

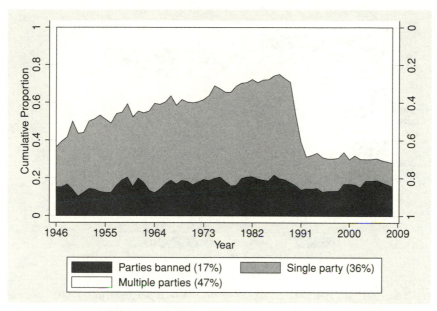

FIGURE 2.4. Restrictions on political parties in dictatorships, 1946–2008. *Note:* Overall distribution of individual categories in parentheses.

1975–2006, to cover my entire sample period 1946–2008 and to match my modified coding scheme. On the conceptual dimension of legislative selection, I distinguish among dictatorships with *no legislature*, an *unelected or appointed legislature*, a *legislature with one party or candidate per seat*, a legislature with multiple parties in which the *largest party controls more than 75 percent of the seats*, a legislature with multiple parties in which the *largest party controls less than 75 percent of the seats*, and dictatorships with elected but *nonpartisan legislatures*.[33] The largest party in authoritarian legislatures is most often what I will call in Chapter 6 a *regime party* – that is, sanctioned by the regime's leadership. Saudi Arabia (1946–2008), Indonesia (1960–1965), Romania (1947–1989), Mexico (1946–1975, 1994–2000), Mexico (1976–1993), and Kuwait (1963–1975, 1982–1985, 1992–2008) are instances of these six respective categories. Figure 2.6 summarizes their distribution throughout the period 1946–2008.

When it comes to executive selection, I distinguish among dictatorships with an *unelected executive*, an executive that is elected but with only *one party or candidate*, an executive that is *selected by a small, unelected body*, an executive that is elected in a competition among multiple candidates and received *more than 75 percent of the vote*, and an executive that is elected in a

[33] I present the 75 percent threshold because I consider it a reasonable (but nonetheless arbitrary) metric of significant oppositional presence. In the complete data, I record the *exact* fraction of legislative seats that the largest party controls. In the case of bicameral legislatures, all percentages refer to the lower house.

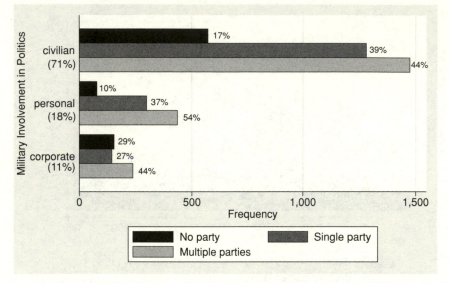

FIGURE 2.5. Joint distribution of restrictions on political parties and military involvement in authoritarian politics, 1946–2008. *Note:* Categories of indirect military involvement and restriction to two parties not included. Percentages under the categories of
military involvement refer to each category's share in the data. Percentages next to bars
refer to each category's share within the corresponding form of military involvement.

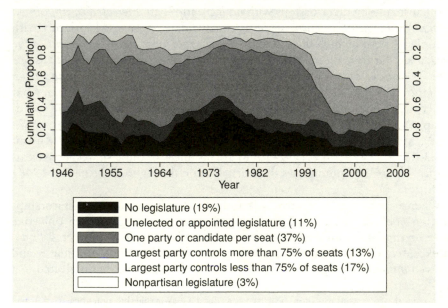

FIGURE 2.6. Legislative selection in dictatorships, 1946–2008. *Note:* Overall distribution of individual categories in parentheses.

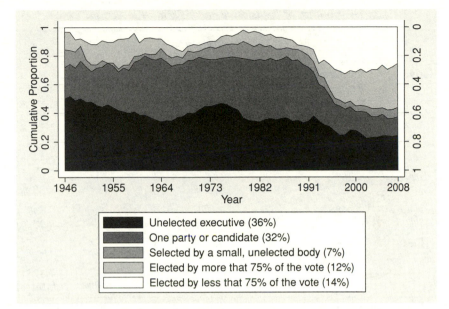

FIGURE 2.7. Executive selection in dictatorships, 1946–2008. *Note:* Overall distribution of individual categories in parentheses.

competition among multiple candidates and received *less than 75 percent of the vote*.[34] Saudi Arabia (1946–2008), Syria (1971–2008), Brazil (1964–1979), Singapore (1979–2005), and Peru (1992–2000) respectively exemplify these five categories. Figure 2.7 portrays the changes in executive selection across dictatorships throughout the period 1946–2008.

Because the two dimensions of legislative and executive selection are based on formal institutional criteria, they jointly provide a directly interpretable indicator of the degree of competitiveness across dictatorships.[35] Table 2.4 displays the joint distribution of these two dimensions. We see that dictatorships in which both the legislature and the executive are elected in a multiparty or multicandidate competition and the largest party or candidate received less than 75 percent of the vote account for about 450 country-years, or only about 10 percent of all country-year observations. These are dictatorships in which political competition is relatively open and are therefore most likely either to be misclassified as dictatorships or barely fail the criteria for democracy that I adopt. Table 2.4 shows that such "competitive" authoritarian regimes make up only about 10 percent of all dictatorships throughout 1946–2008, although they do account for between 20 percent and 30 percent of all dictatorships

[34] In the case of multiple election rounds, these percentages refer to the last round.
[35] This is in contrast to indexed measures or scales such as the Polity Score (Marshall and Jaggers 2008), which lack a direct institutional interpretation. Przeworski et al. (2000) and Cheibub et al. (2010) emphasize such direct interpretability as well as unambiguous operationalization of measurement in their discussion of regime classifications.

TABLE 2.4. *Joint Distribution of Legislative and Executive Selection, 1946–2008*

Legislative Selection	Executive Selection					
	Unelected Executive	One Party	Small Body	Elected by		Total
				>75%	<75%	
No legislature	681 (15%)	17 (<1%)	135 (3%)	24 (<1%)	9 (<1%)	866 (19%)
Unelected or appointed	392 (9%)	54 (1%)	46 (1%)	13 (<1%)	4 (<1%)	509 (11%)
One party or candidate	267 (6%)	1,309 (29%)	66 (1%)	63 (1%)	31 (1%)	1,736 (39%)
Largest more than 75%	48 (1%)	85 (2%)	19 (<1%)	345 (8%)	102 (2%)	599 (13%)
Largest less than 75%	116 (3%)	49 (1%)	40 (1%)	105 (2%)	455 (10%)	765 (17%)
TOTAL	1,504 (34%)	1,514 (34%)	306 (7%)	550 (12%)	601 (13%)	4,475 (100%)

Note: The unit of observation is a country-year. Cell percentages are in parentheses. The legislative-selection category, "nonpartisan legislature," is excluded.

since the end of the Cold War – an increase that was prominently pointed out by Levitsky and Way (2002, 2010).

To summarize, a key advantage of this book's empirical strategy for measuring authoritarian institutions is that categories within each conceptual dimension are *mutually exclusive and collectively exhaustive* and based on transparent coding decisions along a *single conceptual dimension*. Thus, adjudicating whether Syria between 1970 and 2000 was a military, single-party, or personalist dictatorship is unnecessary – it was directly ruled by the military, maintained a single ruling party, had a legislature that was elected within a single party, and had an executive that was elected in single-candidate elections.[36] These aspects of Syrian politics reflect distinct conceptual dimensions that are not mutually exclusive. Because we do not need to adjudicate across incommensurable aspects of authoritarian politics, our coding decisions are more reliable and the resulting categories lend themselves to conceptually valid comparison groups.

As mentioned previously, my decision to measure the conceptual dimensions of military involvement in authoritarian politics, restrictions on political parties, and legislative and executive selection is guided by the need to evaluate

[36] Of course, these elections were not competitive. Hafez al-Asad had himself merely confirmed as head of the government in a single-candidate "plebiscite." Meanwhile, legislative elections allowed for the entry of parties other than the Baath Party, as well as independent candidates. However, all such parties had to be members of the National Progressive Front, which was controlled by the Baath Party, and all independent candidates were vetted by the Baath Party. See, e.g., Seale (1990, 173) and George (2003, 82–99).

key empirical predictions of my theoretical arguments. Chapter 4 uses the data on legislative and executive selection to examine the reasons for the establishment and maintenance of power-sharing institutions in dictatorships. Chapter 5 examines the data on military involvement in authoritarian politics to test my claim that a heavy reliance on repression accounts for the emergence of military dictatorships. And Chapter 6 uses the data on restrictions on political parties to study the role of regime parties in authoritarian co-optation.

2.4 LEADERSHIP CHANGE IN DICTATORSHIPS

The extraordinary institutional diversity of authoritarian politics is not the only challenging aspect of its organization. As I highlighted in Chapter 1, formal institutions in dictatorships cannot be taken at face value and their role in authoritarian politics is an important puzzle itself. This is because authoritarian politics takes place under distinctively dismal conditions: Dictatorships lack an independent authority that would enforce mutual agreements – including the rules according to which formal institutions are supposed to operate. A violent rather than institutional resolution of conflicts is therefore an ever-present possibility in authoritarian politics. In turn, whether and which authoritarian institutions actually matter is far from clear.

This tenuous relevance of formal institutions under dictatorship is one reason why, in addition to country-level data, I collected data at the *leader-level* of observation. The manner by which dictators enter and leave office is an indicator of whether formal institutions actually regulate who holds power: If leaders enter and leave by coups and popular uprisings rather than the institutional procedures that are supposed to regulate their selection, then formal institutions are most likely epiphenomenal or at least secondary to potentially violent, noninstitutional methods of resolving political conflicts. How dictators actually assume and lose power speaks louder than official rules.

As I outlined in the previous chapter, my arguments in Chapter 4 in fact do explain why some dictators accept formal, institutional constraints on their authority. Throughout the book, I also account for the variation in the duration of dictators' tenures, the nature of their entry and exit from office, as well as military intervention in authoritarian politics. To evaluate these claims, I collected detailed data on the timing and manner of entry into and exit from office of all authoritarian leaders who held power for at least one day between 1946 and 2008.

I build on Goemans et al. (2009), who were the first researchers to collect comprehensive data on leader tenures across regime types. Unfortunately, they did not distinguish among the many forms of authoritarian leadership change in detail that would be appropriate for evaluating my claims.[37] I therefore borrowed their leader-identifying information and distinguished among a

---

[37] This is because Goemans et al. (2009) were motivated primarily by empirical questions in international relations, not authoritarian politics.

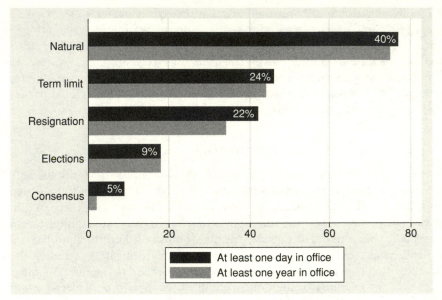

FIGURE 2.8. Constitutional exits from office of authoritarian leaders, 1946–2008. *Note:* Exits of interim leaders are not included. Unambiguous determination of exit was not possible for thirteen leaders.

number of constitutional and nonconstitutional forms of leader entry into and exit from office; coded for the use of violence and the participation of the military in these leadership transitions; and recorded the institutional and political affiliation prior to assuming office of all authoritarian leaders between 1946 and 2008.

As a brief summary of these data, consider dictators' constitutional and nonconstitutional exits from office. Recall from Chapter 1 that a leadership transition is constitutional when it follows an officially endorsed, typically constitutionally mandated process, such as an election, a vote by a ruling body, or a hereditary succession.[38] Figure 2.8 summarizes the form and distribution of such exits. An exit due to *natural* causes – as in the case of a natural death or poor health – is the most frequent form of a constitutional exit from office. The second most frequent category is an exit due a binding *term limit*, followed by *resignation*, which describes those cases in which a dictator steps down without any apparent pressure by his inner circle to do so. Lost *elections* account for about 9 percent of constitutional exits. Cases in which an unelected, small body removes a leader from office account for an additional 5 percent – I refer to

[38] The entries and exits of *interim* leaders – that is, leaders who hold office only temporarily, typically during a constitutional crisis – cannot be unequivocally characterized as constitutional or nonconstitutional; therefore, I treat them as a separate category (see the codebook for details.) With minor differences, my distinction between constitutional and nonconstitutional leadership changes mirrors those between regular and irregular leadership changes in Goemans et al. (2009); see also Goemans (2008).

these exits as *consensus*. Respective examples of these categories include Fidel Castro's 2008 retirement from the Cuban presidency due to failing health; Carlos Salinas's 1994 compliance with the "no reelection" provision that limits the Mexican presidency to a single term; Luis Somoza's 1963 decision to leave the Nicaraguan presidency in favor of a loyal surrogate; apartheid-era departures of South African prime ministers from office after lost elections; and Field Marshal Thanom Kittikachorn's resignation from the post of Thai Prime Minister, which he held briefly in Sarit Thanarat's military regime of 1957–1963.

I reviewed my data on dictators' nonconstitutional exits from office in Chapter 1, where I distinguished among *coups d'état, popular uprisings, transitions to democracy, assassinations,* and *foreign interventions*. In fact, about two-thirds of all leadership transitions in dictatorships are nonconstitutional. Prominent examples of these subcategories include, respectively, Nikita Khrushchev's 1964 removal by the Soviet leadership around Leonid Brezhnev; Fulgencio Batista's 1959 overthrow by Fidel Castro's Cuban Revolution; Reynaldo Bignone's 1983 resignation after the democratic election of Raúl Alfonsín to the Argentine presidency; the 1981 assassination of Egyptian president Anwar al-Sadat; and Saddam Hussein's fall after the 2003 U.S. invasion of Iraq. We saw in Chapter 1 that by far the most frequent form of nonconstitutional leader exit is the coup d'état – which I defined as the removal of an authoritarian leader by his inner circle that is accompanied by the threat or actual use of force.

These data on leadership change allow me to evaluate some of the key arguments in this book. Chapter 3 uses data on the duration of leaders' tenures and the manner by which they leave office to test my claims about the differences in the allies' ability to collectively constrain dictators in contested and established autocracies. I use information on the constitutionality of leadership transitions in Chapter 4, which assesses whether parties and legislatures alleviate commitment and monitoring problems in authoritarian power-sharing. That chapter also uses data on dictators' exits from office due to natural causes as a benchmark for diagnosing potential endogeneity in the adoption of parties and legislatures. Finally, Chapter 5 uses data on military involvement in leaders' entry and exit to test my predictions about the causes of military intervention in politics.

2.5 THE SURVIVAL OF AUTHORITARIAN RULING COALITIONS

The data on institutions and leadership change across dictatorships reviewed so far cover many aspects of authoritarian politics. However, some of my claims in this book – as well as many claims in the extant literature on authoritarian politics – are best assessed not at the country or leader level of observation but rather at the level of what I call the authoritarian ruling coalition. For instance, if we are interested in whether a regime-sanctioned party contributes to authoritarian stability, we want evaluate whether such parties result in the

TABLE 2.5. *Political Affiliation of Authoritarian Leaders, 1946–2008*

Political Affiliation	Frequency	Percentage
Regime	408	60.45
Unaffiliated	135	20.00
Opposition	79	11.70
Independence	53	7.85

Note: The unit of observation is an authoritarian leader. See the codebook for details about coding rules for each category.

continuity in power of the same political coalition – as in the case of Mexico under the PRI. Empirical studies that assess such claims by looking instead at the tenures of individual leaders or the duration of entire authoritarian regimes potentially confound the effect of institutions on the stability of authoritarian ruling coalitions with their effect on the survival of individual dictators or the stability of dictatorship as a regime type.

I overcome this limitation by using information on the political and institutional affiliation of dictators in order to identify authoritarian *ruling coalition spells*. I define the latter as an uninterrupted succession in office of politically affiliated authoritarian leaders. More precisely, a leader was politically affiliated with the previous leader and, hence, from the same ruling coalition if he was a member of the government, a government party, the royal or ruling family, or a military junta under the previous authoritarian leader. The survival of a particular ruling coalition thus corresponds to the continuation in power of what we colloquially refer to as a particular "political regime" or "dictatorship" – as in "the communist regime" in China (1949–), "the PRI regime" in Mexico (1929–2000), or "the military dictatorship" in Brazil (1964–1984).

Table 2.5 summarizes the political affiliation of all authoritarian leaders during the period 1946–2008. It shows that about 60 percent of all dictators come from the same ruling coalition as their predecessor. Prominent examples of ruling coalitions that span multiple leaders include the leadership in Communist and Baathist regimes, Mexican presidents under the PRI, hereditary successions in many Middle Eastern monarchies, and the leadership of the Argentine and Brazilian military governments. As we saw in Chapter 1, however, leadership changes within the same ruling coalition do not always occur peacefully or constitutionally. To name one example, before becoming the president of Syria in 1970, Hafez al-Asad served as a Minister of Defence in the Baath government that came to power in 1966. Al-Asad came to power by staging a coup against the de facto head of government, Salah Jadid, after growing disagreements about the direction of the country between Jadid's ideological and al-Asad's pragmatic faction within the Baath Party and military (Seale 1990, chap. 11).

When recording the political affiliation of those authoritarian leaders who were not affiliated with the previous regime, I distinguish among leaders who were in opposition, unaffiliated leaders, and leaders of newly independent countries. A leader was in *opposition* if he openly opposed the previous leader prior to assuming office, typically as a guerilla leader or an opposition candidate in an executive or legislative election. A leader was *unaffiliated* with the previous authoritarian leader if he did not openly or unambiguously state support or opposition to the preceding government. This was the case with many generals and judges who ultimately took office. As Table 2.5 indicates, these two categories account for approximately 12 and 20 percent of all authoritarian leaders, respectively.

Finally, I separately recorded leaders who came into office at a time when their country gained *independence*. This category is coded separately because the unique nature of political conflicts and alliances during independence struggles. These leaders comprise about 8 percent of all leaders and are a mix of independence fighters who opposed the previous (typically) colonial government (e.g., Hastings Banda in Malawi) and those who actually served in the previous colonial administration or legislature (e.g., Ahmadou Ahidjo in Cameroon).

The information in Table 2.5 allows us to measure the stability of distinct authoritarian ruling coalitions by totaling the lengths of tenures of individual leaders from within the same regime. Thus Cuba, which has been a dictatorship since Fulgencio Batista's 1952 coup d'état, has had two ruling-coalition spells: the first consisting of Batista alone (1952–1959) and the second consisting of the two Castro brothers, Fidel (1959–2008) and Raul (2008–). The complete data contain 374 ruling coalitions whose length varies between one and sixty-three years, with a mean and median duration of sixteen and eight years, respectively. Fifty-four of these ruling coalitions were in existence as of 2008.

I employ data on ruling coalition spells in Chapters 4 and 6. According to my arguments in Chapter 4, parties and legislatures should contribute to the durability of authoritarian ruling coalitions by preventing unnecessary, intra-elite conflicts. I therefore examine whether the presence of either a legislature or a party in fact results in more durable ruling coalition spells and fewer violent, nonconstitutional transitions within individual ruling coalitions. Chapter 6 studies the role of regime parties and uses the ruling coalition data to test my claim that such parties are a particularly effective instrument of authoritarian co-optation.

2.6 CONCLUSION: THE RICH WORLD OF AUTHORITARIAN POLITICS

Popular accounts of authoritarian politics get easily carried away by the eccentricities, longevity, and brutality of a few dictators and their regimes. Thus the crowds in Tahrir or Tiananmen are presented as a dictator's greatest concern; the likes of Saddam Hussein and Kim Jong Il are taken to be the archetypes of authoritarian leadership; and, as George W. Bush's grumbling betrayed, ruling a dictatorship is often thought to be "a heck of a lot easier" than governing a democracy.[39]

Comprehensive, large-N data on authoritarian politics help us uncover the distortions in such impressions. As we saw in Chapter 1, many more dictators lose power in a confrontation with regime insiders than with the masses excluded from power. The comprehensive data on authoritarian leadership transitions reviewed in this chapter further reveal that a typical dictator does not stay in office for much longer than an American president and that the institutional makeup of dictatorships is far too multifaceted to be faithfully summarized by a few descriptive labels.

However, how to organize and summarize the richness of authoritarian politics is not obvious. Because dictatorship is a residual category – defined by what democracy is not – there are no limits to institutional diversity across dictatorships. Quasifeudal and family-ruled Saudi Arabia looks like a relic from a bygone age next to modern and party-ruled Singapore.[40] Whereas democracy has historically followed a few institutional blueprints, dictatorship's richer and longer pedigree combines institutional models from multiple centuries and levels of development.

The study of this institutional diversity is further complicated by the questionable relevance of formal political institutions under dictatorship. As Chapter 1 highlighted, authoritarian politics takes place in the shadow of the threat of violence, and dictatorships inherently lack an independent authority that would enforce compliance with institutional procedures for resolving political conflicts. Whether and which institutional differences across dictatorships actually matter, therefore, is an important question itself. Although many contemporary dictatorships could be easily classified along the many institutional distinctions that political scientists conventionally draw among democracies – like the one among parliamentary, presidential, and semipresidential systems – doing so would betray naïvité about the nature of authoritarian politics. The locus of power in Russia shifted from the post of president to that of prime minister in 2008 not because of a change in the constitution but rather because Vladimir Putin assumed the latter post. Observers anticipate that it will shift back to the presidency in 2012, when Putin is expected to run for president again. That, according to Putin as well as his pliant stand-in, Dimitri Medvedev, had been agreed on "years ago."[41]

This chapter introduces my attempt to organize the diversity in leaders and institutions across dictatorships. This book's data on the political organization of dictatorships cover all authoritarian regimes throughout the period 1946–2008. I use the term *political organization* to jointly label the manifold features

[39] See "Remarks by the President-Elect Following a Meeting with Congressional Leaders," 18 December 2000, at The American Presidency Project.
[40] On Saudia Arabia, see Herb (1999); on Singapore, see Lingle (1996).
[41] See Ellen Barry, "Putin Once More Moves to Assume Top Job in Russia," *The New York Times*, 24 September 2011.

of authoritarian politics that these data describe: legislative and executive selection, restrictions on political parties, and military involvement in authoritarian politics, as well as leadership change and ruling-coalition duration and composition. I also explain why the difference between dictatorship and democracy is best thought of as first one of kind and only then one of degree; why we should abandon the flawed practice of classifying dictatorships into a few ideal types or according to their prominent descriptive features; and why our data on formal institutions need to be complemented by other, more credible measures of their binding power, such as the data on leadership change used throughout this book.

The next two chapters present my substantive arguments about the first of the two conflicts that I argue drive the politics of dictatorships: the problem of authoritarian power-sharing.

2.7 APPENDIX: AUTHORITARIAN SPELLS, 1946–2008

The following table lists all authoritarian spells during the period 1946–2008 that satisfy my definition of dictatorship. Each entry consists of a country name, the first and last year of the authoritarian spell, and its origin and end. The first and last year of each authoritarian spell corresponds to the first and last calendar year that a country entered as a dictatorship, respectively. For instance, 1956 is the first calendar year that Argentina entered as a dictatorship following the military coup that overthrew Juan Perón in September 1955, and 1958 is the last calendar year that Argentina entered as a dictatorship (with a democratic legislative and presidential election taking place that year). A missing last year indicates that a country was a dictatorship as of 2008.

Country	Years	Origin	End
Afghanistan	1946–1977	Continuance	No authority
	1989–1991	No authority	No authority
	1996–2000	No authority	No authority
Albania	1946–1991	Continuance	Democracy
Algeria	1962–1993	Independence	No authority
	2002–	No authority	Continuance
Angola	2002–	No authority	Continuance
Argentina	1956–1958	Democracy	Democracy
	1963–1963	Democracy	Democracy
	1967–1973	Democracy	Democracy
	1977–1983	Democracy	Democracy
Azerbaijan	1991–	Independence	Continuance
Bahrain	1971–	Independence	Continuance
Bangladesh	1971–1991	Independence	Democracy

(continued)

(continued)

Country	Years	Origin	End
Belarus	1997–	Democracy	Continuance
Benin	1962–1991	Democracy	Democracy
Bhutan	1971–	Independence	Continuance
Bolivia	1946–1982	Continuance	Democracy
Brazil	1965–1986	Democracy	Democracy
Brunei	1984–	Independence	Continuance
Bulgaria	1946–1990	Continuance	Democracy
Burkina Faso	1960–	Independence	Continuance
Burundi	1962–1992	Independence	No authority
	1996–1999	No authority	No authority
	2003–2005	No authority	Democracy
Cambodia	1953–1969	Independence	No authority
	1976–1978	No authority	No authority
	1988–	No authority	Continuance
Cameroon	1960–	Independence	Continuance
Cape Verde	1975–1991	Independence	Democracy
Central African Republic	1960–1993	Independence	Democracy
	2004–	Democracy	Continuance
Chad	1960–1977	Independence	No authority
	1984–	No authority	Continuance
Chile	1974–1990	Democracy	Democracy
China	1950–	No authority	Continuance
Colombia	1951–1958	Democracy	Democracy
Comoros	1975–2004	Independence	Democracy
Congo (Brazzaville)	1964–1992	Democracy	Democracy
	1999–	No authority	Continuance
Congo (Zaire)	1966–1995	No authority	No authority
	2001–2006	No authority	Democracy
Costa Rica	1946–1949	Continuance	Democracy
Cuba	1953–	Democracy	Continuance
Cyprus	1960–1962	Independence	No authority
	1968–1983	No authority	Democracy
Czechoslovakia	1949–1990	Democracy	Democracy
Djibouti	1977–	Independence	Continuance
Dominican Republic	1946–1964	Continuance	No authority
	1967–1978	No authority	Democracy
Ecuador	1946–1948	Continuance	Democracy
	1962–1979	Democracy	Democracy
	2001–2002	Democracy	Democracy
Egypt	1946–	Continuance	Continuance
El Salvador	1946–1980	Continuance	No authority
Equatorial Guinea	1968–	Independence	Continuance
Eritrea	1993–	Independence	Continuance
Ethiopia	1946–1979	Continuance	No authority
	1992–	No authority	No authority

Country	Years	Origin	End
Fiji	1988–1991	Democracy	Democracy
	2007–	Democracy	Continuance
Gabon	1960–	Independence	Continuance
Gambia	1965–	Independence	Continuance
Georgia	1991–2004	Independence	Democracy
German Democratic Republic	1954–1990	Independence	Democracy
Ghana	1959–1969	Democracy	Democracy
	1973–1979	Democracy	Democracy
	1982–1992	Democracy	Democracy
Greece	1968–1974	Democracy	Democracy
Grenada	1980–1984	Democracy	Democracy
Guatemala	1955–1986	Democracy	Democracy
Guinea	1958–	Independence	Continuance
Guinea-Bissau	1974–1994	Independence	Democracy
	2000–2000	Democracy	Democracy
	2004–2005	Democracy	Democracy
Guyana	1966–1992	Independence	Democracy
Haiti	1946–1990	Continuance	Democracy
	1992–1994	Democracy	Democracy
	2000–	Democracy	Continuance
Honduras	1946–1958	Continuance	Democracy
	1964–1971	Democracy	Democracy
	1973–1982	Democracy	Democracy
Hungary	1946–1990	Continuance	Democracy
Indonesia	1949–1999	Independence	Democracy
Iran	1946–	Continuance	Continuance
Iraq	1946–2002	Continuance	No authority
Ivory Coast	1960–2001	Independence	No authority
	2007–	No authority	Continuance
Jordan	1946–	Independence	Continuance
Kazakhstan	1991–	Independence	Continuance
Kenya	1963–2002	Independence	Democracy
Korea, North	1948–1949	Independence	No authority
	1954–	No authority	Continuance
Korea, South	1948–1949	Independence	No authority
	1954–1988	No authority	Democracy
Kuwait	1961–	Independence	Continuance
Kyrgyzstan	1991–2005	Independence	Democracy
Laos	1974–	No authority	Continuance
Lebanon	2005–	Democracy	Continuance
Lesotho	1971–1993	Democracy	Democracy
Liberia	1946–1989	Continuance	No authority
	1996–2006	No authority	Democracy
Libya	1951–	Independence	Continuance

(continued)

(continued)

Country	Years	Origin	End
Madagascar	1960–1993	Independence	Democracy
Malawi	1964–1994	Independence	Democracy
Malaysia	1957–	Independence	Continuance
Maldives	1965–	Independence	Continuance
Mali	1960–1992	Independence	Democracy
Mauritania	1960–2007	Independence	Democracy
	2008–	Democracy	Continuance
Mexico	1946–2000	Continuance	Democracy
Mongolia	1946–1990	Continuance	Democracy
Morocco	1956–	Independence	Continuance
Mozambique	1975–1980	Independence	No authority
	1992–	No authority	Continuance
Myanmar	1959–1960	Democracy	Democracy
	1963–1963	Democracy	No authority
	1971–	No authority	Continuance
Namibia	1990–	Independence	Continuance
Nepal	1946–1991	Continuance	Democracy
Nicaragua	1946–1977	Continuance	No authority
	1980–1982	No authority	No authority
	1989–1990	No authority	Democracy
Niger	1960–1993	Independence	Democracy
	1997–1999	Democracy	Democracy
Nigeria	1967–1979	Democracy	Democracy
	1984–1999	Democracy	Democracy
Oman	1971–	Independence	Continuance
Pakistan	1947–1988	Independence	Democracy
	2000–	Democracy	Democracy
Panama	1946–1952	Continuance	Democracy
	1969–1989	Democracy	Democracy
Paraguay	1946–1993	Continuance	Democracy
Peru	1949–1956	Democracy	Democracy
	1963–1963	Democracy	Democracy
	1969–1980	Democracy	Democracy
	1993–2001	Democracy	Democracy
Philippines	1970–1981	Democracy	No authority
Poland	1946–1991	Continuance	Democracy
Portugal	1946–1976	Continuance	Democracy
Qatar	1971–	Independence	Continuance
Romania	1946–1990	Continuance	Democracy
Russia	1946–1991	Continuance	Democracy
	2005–	Democracy	Continuance
Rwanda	1962–	Independence	Continuance
Samoa	1976–	Independence	Continuance
Sao Tome and Principe	1975–1991	Independence	Democracy

Country	Years	Origin	End
Saudi Arabia	1946–	Continuance	Continuance
Senegal	1960–1999	Independence	Democracy
Serbia	1991–2000	Independence	Democracy
Seychelles	1976–1993	Independence	Democracy
Sierra Leone	1968–1997	Democracy	Democracy
Singapore	1965–	Independence	Continuance
Somalia	1970–1989	Democracy	No authority
South Africa	1946–1994	Continuance	Democracy
Spain	1946–1977	Continuance	Democracy
Sri Lanka	1978–1989	Democracy	Democracy
Sudan	1959–1962	Democracy	No authority
	1973–1982	No authority	No authority
	1993–1994	No authority	No authority
	2005–	No authority	Continuance
Suriname	1981–1988	Democracy	Democracy
	1991–1991	Democracy	Democracy
Swaziland	1968–	Independence	Continuance
Syria	1946–1957	Independence	No authority
	1961–	No authority	Continuance
Taiwan	1949–2000	Independence	Democracy
Tajikistan	1991–1991	Independence	No authority
	1994–	No authority	Continuance
Tanzania	1961–	Independence	Continuance
Thailand	1946–1975	Continuance	Democracy
	1977–1979	Democracy	Democracy
	1992–1992	Democracy	Democracy
	2007–	Democracy	Democracy
Togo	1960–	Independence	Continuance
Tonga	1999–	Independence	Continuance
Tunisia	1956–	Continuance	Continuance
Turkey	1946–1961	Continuance	Democracy
	1972–1973	Democracy	Democracy
	1981–1983	Democracy	Democracy
Turkmenistan	1991–	Independence	Continuance
Tuvalu	2000–	Independence	Continuance
Uganda	1967–1980	Democracy	No authority
	1990–	No authority	Continuance
United Arab Emirates	1971–	Independence	Continuance
Uruguay	1974–1985	Democracy	Democracy
Uzbekistan	1991–	Independence	Continuance
Venezuela	1946–1959	Continuance	Democracy
Vietnam, North	1954–1964	Independence	No authority
	1976–	No authority	Continuance
Vietnam, South	1954–1954	Independence	No authority

(continued)

(continued)

Country	Years	Origin	End
Yemen	1990–	Independence	Continuance
Yemen Arab Republic	1946–1961	Continuance	No authority
	1968–1989	No authority	No authority
Yemen People's Republic	1967–1989	Independence	No authority
Yugoslavia	1946–1991	Continuance	Independence
Zambia	1964–1991	Independence	Democracy
Zimbabwe	1965–1975	Independence	No authority
	1980–	No authority	Continuance

PART I

THE PROBLEM OF AUTHORITARIAN POWER-SHARING

3

And Then There Was One! Authoritarian Power-Sharing and the Path to Personal Dictatorship

> [A]ll principalities known to us are governed in two different ways: either by a prince with all the others his servants, who as ministers (through his favor and permission) assist in governing that kingdom; or by a prince and by barons, who hold that rank not because of any favor of their master but because of the antiquity of their bloodline.
>
> Niccolò Machiavelli, *The Prince*

> As democracies are subverted when the people despoil the senate, the magistrates, the judges of their functions, so monarchies are corrupted when the prince insensibly deprives societies or cities of their privileges. In the former case the multitude usurp the power, in the latter it is usurped by a single person.
>
> Montesquieu, *The Spirit of the Laws*

> Although numerous distinct stages can be identified in Soviet history, in terms of the structure of supreme authority there are only two periods: oligarchy and dictatorship. The latter existed only under Stalin.
>
> Khlevniuk, *Master of the House* (2009, p. 246)

Joseph Stalin's ascent to the pinnacle of Soviet power continues to astonish casual observers and to intrigue historians. By the time of his death, Stalin arguably held "the greatest power over the greatest number of people in history" (Suny 1998, 167), an assessment all too grimly affirmed by the millions who perished in the government-directed terror, punitive famines, and deportations during Stalin's rule (see, e.g., Snyder 2010). Stalin, initially just "an obscure associate of more radiant revolutionaries" (Suny 1998, 167), gradually defeated actual and potential contenders within the Soviet leadership and eventually subordinated key institutions within the Soviet political system to his personal authority. By the end of the 1920s, Stalin had eliminated rival factions headed by Leon Trotsky, Gregory Zinoviev, and Nikolai Bukharin; by the end of the 1930s, the Great Purges decimated any independent,

Parts of this chapter draw on Svolik (2009).

collective power of the Communist Party, the Red Army, and Soviet officialdom (Suny 1998, chap. 11).

Particularly perplexing then is the equally spectacular downfall of Stalin's erstwhile political allies. The historian Oleg Khlevniuk begins his account of the power struggles within the Soviet Politburo after Vladimir Lenin's death with a telling narrative of the relationship between Stalin and one of his closest associates, Vyacheslav Molotov.[1] In 1929, Molotov apparently had enough personal influence within the Soviet leadership to compel Stalin to apologize for not writing to him frequently enough.[2] By the time of Stalin's death in 1953, Molotov had been forced to denounce his wife (who was later arrested for treason), saw many of his protegés purged, and had been himself almost entirely dismissed from the Soviet leadership (Khlevniuk 2009, xiii–xiv). Although Molotov was fortunate enough to have Stalin's death arrest his political demise, more than half of the full or candidate members of the Soviet Politburo between 1924 and 1952 either were imprisoned, assassinated, executed, or had committed suicide.[3] Stalin managed to turn the Politburo, originally an institution of collective leadership, into an instrument of his personal rule (Suny 1997; Gorlizki and Khlevniuk 2004; Khlevniuk 2009).

How did Stalin manage to consolidate absolute power among a sea of strongmen? This chapter clarifies the logic behind the transition from collective authoritarian rule to personal autocracy, as epitomized by Stalin's rise to uncontested power. Such transitions represent the degeneration of a process I call authoritarian power-sharing: the sharing of the spoils from joint rule between the dictator and his allies. Stalin and Molotov's parallel yet opposite political trajectories highlight the stakes at the heart of authoritarian power-sharing.

The key obstacle to successful power-sharing is any dictator's desire and opportunity to acquire more power at the expense of his allies. Under dictatorship, an effective deterrent against such opportunism must be backed by a credible threat of the dictator's removal by his inner circle. Throughout this

---

[1] According to Khlevniuk (2009, 4), for instance, Molotov's "unconditional loyalty was one of Stalin's greatest advantages" during the power struggles of the 1920s. In return for his loyalty, Molotov was rewarded with some of the most prominent political posts in the Soviet Union: Chairman of the Council of People's Commissars (1930–1941), Minister of Foreign Affairs (1939–1949), and a key member of the Politburo (1927–1956). In fact, Milovan Djilas, the Yugoslav envoy to Moscow in the 1940s, observed that Molotov was the only member of the Politburo whom Stalin addressed using the familiar pronoun *ty* (Djilas 1962, 62).

[2] According to Khlevniuk (2009, xiii), Stalin's letter begins, "Hello, Viacheslav. Of course I got your first letter. I know you are cursing me in your heart for my silence. I can't deny that you are fully within your rights to do so. But try to see things my way: I'm terribly overloaded and there's no time to sleep (literally!). Soon I will write a proper letter..."

[3] After the 19th Party Congress in 1952, according to Khrushchev, Stalin planned to "finish off" Molotov along with the rest of the veterans in the Politburo (Taubman 2004, 272) and replace them with a new generation of loyal followers (Gorlizki and Khlevniuk 2004, 148–9). My summary of Politburo members's violent fate under Stalin is based on Appendix 1 in Rees (2004, 240–2); I am not counting Lenin and Stalin.

book, I refer to such attempts as allies' rebellions. Because rebellions may fail and the allies typically have only limited information about the dictator's actions, they will be reluctant to rebel under most circumstances, thereby giving the dictator an incentive to try his luck and attempt to acquire power at their expense. If he succeeds in several power grabs without being stopped, the dictator may accumulate enough power that the allies will no longer be able to stage a rebellion that could topple him. It is precisely this type of dynamic that allows for the emergence of a personal autocracy.

This chapter thus answers one question that Stalin's rise to the pinnacle of Soviet power frequently evokes: Why didn't anyone stop him before it was too late? The short answer is as follows: The allies tried but failed. Indeed, shortly before his death in 1924, Vladimir Lenin was one of the first to warn about Stalin's appetite for power (Suny 1998, 143–4); Martemian Riutin's failed 1932 attempt to organize resistance against Stalin's emergent dictatorship was the last before the Great Purges cemented Stalin's personal autocracy (Suny 1998, 254–6). After the Purges, Stalin achieved "limitless power over the fate of every Soviet official, including the top leaders" (Khlevniuk 2009, 247).

However, this answer – they tried but failed – is too short and this chapter clarifies why: The answer fails to appreciate that the reasons for the emergence of personal autocracy are structural. As emphasized in Chapter 1, authoritarian elites operate under distinctly hazardous conditions. They cannot rely on an independent authority to enforce mutual agreements, and violence is the ever-present, ultimate arbiter of their conflicts. These dismal circumstances ensure that any dictator's aspiration to become the next Stalin is matched by the opportunity to do so. In fact, we will see that even if a dictator's allies do their best to deter him from usurping power at their expense, their ability to reign him in will be limited and intimately tied to the distinctive conditions under which authoritarian elites operate. Rather than an accident of history, the emergence of personal autocracy is a systematic phenomenon.

This chapter's analysis of the emergence of personal autocracy also clarifies that authoritarian power-sharing across dictatorships generally takes two qualitatively distinct forms. In the first, which I call *contested autocracy*, politics is one of balancing between the dictator and his allies, and the latter are capable of using the threat of a rebellion to deter the dictator's opportunism, even if imperfectly. By contrast, *established autocrats* have acquired enough power so they can no longer be credibly threatened by an allies' rebellion. Thus, even if the distribution of power between the dictator and his allies spans a continuum – as in the selectorate theory of Bueno de Mesquita et al. (2003) – there are, in fact, only two qualitatively distinct power-sharing regimes: Contested autocrats can be credibly threatened with a removal; established autocrats have effectively monopolized power.[4] This theoretical difference between contested

---

[4] In the next chapter, we will see that further distinctions can be drawn among contested autocracies depending on the role of institutions in power-sharing. In this chapter, I intentionally do not consider the potential role of institutions in power-sharing.

and established autocracy corresponds to the empirical difference between oligarchy and personal autocracy.

Dictators with seemingly unlimited powers have been labeled alternatively as *personalist* (Geddes 1999a), *patrimonial* (Zolberg 1966; Roth 1968), *neopatrimonial* (Jackson and Rosberg 1982; Snyder 1992; Bratton and Van de Walle 1997; Brownlee 2002), and *sultanistic* (Linz and Chehabi 1998). Thus the theoretical equilibrium of established autocracy naturally corresponds to these notions and clarifies why such dictators typically enjoy long tenures and die in their bed: They have effectively eliminated any threats from their inner circle. Nevertheless, I intentionally refer to dictatorships in which a dictator's inner circle cannot credibly threaten him with removal as established rather than personalist, neopatrimonial, or sultanistic: I emphasize that the former label is a theoretical equilibrium, whereas the latter three are empirical categories that carry additional connotations, such as charismatic leadership, reliance on traditional institutions rather than modern bureaucracy, or the lack of clear boundaries between the state and the leader's personal domain. Such empirical connotations may be implied by but are neither necessary nor do they define the analytical distinction between contested and established autocracy.

The category of a personalist dictatorship was introduced by Geddes (1999a), who distinguishes such regimes from military and single-party dictatorships. Unfortunately, she did not temporally distinguish the type of dictatorship that existed prior to any personalist regime – which would correspond to the equilibrium of contested autocracy herein – from the period of the personalist regime proper. Nevertheless, we do observe the consolidation of power that culminates in what Geddes calls a personalist dictatorship across all types authoritarian regimes.[5] Prominent examples include both military and single-party regimes, as exemplified by Francisco Franco and Joseph Stalin. The theory presented here provides the theoretical microfoundations that explain why such degeneration into personal rule – to borrow Brooker's expression (2000, Chap. 6) – occurs across various types of dictatorships: All dictatorships operate in a setting that lacks an independent authority that can enforce mutual agreements and in which violence is the ultimate arbiter of political conflicts.

The transition from contested to established autocracy analytically mirrors the rise to uncontested power by some of the most iconic personalist dictators: Mao Zedong, Saddam Hussein, and "Papa Doc" Duvalier, to name a few.[6] On any of these trajectories, an authoritarian leader assumes office as the "first among equals" and succeeds over time in accumulating enough power to become an invincible autocrat. The logic outlined previously explains why such a trajectory is possible but at the same time highly unlikely. Thus, however fascinating Mao's, Hussein's, and Duvalier's path to power may be, they should also be highly unrepresentative of the "average dictator." The average dictator

---

[5] See also Brooker (2000, 37), Hadenius and Teorell (2007), and Slater (2003).
[6] See Khlevniuk (2009) and Gorlizki and Khlevniuk (2004) on Stalin; MacFarquhar (1997a) and MacFarquhar and Schoenhals (2006) on Mao; and Makiya (1998) and Karsh (2002) on Hussein.

does not survive in office long enough to have the privilege of becoming a household name.

This empirical insight is developed in Section 3.3, which examines the statistical implications of my theoretical arguments. The long-run statistical distributions of several quantities of political interest – including the duration of tenure before a dictator is removed by a rebellion and the time in office until he becomes established, among others – can be derived directly from the theoretical model in this chapter. In fact, when actual data on tenures of authoritarian leaders are discussed in Section 3.4, I show that the probability density of the time that a dictator stays in office implied by the present model closely mirrors the actual distribution of dictators' tenures. Consistent with the arguments in this chapter, I also find that the longer an authoritarian leader stays in office, the less likely he is to be removed by a rebellion as opposed to one manner certainly unrelated to interaction with his inner circle: a natural death.

The next section outlines why and how power-sharing fails in dictatorships. It also explains why the emergence of established autocracy is a rare but systematic feature of authoritarian politics and why its occurrence depends in part on plain luck and crucially on an endogenously evolving balance of power between a dictator and his allies. Section 3.2, develops a game-theoretic model that highlights limits to the allies' ability to deter the dictator's opportunism under conditions that are characteristic of most dictatorships: the lack of an independent authority that would enforce agreements among the elites, the ever-present option of resorting to violence, and widespread secrecy. Section 3.3 derives the empirical implications of my arguments, which I evaluate by examining data on leadership change across dictatorships in Section 3.4. I conclude by discussing the rationale behind several distinctive practices used by established autocrats: personality cults as well as arbitrary and unexpected rotations, dismissals, and promotions of their key administrators or military commanders. I explain why personality cults as well as these other more peculiar practices are aimed not at the ideological conversion of the masses but rather as a public signal of the dictator's paramount political status under established autocracy.

3.1 AUTHORITARIAN POWER-SHARING AND THE EMERGENCE OF PERSONAL AUTOCRACY

This chapter studies a political setting with two key players, the *dictator* and the *ruling coalition*. The latter is composed of the dictator's allies who jointly, with him, hold enough power to be both necessary and sufficient for a regime's survival.[7] For instance, the Syrian government of Hafiz al-Asad (1971–2000)

---

[7] I use the term *power* very broadly: Both the dictator and members of the ruling coalition may derive power from economic or military resources or by having a large number of loyal followers. Loyalty in turn may be the result of ethnic, sectarian, or tribal ties or patronage or it may have more elusive foundations, as in the case of personal charisma.

relied throughout most of its existence on the support of two groups: military officers of the Alawi sect and al-Asad's family and friends.[8] In another case, Leonid Brezhnev's position at the helm of the Soviet government depended on loyal followers from his former posts in Dnepropetrovsk and Moldova, whom he elevated into key positions in the Politburo, the Central Committee, and various government ministries (Tompson 2003; Hanson 2006).[9]

The joint desire of the dictator and the ruling coalition to share power is complicated by a fundamental conflict of interest between them: Members of the ruling coalition worry that the dictator could use his position at the helm of the regime to acquire more power and later eliminate them from the ruling coalition.[10] Consider, for instance, the fate of Abdel al-Hakim Amir, who was a key member of the Free Officers Movement that brought Gamal Abdel Nasser to power in Egypt in 1952. Amir held key political posts in the Egyptian government, including the Supreme Control Committee that oversaw the Egyptian public sector and the Committee to Liquidate Feudalism that presided over agrarian reforms, culminating in his appointment as head of the Egyptian military. Nasser used Egypt's defeat in the Six-Day War of 1967 as a pretext for removing Amir from office and arrested Amir shortly thereafter for allegedly plotting to overthrow him. Amir eventually committed suicide under unclear circumstances (Waterbury 1983, 98, 279, 336–8).

Under dictatorship, the only effective deterrent against such opportunism is the ruling coalition's threat to replace the dictator. As discussed in the introduction, I refer to such collective attempts by the dictator's inner circle as allies' *rebellions*, mirroring the language of the Magna Carta of 1215, one of the first written recognitions of the right to such "baronial rebellions." However, my choice of the word *rebellion* should not be taken too literally: Most such rebellions are typically labeled coups d'état, plots, or even revolutions, as in the 17 July Revolution that brought the Baath Party to power in Iraq in 1968.

The key challenge that members of the ruling coalition face when they threaten a rebellion to discourage the dictator from usurping power is to establish the *credibility* of that threat. The threat of a rebellion may lack credibility for two reasons. First, if the balance of power between the dictator and the ruling coalition favors the dictator to the extent that a rebellion will most likely fail, the ruling coalition would rather be at the mercy of the dictator than rebel against him – even if they are certain that the dictator is usurping power. When this is the case, a rebellion lacks *ex-ante credibility*.

---

[8] See, e.g., Batatu (1981), Hinnebusch (1990, Chap. 5), Hinnebusch (2002, Chap. 4), Perthes (1995, Chap. 4), Seale (1990), Van Dam (1979, Chap. 5), and Zisser (2001, Chap. 2).

[9] Hence the concept of the ruling coalition is close to the concept of "winning coalition" in Bueno de Mesquita et al. (2003). Besley and Kudamatsu (2007), Haber (2007), and Pepinsky (2009) also examine settings in which a dictator relies on a group of core supporters.

[10] Although some members of the ruling coalition may attempt to strengthen their position as well, the dictator's control of the executive presents him with the greatest opportunity to do so. I therefore analytically focus on the dictator's potential opportunism as the central obstacle to successful authoritarian power-sharing.

Understandably, the consequences of failed rebellions are dire. By far, the most frequent fate of unsuccessful plotters is death. More fortunate defeated rebels may get away with house arrest, as did Armengol Ondo Nguema – the head of internal security and the half-brother of the president of Equatorial Guinea – after the last in a series of failed coups against him in 2004; ambassadorship to Outer Mongolia, as in the case of Vyacheslav Molotov after a failed attempt to depose Nikita Khrushchev in 1957; or "rustication," which was one of Mobutu's methods of punishing suspicious government officials by exiling them to their home village.

However, the threat of a rebellion also lacks credibility in a more fundamental, strategic sense, which is at the heart of the arguments developed in this chapter. A rebellion's deterrent effect is compromised by the interplay of two factors: the rebellion's potential failure and the allies' imperfect information about the dictator's actions.

Dictators have understandable tactical reasons for concealing their ambitions to consolidate power. The first salvos of the Cultural Revolution – Mao Zedong's monumental campaign against "revisionist" opponents that eventually destroyed most of the Party and state apparatus – began in 1965 with the critique of a historical theatrical play about a Ming emperor that Mao interpreted as criticism of his leadership (MacFarquhar and Schoenhals 2006, Chap. 1). Even well into the Cultural Revolution, Mao's ultimate intentions were unclear to both his followers and his opponents (Teiwes 2010, 86).

More generally, however, the autonomy associated with delegated power in most political systems is amplified by the secrecy and back-channel politics that are typical in dictatorships. During the struggle for Soviet leadership after Vladimir Lenin's health deteriorated between 1921 and 1924, Joseph Stalin's maneuvers to accumulate influence by securing key appointments for himself and his loyal followers in the Party hierarchy at first went unnoticed by many powerful figures (Suny 1998, 143–8).

In Section 3.2, I formalize this aspect of authoritarian politics by assuming that the ruling coalition observes an informative yet imperfect signal of whether the dictator is attempting to strengthen his position. In dictatorships that rely heavily on their bureaucracy or party to govern, the dictator's attempt to solidify power may manifest as the ruling coalition members' loss of influence within these structures. During the struggle for Soviet leadership after Stalin's death in 1953, for instance, Lavrentiy Beria took control of internal security by merging the Ministries of Internal Affairs (i.e., NKVD) and State Security (i.e., MGB), appointing men loyal to him, and deploying large contingents of the secret police to Moscow and other major cities. The danger of too much power in the hands of one man prompted a reaction so strong that even his ally Georgy Malenkov joined Nikita Khrushchev's Party faction and Marshal Georgy Zhukov in deposing Beria. Within a few months, Beria was arrested, tried, and executed (Suny 1998, Chap. 17).

But in most dictatorships, politics is highly informal. In these settings, the relevant signal about a dictator's actions is the loyalty of the individuals within the bureaucracy rather than formal changes in the bureaucratic hierarchy. Such loyalties often develop institutionally, as in the case of many military dictators, but also may be tribal, ethnic, or sectarian (see, e.g., Bratton and Van de Walle 1997; Van de Walle 2001). An important step in Saddam Hussein's rise in power, for instance, was the gradual elimination of the Baath Party's independent institutional influence on the regime via the appointment of individuals from Tikrit – his place of origin – into key positions in the bureaucracy. In the late 1970s, the entrenchment of the Tikritis in the government reached such major proportions that Hussein felt the need to conceal it from public view by abolishing family names denoting place of origin (Karsh 2002, 182).

The allies' imperfect information about the dictator's actions and a rebellion's potential failure jointly undermine its *ex-post credibility*. This is how the two factors interact: The potential failure of any rebellion makes its staging costly – even if it is expected to succeed. The dictator's allies would therefore like to avoid staging it unless they are certain that the dictator is indeed trying to usurp power at their expense. But, because they observe only an imperfect signal of the dictator's actions, they never have such certainty. Stated simply, the allies would like to threaten a rebellion but will be reluctant to carry it out.

Importantly, because the dictator anticipates this dilemma, the allies' ability to deter his opportunism will be limited. The model in Section 3.2 clarifies that the more precise the allies' information about the dictator's actions or the closer the dictator is to consolidating power, the more willing the allies will be to act on their threat to rebel. Crucially, however, the allies' reluctance to rebel will invariably tempt the dictator to usurp power in the hope that the allies will fail to either detect or act on it. More technically, the dictator will try to usurp power with a positive probability.

This tenuous ex-post credibility of the allies' threat of a rebellion, caused by an interplay of the allies' imperfect information about the dictator's actions and the potential failure of any rebellion, is a key obstacle to successful authoritarian power-sharing: Even if the ruling coalition acts optimally, the dictator may be sufficiently fortunate to accumulate enough power to eliminate them altogether.

I investigate this possibility in a dynamic setting in which the balance of power between the dictator and the ruling coalition evolves endogenously. In some periods, the dictator will be fortunate enough that even when he behaves opportunistically, a rebellion will either not be staged or fail, thereby shifting the balance of power in the dictator's favor. If the dictator succeeds in several power grabs, he may accumulate enough power that the ruling coalition will no longer be willing to rebel – the threat of a rebellion will lose ex-ante credibility. This, according to the *Resolution on Party History (1949–81)*, is what happened during Mao Zedong's rule. The *Resolution*, which after the Chairman's death summarized the Chinese Communist Party's lessons from the Party's total subjugation to Mao's whims, explains that his growing arrogance and arbitrariness "took place only gradually" and that "the Central Committee of the Party should be held partly responsible" for failing to prevent it (cited in MacFarquhar and Schoenhals 2006, 458).

In the formal model examined in the next section, I show that this dynamic results in the emergence of two qualitatively distinct power-sharing regimes. Under *contested autocracy*, a rebellion threatened by the ruling coalition has sufficient ex-ante credibility to deter his opportunism, even if only partially. Thus, contested autocracy is an equilibrium in which authoritarian politics is characterized by power-sharing – albeit imperfect – between the dictator and the ruling coalition. Although the dictator may be the most powerful member of the ruling coalition, he rules in the shadow of the threat of a rebellion. This type of power-balancing appears to have characterized the interaction between the General Secretary of the Communist Party and the Politburo after Stalin's death. In Zemtsov's (1991, 133) depiction, for instance,

... the general secretary's power or potential is inversely proportional to the influence of the Politburo members, who aim at maintaining a delicate balance between his power and theirs. They cannot let the general secretary accumulate too much power, for they would they find themselves devoid of influence in decision-making....

I call the second power-sharing regime *established autocracy*, which emerges after a dictator succeeds in consolidating enough power that he can no longer be credibly threatened by the ruling coalition. Under this "degenerated" power-sharing regime, rebellions do not occur and the dictator has effectively eliminated the ruling coalition, whose support is no longer necessary for his survival. In their study of personal rule in Africa, Jackson and Rosberg (1982, 143) call such dictators "African Autocrats" and emphasize – as I do herein – that what distinguishes the African Autocrat is

... not ideology or ruling style but by his greater freedom to act as he sees fit. He is freer to break agreements (or not to make them in the first place) because those with whom he may have them are in no position to enforce them. There are no powerful rivals with whom he must contend.

The transition from contested to established autocracy therefore can be seen as one from oligarchy to autocracy: Instead of allies who share power with the dictator and may constrain his choices, members of the ruling coalition become administrators who are fully subservient to the dictator and do not share power with him in any meaningful sense.

In fact, historical accounts of authoritarian politics identify precisely such a dichotomy in the power trajectories of dictators.[11] According to Teiwes (2001, 79), Mao Zedong's tenure "can essentially be divided between the period before 1958 when the Chairman listened to interests within the system and sought results that took those interests into account..., and the subsequent 'later Mao' period when he simply overrode interests...." In Jackson and Rosberg's

---

[11] Meanwhile, classical philosophers have drawn distinctions between political regimes that parallel the difference between contested and established autocracy. In *Politics*, Aristotle distinguished between the government of one or of a few; in *The Spirit of the Laws*, Montesquieu differentiated between monarchical and despotic regimes; and in *The Prince*, Machiavelli separated limited and absolute princes.

account (1982, 170–1), Mobutu Sese Seko's tenure in office consists of the period before 1970, when he was consolidating power, and the period after 1970, when his "personal autocracy was firmly established" and "old political allies . . . who exhibited the slightest sign of independence were purged." Finally, as Khlevniuk's (2009, 246) summary in the epigraph at the beginning of this chapter highlights, the same can be said about Stalin's trajectory in power – there were only two periods in terms of the structure of supreme authority: oligarchy and dictatorship.

Among the possible power trajectories explained by the arguments in this chapter is one on which an authoritarian leader assumes office as the "first among equals" but over time, as a result of opportunism and luck, accumulates enough power to become an invincible autocrat. Observers are often puzzled by how – typically in several distinct stages along such a trajectory – the dictator's old allies become his new enemies. Consider Karsh's characterization of Saddam Hussein's position as the apparent successor of Ahmed Hassan al-Bakr, after the latter resigned his presidency:

[Saddam] was not content with the comfortable majority he enjoyed in the state's ruling institutions. . . . He was at once far more powerful than all his comrades put together, and far more vulnerable to attack from them. (2002, 113)

This chapter explains this dynamic: After every successful power grab by the dictator, members of the ruling coalition become more concerned about the possibility that he will become established and eliminate them. As discussed in the next section, the dictator's appetite for power also grows as he strengthens his position. Meanwhile, the ruling coalition counters this expanding appetite by rebelling with an increasing probability. The ladder to ultimate power becomes more slippery as the dictator advances to the top.

As suggested at the beginning of this chapter, Stalin's rise to power is perhaps the most prominent example of the transition from contested to established autocracy. Stalin rose from the position of an "obscure party functionary" (Suny 1998, 49) in the 1920s to an indomitable autocrat by the end of the 1930s. By the end of the 1920s, Stalin eliminated from the Communist Party the key opposition groups associated with Trotsky, Zinoviev, and Bukharin (Suny 1998, 165–6). In 1924, when the terminally ill Lenin warned that Stalin had accumulated too much power, the Party ignored him, and Stalin was retained as the general secretary (Suny 1998, 146–8). Ten years later, in another push to consolidate his power, Stalin's Purges transformed the Communist Party from an ideological organization of elites and intellectuals, whose primary political interest was the promotion of Communism, into a party in which power rested in the hands of people of low-class origins whose primary personal loyalty was to Stalin. Stalin eliminated more than one-half of the 1,961 delegates and more than two-thirds of the 139 Central Committee members elected at the 17th Party Congress in 1934, the last such Congress before the Great Purges. He purged about one-half of the officer corps from the army and executed more Soviet generals than would be killed in World War II (Suny 1998, 261–8). In a series of steps, Stalin first defeated rival factions within the Soviet leadership; later, he eliminated the Communist Party and the army as independent political forces. At the end of this process, according to Nikita Khrushchev, "all of us around Stalin were temporary people. As long as he trusted us to a certain degree, we were allowed to go on living and working."[12]

Whereas the transition from contested to established autocracy happens with a positive (if small) probability, there is no return from established to contested autocracy. Once a dictator is established, he may, of course, still lose power, but such instances should be rare and occur primarily by a process that is politically divorced from the interaction between the dictator and his ruling coalition. Hence, rather than by the hands of their inner circle, established dictators should more often lose power by popular uprisings – as in the case of Tunisian President Zine El Abidine Ben Ali – or by foreign interventions – as in the case of Jean-Bédel Bokassa of the Central African Republic. In terms of the dictator's position vis-à-vis his ruling coalition, established autocracy is one in which all ends are tied up ("atado y bien atado"), to paraphrase Franco's assurance about the continuity of his regime (Payne 1987, 575).

3.2 A FORMAL MODEL

This section presents a game-theoretical model of authoritarian power-sharing that generates the key results discussed so far. Consider a polity governed by a *ruling coalition* of allies and a *dictator*. Jointly with the dictator, members of the ruling coalition hold enough power to be both necessary and sufficient for the survival of the government. I normalize this amount of power to 1. I denote the dictator's share of power by $b \in (0, 1)$ and the ruling coalition's share of power by $1 - b$. Thus the term b measures the balance of power between the dictator and the ruling coalition.

The dictator's position allows him to *renege* on his promise to share power – for example, by appointing loyal followers to key policy-making positions – and thus increase his share of power relative to the power of the ruling coalition. Once he acquires enough power, he may eliminate members of the ruling coalition who are no longer necessary for the survival of the government. Therefore, the ruling coalition prefers to deter such behavior and have the dictator *comply* with the status quo.

However, the ruling coalition observes only an imperfect signal $\theta \in \{H, L\}$ of the dictator's actions. More specifically, the conditional probability that the observed signal θ is *high* (H) or *low* (L) is $\pi_{\theta a}$, where $a \in \{c, r\}$ denotes the dictator's actions: comply and renege, respectively. Thus if the dictator reneges, the probability that the ruling coalition observes a high signal is π_{Hr}. I assume that the signal θ is informative about the dictator's actions in the sense of the monotone likelihood ratio property: $\pi_{Hr} > \pi_{Hc}$. In other words, when the signal is H, the ruling coalition knows that it is more likely that

---

[12] Khrushchev (1970, 307), cited in Suny (1997, 51).

the dictator has reneged than complied and vice versa, but it is never certain. Setting $0 < \pi_{\theta a} < 1$ for all θ and a ensures that the dictator's actions cannot be perfectly inferred from the observed signal.

To deter the dictator from reneging, the ruling coalition may threaten to stage a *rebellion*, the success of which depends on the balance of power between the dictator and the ruling coalition. I denote the probability that a rebellion succeeds by $\rho \in (0, 1)$. To keep the model tractable, I assume $\rho = 1 - b$.[13] Thus, the stronger the ruling coalition is relative to the dictator, the more likely it is that a rebellion succeeds. At this point, I assume away any collective-action problems that the ruling-coalition members may face when staging a rebellion and simply treat the ruling coalition as a unitary actor. I focus on the collective-action problem of replacing a dictator in the context of authoritarian power-sharing in the next chapter and, in fact, show that these simplifying assumptions are warranted.

The payoffs to the dictator and the ruling coalition depend on three consecutive outcomes: whether the dictator reneges, whether the ruling coalition rebels, and whether the rebellion succeeds. If the dictator complies and is not removed by a rebellion, the status quo is maintained and he receives the payoff b. Ideally, however, the dictator would renege and not be removed by a rebellion. I denote the amount of power that the dictator acquires when he reneges by $\mu > 0$.[14] Then, if the dictator reneges and a rebellion is either not staged or fails, his power (and payoff) grows from b to $b + \mu b$.[15] Because the amount of power that the dictator can hold is at most 1, μ must be such that $b + \mu b \leq 1$. Finally, if a rebellion succeeds, the dictator is removed from power and receives the payoff 0.

Each member of the ruling coalition would ideally like to preserve the status quo and share power with the dictator. This occurs when the dictator complies and a rebellion is not staged or when a rebellion is staged and succeeds, regardless of whether the dictator reneged.[16] In that case, each member of the ruling coalition obtains a payoff 1. If a rebellion fails, the entire ruling coalition is eliminated and each member receives the payoff 0. Finally, if the dictator reneges and a rebellion is not staged, the dictator eliminates a member of the ruling coalition with the probability $\epsilon \in (0, 1)$. In that case, the expected payoff to each member of the ruling coalition is $1 - \epsilon$. Thus we allow for the possibility that a member of the ruling coalition survives even if the dictator reneges and a rebellion is not staged. More precisely, $1 - \epsilon > 0$ implies that a

---

[13] Hirshleifer (1989) and Skaperdas (1996) discuss more general forms for a contest success function.

[14] In a more realistic setting, μ would be the dictator's choice rather than fixed. Here, we can think of μ as the maximum amount of power that the dictator can acquire by reneging without it being perfectly observed.

[15] Thus if the dictator reneges and a rebellion fails, the dictator still needs a ruling coalition with the power $1 - (b + \mu b)$ for his regime to stay in power.

[16] If a rebellion is staged and succeeds, the ruling coalition renegotiates the power-sharing agreement and chooses a new dictator.

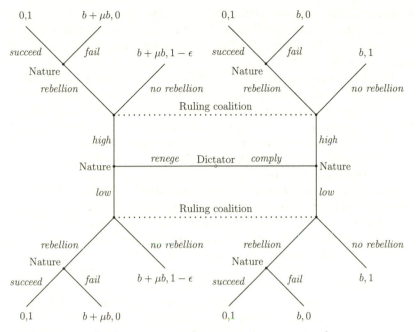

FIGURE 3.1. Authoritarian power-sharing game in extensive form.

member of the ruling coalition prefers being at the mercy of a dictator who reneged to participating in a failed rebellion.

Figure 3.1 portrays the timing of the actions and the payoffs in this authoritarian power-sharing game. First, the dictator chooses whether to renege or comply. Second, the ruling coalition observes an imperfect signal of the dictator's action and decides whether to rebel. Finally, if a rebellion is staged, then it either succeeds or fails.

3.2.1 Authoritarian Power-Sharing

Can the ruling coalition deter the dictator's opportunism using only the threat of a rebellion? The threat of a rebellion would certainly deter the dictator's opportunism if his actions were *perfectly observable*. The dictator would anticipate that if he reneged, the ruling coalition would plainly observe his actions and have no choice but to rebel. He would therefore always comply.

This reasoning does not extend to the present setting, in which a dictator's actions are not perfectly observable. Recall that the likelihood of a successful rebellion depends on the balance of power between the dictator and the ruling coalition. Thus staging a rebellion is costly to the ruling coalition because it may fail. As a result, the ruling coalition would prefer to threaten a rebellion if it observes a high signal, have the dictator believe this threat and therefore comply from the outset, but ultimately *not* carry out the rebellion despite having observed a high signal. Of course, believing such a threat on the dictator's part would not be consistent with the ruling coalition's strategy. Instead, the dictator would anticipate the ruling coalition's line of reasoning, not consider the threat of a rebellion credible, and thus renege.

The threat of a rebellion is credible only if the ruling coalition has an incentive to carry out its threat *after* the dictator has acted and the ruling coalition has observed an imperfect signal of his action. This incentive exists only if the possibility that the dictator reneged is real. In other words, the threat of a rebellion is *credible* only if the dictator reneges with a positive probability. This logic can be verified by examining the perfect Bayesian equilibrium of this authoritarian power-sharing game.

Allowing for mixed strategies, this game proceeds in four stages. First, the dictator reneges with probability α. Second, depending on the dictator's action, nature determines the realization of the signal θ with probability $\pi_{\theta a}$. Third, the ruling coalition rebels with probability β_θ after it observes the signal θ. For example, β_H is the probability that the ruling coalition rebels when it observes a high signal. Fourth, if a rebellion is staged, it succeeds with probability ρ.

First, consider the ruling coalition's equilibrium strategy β_θ. Based on the previous discussion, we may verify that there is no equilibrium in which the dictator uses a pure strategy *and* the ruling coalition conditions its decision to rebel on the observed signal.[17] In a mixed-strategy equilibrium, the ruling coalition rebels with probability β_θ such that, given the correlation between his actions and the signal θ, the dictator is indifferent between reneging and complying. Thus we have

$$\sum_{\theta \in \{H,L\}} \pi_{\theta c} \left[\beta_\theta (1-\rho) b + (1-\beta_\theta) b \right]$$

$$= \sum_{\theta \in \{H,L\}} \pi_{\theta d} \left[\beta_\theta (1-\rho)(b+\mu b) + (1-\beta_\theta)(b+\mu b) \right],$$

or, equivalently,

$$\sum_{\theta \in \{H,L\}} \pi_{\theta c}(1 - \beta_\theta \rho) b = \sum_{\theta \in \{H,L\}} \pi_{\theta d}(1 - \beta_\theta \rho)(b + \mu b). \tag{3.1}$$

Solving (3.1) for β_H, we obtain

$$\beta_H = \frac{\mu}{\pi_{Hr}(1+\mu) - \pi_{Hc}} \left(\frac{1}{\rho} - \beta_L \right) + \beta_L,$$

which implies that $\beta_H > \beta_L$. Intuitively, the ruling coalition rebels with a greater probability after observing a high signal than a low signal. Among the possible pairs (β_L, β_H) that satisfy equality (3.1), only the pairs $(\beta_L = 0, \beta_H > 0)$ and

---

[17] As is the case with many extensive games with imperfect information, this game also has an implausible equilibrium in which the ruling coalition ignores the information conveyed by the signal θ, rebels with probability 1, and the dictator reneges with probability 1.

($\beta_L > 0, \beta_H = 1$) constitute an equilibrium.[18] Moreover, the equilibrium in which $\beta_L = 0$ and $\beta_H > 0$ is focal from the point of view of a dictator and a ruling coalition who would like to share power: *Both* actors prefer this equilibrium to that in which $\beta_L > 0$ and $\beta_H = 1$.[19] Therefore the remainder of this chapter restricts attention to the relevant equilibrium, in which $\beta_L = 0$ and $\beta_H > 0$.

In this equilibrium, the ruling coalition rebels with a positive probability *only* after observing a high signal,

$$\beta_L^* = 0 \quad \text{and} \quad \beta_H^* = \frac{\mu}{\rho\left[\pi_{Hr}(1+\mu) - \pi_{Hc}\right]} > 0. \tag{3.2}$$

Furthermore, (3.2) implies that the equilibrium probability that the ruling coalition rebels after observing a high signal β_H^* is decreasing in both the probability that a rebellion succeeds (ρ) and the informativeness of the signal θ about the dictator's actions (π_{Hr}/π_{Hc}), whereas it is increasing in the amount of power μ that the dictator acquires by reneging. This raises the possibility that μ could be so large that the dictator would renege even if $\beta_H = 1$. That is, the dictator would renege even if the ruling coalition *always* rebelled after observing a high signal. To focus on settings in which a dictator is potentially deterrable, I make the following assumption.

Assumption 3.1 (Limited Temptation to Consolidate Power). *The additional power μ that the dictator acquires by reneging cannot be so large that the dictator reneges for all $\beta_H \leq 1$,*

$$\mu < \frac{\rho(\pi_{Hr} - \pi_{Hc})}{1 - \rho\pi_{Hr}}.$$

Assumption 3.1 admits a larger μ by the dictator when the signal θ is more informative about his actions and when the probability that a rebellion succeeds ρ is larger.

Finally, what is the dictator's equilibrium strategy α? In a mixed-strategy equilibrium, α must be such that the ruling coalition is indifferent between rebelling and not rebelling after observing a high signal. Although the ruling coalition does not directly observe the dictator's actions, we can compute the conditional probability that the dictator reneged given the signal that the ruling coalition observes. I denote this probability as $\Pr(a|\theta)$. For example, $\Pr(d|H)$ is the probability that the dictator reneged, given that the ruling coalition observes a high signal. Using Bayes' rule, we see that

$$\Pr(d|H) = \frac{\pi_{Hr}\alpha}{\pi_{Hr}\alpha + \pi_{Hc}(1-\alpha)}. \tag{3.3}$$

---

[18] In any equilibrium in mixed strategies, the ruling coalition is indifferent between rebelling and not rebelling after observing a high signal or a low signal but not both. Therefore, in an equilibrium in mixed strategies, either $\beta_L = 0$ or $\beta_H = 1$.

[19] A detailed proof of this claim, as well as of all the propositions that follow, is in the appendix to this chapter.

Then, the ruling coalition is indifferent between rebelling and not rebelling after observing a high signal whenever

$$\rho = \Pr(d|H)(1 - \epsilon) + 1 - \Pr(d|H),$$

where ρ is the expected payoff to the ruling coalition from rebelling, whereas $\Pr(d|H)(1 - \epsilon) + 1 - \Pr(d|H)$ is the expected payoff from no rebellion. Substituting $\Pr(d|H)$ from (3.3), the equilibrium probability with which the dictator reneges is

$$\alpha^* = \frac{\pi_{Hc}}{\pi_{Hc} + \pi_{Hr}\left(\frac{\epsilon}{1-\rho} - 1\right)}. \tag{3.4}$$

3.2.2   Balance of Power and Authoritarian Power-Sharing

I intentionally reserved the discussion of the effect of the balance of power between the dictator and the ruling coalition on their equilibrium behavior until now because it is central to the dynamics of authoritarian power-sharing. As outlined previously, depending on the balance of power between the dictator and the ruling coalition, two distinct power-sharing regimes may emerge.

First, a *contested autocracy* is an equilibrium in which a rebellion staged by the ruling coalition succeeds with a sufficiently high probability to credibly threaten the dictator. Despite the fact that the dictator reneges with a positive probability and rebellions do occur, the dictator's opportunism is at least partially deterred in this equilibrium. On the other hand, in an *established autocracy*, the balance of power between the dictator and the ruling coalition favors the dictator to the extent that a rebellion is so unlikely to succeed that he correctly anticipates that the ruling coalition will not stage one. In this regime, rebellions do not occur and the dictator has effectively eliminated the ruling coalition.

Equilibrium conditions (3.2) and (3.4) imply that as the balance of power between the dictator and the ruling coalition shifts in favor of the dictator, the ruling coalition rebels and the dictator reneges with increasing probability. That is, as the dictator becomes more powerful, his appetite for power grows and the ruling coalition counters it by rebelling with greater probability. This dynamic can be seen by substituting $\rho = 1 - b$ into (3.4),

$$\alpha^* = \frac{\pi_{Hc}}{\pi_{Hc} + \pi_{Hr}\left(\frac{\epsilon}{b} - 1\right)}.$$

How much power must the dictator acquire before the ruling coalition can no longer credibly threaten a rebellion? We may say that the threat of a rebellion lacks *ex-ante credibility* when the balance of power favors the dictator to the extent that the ruling coalition would not rebel even if it were certain that the dictator actually reneged. Thus the threat of a rebellion will be ex-ante credible as long as after the dictator reneges, the ruling coalition's expected payoff from rebelling is greater than the expected payoff from not rebelling, $\rho \geq 1 - \epsilon$, or equivalently, $\epsilon \geq b$. When the threat of a rebellion lacks ex-ante credibility, each member of the ruling coalition would rather do nothing and hope that the dictator does not eliminate him than stage a rebellion that would most likely fail.

Therefore, $b = \epsilon$ is the largest share of power held by the dictator under which the threat of a rebellion is ex-ante credible. Then as long as $b \in (0, \epsilon]$, the strategies of the dictator and the ruling coalition summarized by expressions (3.2) and (3.4) constitute an equilibrium of this power-sharing game. We can check that, given the equilibrium probability with which the dictator reneges α^* and as long as $\rho \geq 1 - \epsilon$, the ruling coalition prefers not to rebel when it observes a low signal,

$$\rho \leq \Pr(d|L)(1 - \epsilon) + 1 - \Pr(d|L).$$

Thus, the ruling coalition has no incentive to deviate from its equilibrium strategy of rebelling with a positive probability only when it observes a high signal $(\beta_L^* = 0, \beta_H^* > 0)$, as long as the threat of a rebellion is ex-ante credible. This condition also guarantees that $0 < \alpha^* \leq 1$. I call this equilibrium a *contested autocracy*.

Now consider the case when $b > \epsilon$. In this case, the success of a rebellion is so unlikely that the ruling coalition would not stage one even if it knew that the dictator reneged. Thus we have $\beta_L^* = \beta_H^* = 0$. In turn, there is nothing to deter the dictator from reneging and $\alpha^* = 1$. I call this equilibrium *established autocracy*. These results are summarized in the following proposition.

Proposition 3.1 (Authoritarian Power-Sharing). *In a perfect Bayesian equilibrium of the authoritarian power-sharing game,*

$$\alpha^* = \frac{\pi_{Hc}}{\pi_{Hc} + \pi_{Hr}\left(\frac{\epsilon}{1-\rho} - 1\right)}, \quad \beta_L^* = 0,$$

and

$$\beta_H^* = \frac{\mu}{\rho\left[\pi_{Hr}(1 + \mu) - \pi_{Hc}\right]} \quad if \quad b \in (0, \epsilon];$$

and $\alpha^* = 1$, $\beta_L^* = \beta_H^* = 0$ *if* $b \in (\epsilon, 1]$.

Does the ability of the dictator and the ruling coalition to share power under contested autocracy deteriorate as the dictator acquires more power? Power-sharing is successful when the dictator complies and the ruling coalition does not rebel,

$$\Pr(\text{Successful Power-Sharing}) = (1 - \alpha^*)\left[\pi_{Hc}(1 - \beta_H^*) + (1 - \pi_{Hc})\right].$$

We may check that the probability of successful power-sharing is decreasing in the dictator's power.

Furthermore, we have seen that under contested autocracy, both the probability that the dictator reneges and the probability that the ruling coalition rebels increase as the balance of power shifts in the dictator's favor. However, does the probability that a dictator reneges *successfully* also increase when he has accumulated more power? Under contested autocracy, the dictator reneges successfully when he reneges and (1) the ruling coalition observes a low signal; (2) the ruling coalition observes a high signal but does not rebel; or (3) the ruling coalition observes a high signal and stages a rebellion that fails. Thus the probability that the dictator gets away with reneging is

$$\text{Pr(Successful Reneging)} = \alpha^* \left[\pi_{Ld} + \pi_{Hr}(1 - \beta_H^*) + \pi_{Hr}\beta_H^*(1 - \rho) \right].$$

The appendix to this chapter confirms that the probability that the dictator successfully reneges is indeed increasing in the dictator's power. In other words, the moral hazard associated with authoritarian power-sharing intensifies as the dictator gains more power.

Proposition 3.2 (Balance of Power). *If $b \in (0, \epsilon]$, then α^*, β_H^*, and Pr(Successful Reneging are all increasing in b, whereas Pr(Successful Power-Sharing) is decreasing in b.*

We may also examine how the likelihood of successful power-sharing and the dictator's successful reneging depend on the precision of the signal θ about his actions. We can check that the equilibrium probabilities α^* and β_H^* are decreasing in π_{Hr} and increasing in π_{Hc}. Therefore, when the signal θ about the dictator's actions is more informative (i.e., π_{Hr}/π_{Hc} increases), the likelihood of successful power-sharing is greater. On the other hand, the relationship between the dictator's probability of successfully reneging and the informativeness of the signal θ is nonmonotonic.

Proposition 3.3 (Transparency). *If $b \in (0, \epsilon]$, then Pr(Successful Power-Sharing) is increasing in the informativeness of the signal θ about the dictator's actions, π_{Hr}/π_{Hc}.*

Finally, observe that the equilibrium probability with which the dictator reneges α^* is decreasing in ϵ, the probability with which he eliminates a member of the ruling coalition if he successfully reneges. Although not an explicit part of this model, if larger ruling coalitions are associated with a lower probability of any ruling-coalition member being eliminated and, therefore, a lower ϵ, then larger ruling coalitions may be better able to deter the dictator's opportunism and thus successfully share power.

To illustrate the findings in this section, consider the following numerical example. When $\pi_{Hr} = 0.8$, $\pi_{Hc} = 0.2$, $\mu = 0.2$, $b = 0.45$, and $\epsilon = 0.5$, a rebellion succeeds with the probability $\rho = 0.55$; the ruling coalition never rebels when the signal θ is low ($\beta_L^* = 0$) but rebels when the signal θ is high with the probability $\beta_H^* = 0.48$; and the dictator reneges with the probability $\alpha^* = 0.69$. The probability of successful power-sharing under these conditions is 0.28 and the probability that the dictator successfully reneges is 0.55. This is an example of contested autocracy because $b < \epsilon$. However, if the dictator successfully reneges, his power grows to $b = 0.54 > \epsilon = 0.5$. In that case, this regime becomes established with $\beta_L^* = \beta_H^* = 0$ and $\alpha^* = 1$.

3.2.3 A Model with Endogenously Evolving Balance of Power

Although the results so far are based on a single-period extensive game, they suggest a dynamic interpretation of the dictator's power trajectory. That is, we could conceive of a repeated game in which the balance of power between the dictator and the ruling coalition in each period depends on whether the dictator successfully reneged in the previous period. Proposition 3.1 implies that, under contested autocracy, the dictator will act opportunistically with a positive probability and the ruling coalition will rebel with a positive probability as well. Proposition 3.2 implies that the probability that the dictator indeed acquires more power is always positive and, in fact, increases with that power. Any contested autocrat therefore may become established if he succeeds in acquiring a sufficient amount of power, although such a trajectory is unlikely.

I now examine such a multiperiod game. In an equilibrium of this game, the balance of power between the dictator and the ruling coalition evolves *endogenously*. The dynamic in this multiperiod game is qualitatively identical to that in the single-period game. In the next section, I use this multiperiod game to examine the implications of my theory for the statistical analysis of leaders tenures in authoritarian regimes.

Periods are indexed by $t = \{T, T - 1, \ldots, 1, 0\}$ so in any period, T is the number of times the dictator must successfully renege to become an established autocrat. Thus, $t = 1$ denotes the period in which a single successful reneging turns contested into established autocracy. The game ends in period $t = 0$ in which $b_0 > \epsilon$ and the ruling coalition's threat to rebels is no longer ex-ante credible.

In each period, the dictator and the ruling coalition receive one of the three possible payoffs portrayed in Figure 3.1. Recall that these payoffs depend on whether the dictator reneges, whether the ruling coalition rebels, and whether a rebellion succeeds. In any period, the existing balance of power b_t summarizes the payoff-relevant history of play. Then

$$V^t = (b_t + \delta V^t)(1 - \alpha_t) \left[\pi_{Hc} \beta_t (1 - \rho_t) + \pi_{Hc}(1 - \beta_t) + 1 - \pi_{Hc} \right]$$
$$+ (b_t + \mu b_t + \delta V^{t-1})\alpha_t \left[\pi_{Hr} \beta_t (1 - \rho_t) + \pi_{Hr}(1 - \beta_t) + 1 - \pi_{Hr} \right],$$

and

$$U^t = (1 + \delta U^t)[\alpha_t \pi_{Hr} \beta_t \rho_t + (1 - \alpha_t)\pi_{Hc}\beta_t \rho_t + (1 - \alpha_t)\pi_{Hc}(1 - \beta_t)$$
$$+ (1 - \alpha_t)(1 - \pi_{Hc})] + (1 - \epsilon + \delta U^{t-1}) \left[\alpha_t \pi_{Hr}(1 - \beta_t) + \alpha_t(1 - \pi_{Hr}) \right]$$

are the discounted expected payoffs to the dictator and any member of the ruling coalition in period t, respectively, and $\delta \in (0, 1)$ is a discount factor. When the dictator becomes established, $V^0 = 1$ and $U^0 = 1 - \epsilon$.

Suppose that given an existing balance of power, the ruling coalition uses the threat of a rebellion in a way that is optimal from that period onward and ignores any previous history of play. That is, we examine a Markov perfect equilibrium of this multiperiod, authoritarian power-sharing game. Optimal strategies can be computed using backward induction by starting in period

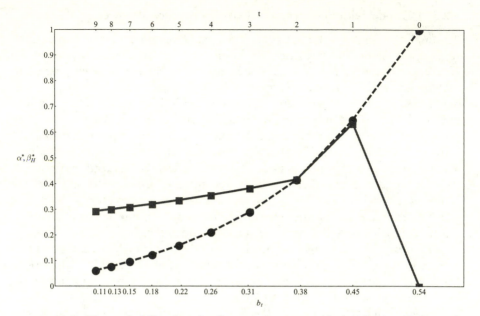

FIGURE 3.2. The probability that the dictator reneges, α^* (dashed line), and the probability that the ruling coalition rebels if it observes a high signal, β_H^* (solid line), in an equilibrium of the multiperiod authoritarian power-sharing game.

$t = 1$ and then proceeding recursively for the remaining periods. Explicit solutions obtained in this way are far too complicated algebraically to be useful. I therefore present a numerical example here instead.

Suppose that $\pi_{Hr} = 0.8$, $\pi_{Hc} = 0.2$, $\mu = 0.2$, $\epsilon = 0.5$, and $\delta = 0.1$ and the initial balance of power is 0.11. In this case, the dictator must renege successfully nine times to become established, $T = 9$ and $b_t = (0.11, 0.13, 0.15, 0.18, 0.22, 0.26, 0.31, 0.38, 0.45)$ for $t = 9, \ldots, 1$. The equilibrium probabilities with which the dictator reneges and the ruling coalition rebels, α_t^* and β_{Ht}^*, are portrayed in Figure 3.2. The horizontal axis denotes both the periods t (i.e., upper axis) and the balance of power b_t (i.e., lower axis) in these periods. We see that the equilibrium probabilities that the dictator reneges and the ruling coalition rebels are increasing as he acquires more power until period 1, when $b_1 = 0.45$. If the dictator successfully reneges in that period, he becomes established and the ruling coalition prefers to be at his mercy to staging a rebellion. This numerical example can be easily generalized to any number of periods T.

3.3 IMPLICATIONS FOR THE EMPIRICAL STUDY OF AUTHORITARIAN TENURES

Some of the key theoretical results so far have been stated with respect to the balance of power between the dictator and the ruling coalition – a factor that is difficult to measure in large-N data. An advantage of the model in Section 3.2 is that it has unambiguous implications for another outcome that is easily observable and of substantial political interest: the amount of time that a dictator stays in power.[20] We can derive the statistical distribution of an authoritarian leader's time in office until a successful rebellion, the time until an autocracy becomes established, and the distribution of the time that a leader is expected to spend at each step of his power trajectory. In fact, a convenient feature of the equilibrium in mixed strategies examined in Section 3.2 is that statistical distributions of these quantities can be derived directly from the multiperiod model. Furthermore, these distributions correspond to standard survival distributions. The claims advanced in Section 3.2 therefore can be evaluated within a well-specified statistical framework.

As previously, periods are indexed by $t = \{T, T-1, \ldots, 1, 0\}$, where $T > 0$ denotes the number of times that the dictator must successfully renege to become established. Then along the dictator's equilibrium-power trajectory, three possible outcomes – successful power-sharing, a successful rebellion, or successful reneging – occur with the following probabilities:

$$\Pr(\text{Successful Power-Sharing}_t) = (1 - \alpha_t)(1 - \pi_{Hc}$$
$$+ \pi_{Hc}[1 - \beta_{Ht} + \beta_{Ht}(1 - \rho_t)]),$$
$$\Pr(\text{Successful Rebellion}_t) = [\alpha_t \pi_{Hr} + (1 - \alpha_t)\pi_{Hc}]\beta_{Ht}\rho_t,$$
$$\Pr(\text{Successful Reneging}_t) = \alpha_t(1 - \pi_{Hr} + \pi_{Hr}[\beta_{Ht}(1 - \rho_t)$$
$$+ 1 - \beta_{Ht}]) \quad \text{for} \quad t = T, \ldots, 1.$$

The probability of each outcome depends only on the current balance of power between the dictator and the ruling coalition, b_t. Therefore, the equilibrium path in this game can be statistically represented by a discrete-time absorbing Markov chain in which the states $t = T, \ldots, 1$ are transient, whereas the states established and rebellion are absorbing. Using the canonical form, the transition matrix is

$$\mathbf{P} = \begin{pmatrix} \mathbf{Q} & \mathbf{C} \\ \mathbf{0} & \mathbf{I} \end{pmatrix},$$

where $\mathbf{Q}$ is a $T \times T$ matrix of transition probabilities for the states $t = T, \ldots, 1$; $\mathbf{C}$ is a $T \times 2$ matrix of transition probabilities from the T transient into the two absorbing states; $\mathbf{0}$ is a $2 \times T$ matrix of zeros; and $\mathbf{I}$ is a 2×2 identity matrix.

The fundamental matrix $\mathbf{M} = (\mathbf{I} - \mathbf{Q})^{-1}$ exists and its first row denotes the expected time the dictator spends at each step of the power trajectory before he is either removed by a rebellion or becomes established.[21] Continuing with the numerical example in the previous section, these expected times are 8.98, 3.49,

[20] On the study of the duration of dictators' tenures, see Bueno de Mesquita et al. (2003), Gandhi and Przeworski (2006, 2007), Gandhi (2008, Chap. 6), and Goemans (2008).

[21] See, e.g., Trivedi (2002, Chap. 7).

1.47, 0.67, 0.32, 0.16, 0.08, 0.04, 0.02 for states $t = T, \ldots, 1$, respectively. The distribution of these expected times illustrates how the ruling coalition's concern that the dictator may become established intensifies as he acquires more power. In terms of the expected time that the dictator spends at each step of his power trajectory, his transition from one step to the next accelerates as he acquires more power. Adding these expected times, we obtain the total expected time before the dictator is removed by a rebellion or becomes established; in our numerical example, this time is 15.23.

The first row of the product **MC** contains the long-run distribution of the two absorbing states, *established* and *rebellion*. In the numerical example, we should expect that only 1 percent of dictators will become established autocrats, whereas the remaining 99 percent will be removed by a rebellion. However, this distribution depends on the number of steps that the dictator must take to become established. In our numerical example $T = 9$, but as many as 23 percent of dictators would become established if the dictator had to successfully renege only four times to become an established autocrat.

An important implication of this result for the statistical analysis of dictator tenures is that a positive fraction of dictators may stay in office for an arbitrarily long period. In real-world cases, of course, a dictator may be removed not only by a rebellion but also via alternative forms of exit, such as natural death, foreign intervention, or transition to democracy. Nevertheless, the present analysis implies that a positive fraction of existing dictators may at any time no longer be at the risk of losing power in a rebellion. Ignoring this possibility may lead to incorrect inferences about the effects of covariates on leader survival.[22]

The probability distribution of time-to-rebellion implied by the present model is of particular empirical interest because of available data on the timing of dictators' removal from office. The coup d'état, defined in Chapter 2 as the removal of an authoritarian leader by his inner circle, is the closest empirical counterpart to allies' rebellions in this chapter. The probability distribution of time-to-rebellion can be obtained using the power method. For time $\tau = \{1, 2, \ldots, \infty\}$, the probability distribution of time-to-rebellion is given in position $T + 2$ of the vector $\mathbf{p_0 P}^\tau$, where $\mathbf{p_0}$ is the initial $1 \times (T + 2)$ probability vector $\mathbf{p_0} = (1, 0, \ldots, 0)$.[23] Thus under contested autocracy, the distribution of time-to-rebellion follows a generalized geometric distribution with a probability of success that decreases for $t = T, \ldots, 1$. Its continuous-time analogue is the Weibull distribution with an increasing hazard rate (Ali Khan et al. 1989).[24] On the other hand, the probability density of time-to-established autocracy is given in position $T + 1$ of the vector $\mathbf{p_0 P}^\tau$. It follows the

---

[22] Survival techniques that account for the possibility that a fraction of observations may not be subject to the relevant risk – such as cure rate or split-population models – have been applied in political science by Box–Steffensmeier et al. (2005) and Svolik (2008).

[23] This result can be easily extended to the case of an arbitrary distribution of starting points by working with an initial vector that describes that distribution.

[24] This is the distribution of successful rebellions, but it is easy to see that the distribution of failed rebellions is also Weibull.

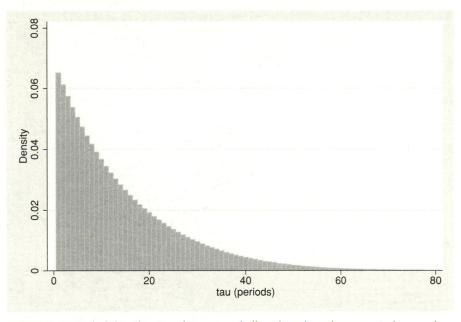

FIGURE 3.3. Probability density of time-to-rebellion based on the numerical example.

generalized negative-binomial distribution with T successes and a probability of success that decreases with $t = T, \ldots, 1$. The equivalent continuous-time distribution is the generalized Gamma distribution (Gerber 1991).

To illustrate these results, I continue with the numerical example from Section 3.2 and plot the probability density of time-to-rebellion and time-to-established autocracy in Figures 3.3 and 3.4, respectively. We may compare this numerical illustration with the distribution of successful coups d'état based on actual data in Figure 3.5. The model in Section 3.2 implies a distribution of successful coups that reasonably reflects real-world data.[25]

3.4 THE PATH TO PERSONAL AUTOCRACY AND AUTHORITARIAN EXIT FROM OFFICE

A key implication of the theoretical analysis in this chapter concerns the empirical association between the length of dictators' tenures and the manner by which they leave office.[26] The longer a dictator is in office, the more likely it is

---

[25] Understandably, existing large-N data do not record whether an autocracy is contested or established. We therefore should expect that observations of dictators' tenures contain both contested and established autocrats. Whereas both the hazard of time-to-established autocracy and time-to-rebellions are increasing over time, the hazard of a successful rebellion declines relative to that of the dictator becoming established after a certain threshold time. In my numerical example, that time is thirty-five years. We therefore should expect the hazard of successful rebellions to be first increasing and then decreasing in actual real-world data.

[26] Goemans (2008) comprehensively studies the manner in which leaders lose office across regime types.

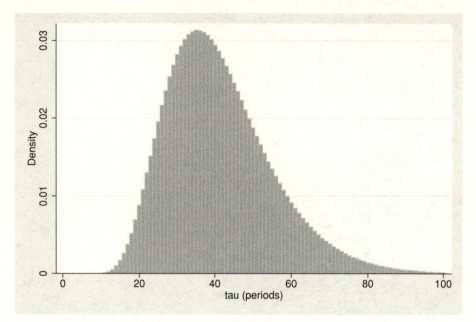

FIGURE 3.4. Probability density of time-to–established autocracy based on the numerical example.

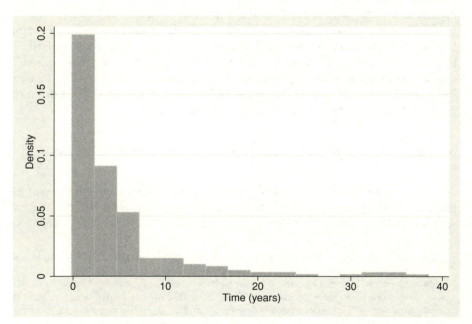

FIGURE 3.5. The empirical density of coups d'état, 1946–2008.

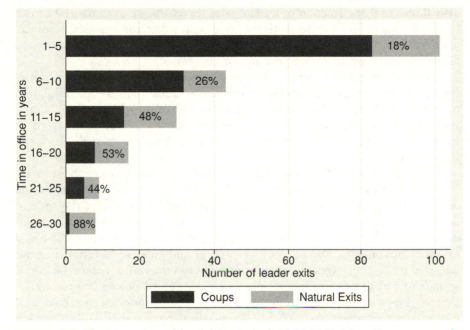

FIGURE 3.6. The improving odds of dying in bed, 1946–2008. *Note:* Percentages refer to natural exits as a fraction of both types of exits in each tenure interval.

that he is an established rather than a contested autocrat and the less likely it is that he will be removed from office by his inner circle. Hence long-lived authoritarian leaders should leave office more often in ways that are unrelated to their interaction with their inner circle, such as natural death, foreign intervention, or popular uprising.[27]

To evaluate this prediction, consider how the relative risk of coups d'état and natural deaths varies across dictators with different tenure durations.[28] Figure 3.6 contrasts exits by coups to exits due to natural causes across six ordered, five-year intervals of tenure durations. Leaders who stayed in office for less than a year are not plotted because they may have been particularly vulnerable to coups. Leaders who stayed in office for more than thirty years also are excluded because only few of such long-serving leaders survive in any five-year tenure interval above thirty years and therefore may be unrepresentative.[29]

Consistent with the model in this chapter, the total number of leaders that manage to survive in office declines over time. More importantly, Figure 3.6

---

[27] Nevertheless, there are examples of leaders (e.g., Haile Selassie of Ethiopia) who ruled for an unusually long time and managed to consolidate power in their hands but were later removed from office by their inner circle. The model in this chapter implies that such cases may occur but should be the exception rather than the rule.

[28] Luttwak (1968), O'Kane (1981), Londregan and Poole (1990), Galetovic and Sanhueza (2000), and Belkin and Schofer (2003) examine coups d'état empirically.

[29] There are 16, 44, and 4 leaders in the 31–35, 36–40, and 41–45 tenure intervals, respectively.

also shows that the fraction of leaders who leave office due to natural causes rather than a coup increases with the time that a dictator has been in office. This pattern is directly implied by the conceptual difference between contested and established autocracy outlined in this chapter.

Could the observed increase in natural exits from office be the consequence of an age-related increase in mortality rather than the consolidation of power by long-serving dictators? This is unlikely to be the case. Long-serving dictators are indeed older on average; the average age grows from 54 to 57, 60, 63, 67, and 68 across the six tenure-duration intervals shown in Figure 3.6.

However, an age-related increase in mortality is unlikely to be the primary cause of the observed increase in natural exits from office. Using information on dictators' dates of birth and death, I calculated their age at the time of death and estimated the age-related mortality among those who died of natural causes – whether in office or after leaving office. These estimates are based on the nonparametric Kaplan–Meier estimator and indicate that the difference between the average ages of two adjacent tenure intervals in Figure 3.6 corresponds to a mortality increase of only 5, 2, 6, 11, and 1 percent, respectively – that is, 5 percent on average. By contrast, the corresponding percentage of natural exits increases by 7, 22, 5, −8, and 43 percent – that is, 13.8 percent on average. Therefore, the most likely, primary cause of the improving odds of dying in bed observed among long-serving dictators is not related to their age but rather to the consolidation of power by established autocrats explored throughout this chapter.

3.5 CONCLUSION: THE MANAGEMENT OF ESTABLISHED AUTOCRACY

All principalities, Niccolò Machiavelli wrote in *The Prince*, are governed in two different ways. The first are governed "by a prince with all others as his servants" who merely assist him in governing and, if they are obeyed, it is "because they are his ministers and officials"; the second are governed "by a prince and by barons" who have their "own dominions" and "are recognized by their subjects." In the Kingdom of the Turk, which is an example of the former according to Machiavelli, all ministers are "his slaves and bound to him." However, the King of France, who is an example of the latter, cannot take away the privileges of the barons "without endangering himself" (Machiavelli 2005[1513], 16–17).

Machiavelli's distinction between these two types of principalities mirrors the two authoritarian power-sharing regimes examined in this chapter. Under contested autocracy, the dictator's allies are genuine political players who share power with him and constrain his choices. In established autocracies, they are in a position of fully subservient administrators and do not share power with the dictator in any meaningful sense. The analysis in this chapter highlights that the difference between the two comes down to answering a simple question: Are the dictator's allies capable of replacing him? This is a distinction that may be obscured by the descriptively richer but also less analytically focused notions of personalist, neopatrimonial, and sultanistic regimes.

Nevertheless, no dictator governs alone. Even established autocrats – like Machiavelli's Turk – depend on their ministers and officials for governing: administration, repression, taxation, and so on. As Lewis (1978, 622) stated in his study of Antonio Salazar's ministerial elite, "regardless of how powerful dictators are, the complexities of modern society and government make it impossible for them to rule alone."

Hence even established autocrats are not entirely free of constraints on their authority. Even at the height of Stalin's dictatorship, according to Gorlizki and Khlevniuk (2006, 254), built-in forces continued pushing toward oligarchic or collegial rule and "found their expression in the relative autonomy of Politburo leaders in dealing with everyday operational issues. . . ." Such operational dependence raises the possibility that a talented vizier or general may turn into a rival if he becomes admired or perceived as indispensable. The dictator's operational dependence on his administrators thus contains the seeds of his political dependence.

Established autocrats counter that danger with a number of instruments: key administrators or military commanders are periodically purged, publicly humiliated, rotated across posts, or dismissed and later reappointed. Reports of systematic use of such practices date back to at least Mughal India and the Ottoman Empire (see, e.g., Debs 2007). One of the most prominent twentieth-century applications of these practices occurred in Mobutu Sese Seko's Zaire. According to a report by the journalist Blain Harden:

Conventional wisdom in Kinshasa says that besides Mobutu and his family only 80 people in the country count. At any one time, 20 of them are ministers, 20 are exiles, 20 are in jail and 20 are ambassadors. Every three months, the music stops and Mobutu forces everyone to change chairs.[30]

Likewise, Gabonese President Omar Bongo frequently and unpredictably rotated, promoted, and dismissed his governors; Benito Mussolini referred to his cabinet reshuffles as "changing the guard" (Lewis 2002, 23); and Rafael Trujillo's penchant for arbitrary purges and reinstatements of leading government officials underpins the plot of Mario Vargas Llosa's celebrated novel, *The Feast of the Goat.*

According to most existing explanations, these practices protect the dictator by preventing administrators from establishing an independent power base (Jackson and Rosberg 1982; Migdal 1988; Quinlivan 1999; Debs 2007).[31] Yet the analytical difference between contested and established autocrats outlined in this chapter suggests an alternative explanation, one that more closely mirrors the distinctive features of these practices.

---

[30] "Zaire's President Mobutu Sese Seko: Political Craftsman Worth Billions," *The Washington Post*, 10 November 1987.

[31] Debs (2007) also examines the implication of these practices for economic development.

The conspicuous feature of these practices is not only the temporariness of political appointments but also the arbitrary and public nature of their abrogation: In most accounts, rotations, dismissals, or personal attacks come unexpectedly, without an objective rationale, and are accompanied by a campaign of public humiliation. This suggests that the common primary purpose behind these practices is to *publicly signal* the dictator's independence from his administrators. Thus following World War II, after the war's exigencies conferred a measure of bureaucratic autonomy on Stalin's associates, Stalin conducted a series of humiliating, arbitrary, and public attacks against his inner circle to restore the absolute leadership that prevailed before the war (Gorlizki and Khlevniuk 2004, Chap. 1).

That is, even if established autocrats depend on their administrators as a collective, they ensure that such dependence does not translate into the public perception that any *individual* administrator is indispensable. Hence whereas Saddam Hussein depended on the loyalty of the many Tikritis he favored in the country's administration, he nevertheless ensured that

... no single one of them or indeed grouping amongst them should be in a position to challenge him. Nor should any of them assume that they have a right to the favors dispensed by [him]. On the contrary, they are constantly reminded, through reassignment and through the granting of land and of economic concessions, as well as through the withdrawal of the same, that they are all creatures of the president. (Tripp 2000, 266–7)

Under established autocracy, the dictator's outward appearance of invincibility is as important as his actual power.

This is why personality cults are the hallmark – and primarily a consequence rather than the cause – of established autocracy. According to Suny (1997, 38), Stalin – who was short in stature, a mediocre speaker, and the "ultimate man of the machine" – did not project an image of a leader until one was created for him. Unlike regime propaganda, the purpose of which is to disseminate ideology, a personality cult aims to reinforce the dictator's paramount political standing. Thus Hafez al-Asad was the twentieth-century's Saladin (Wedeen 1999, 1); Saddam Hussein was the new Nebuchadnezzar (Karsh 2002, 152–3); and His Excellency, the Generalissimo, Doctor Rafael Léonidas Trujillo Molina, Honorable President of the Republic, Benefactor of the Nation, Restorer of the Financial Independence of the Country, and Commander-in-Chief of the Armed Forces was right next to God when his regime ordered that even churches display the slogan "God in Heaven, Trujillo on Earth" (López-Calvo 2005). Even more than that: The self-dubbed Light of Human Genius Kim Il Sung could control the weather with his mood (Oh and Hassig 2000, 4); Chairman Mao could swim nearly four times the world record (Harding 1997, 176); and Togo's Gnassingbé Eyadéma commanded superpowers in the comic books that his regime commissioned (Lamb 1984, 48).

Whereas an established autocrat boasts of supernatural powers, everyone else fades into anonymity. Thus at the peak of Mobutu Sese Seko's personality cult in 1974–1975, official media were banned from mentioning by name any government figure other than Mobutu (Young 1985, 168). As one of Mobutu's ministers explained,

In our religion, we have our own theologians. In all religions, and at all times there are prophets. Why not today? God has sent a great prophet, our prestigious Guide Mobutu – this prophet is our liberator, our Messiah. Our Church is the [Popular Movement of the Revolution]. Its chief is Mobutu, we respect him like one respects the Pope. Our gospel is Mobutuism. This is why crucifixes must be replaced by the image of our Messiah. (Young 1985, 168–9)

The arguments in this chapter illuminate why the astounding absurdity of personality cults fails to undermine their effectiveness, as observers frequently wonder.[32] On the contrary, it serves to reinforce the political message behind personality cults: "In this regime, only one person counts!"

This is the first of two chapters that focus on the problem of authoritarian power-sharing. Throughout this chapter, I have focused on the threat of an allies' rebellion as the unique, coercive mechanism available to a ruling coalition that faces an opportunistic dictator. We saw that even under contested autocracy, the threat of rebellion by the ruling coalition remains tenuous, only imperfectly deterring a dictator's opportunism. It thus echoes Aristotle's warning in the epigraph to Chapter 1 about the dangers of oligarchs falling out among themselves. The instability of power-sharing is a consequence of the distinctive, dismal conditions under which authoritarian power-sharing takes place. Authoritarian elites cannot rely on an independent authority to enforce their agreements about sharing power, they may use violence to resolve mutual conflicts, and they typically operate under a shroud of secrecy.

Although the first two of these factors are beyond the control of authoritarian elites, the last – secrecy in power-sharing – might be reduced, if not eliminated, by adopting appropriate political institutions. Section 3.2, for instance, explains that secrecy exacerbates the moral hazard in authoritarian power-sharing, thereby undermining its success. The equilibrium dynamics under contested and established autocracies therefore may be considered a benchmark for feasible authoritarian power-sharing in settings that lack political institutions, suggesting one rationale for political institutions in dictatorships: Regular interaction within governing councils, legislatures, or parties may allow the governing authoritarian elite to reassure one another that none of them is trying to acquire more power at the others' expense. I investigate this potential contribution of institutions to the stability of authoritarian rule in the next chapter.

3.6 APPENDIX: PROOFS

This appendix provides details of the formal results in Section 3.2.

---

[32] See, e.g., "Toughs at the Top," *The Economist*, 18 December 2004.

Proposition 3.1. *As explained previously, there is no equilibrium in which the dictator uses a pure strategy and the ruling coalition conditions its decision to rebel on the observed signal.*

In any equilibrium in mixed strategies, (1) the ruling coalition rebels with probability β_θ such that given the correlation between his actions and the signal θ, the dictator is indifferent between reneging and complying; and (2) the dictator reneges with probability α such that the ruling coalition is indifferent between rebelling and not rebelling after observing a high signal or a low signal, but not both.

Note that the ruling coalition cannot be indifferent between rebelling and not rebelling after both a high and a low signal: If the dictator chooses such α as to make the ruling coalition indifferent between rebelling and not rebelling after observing a high signal, then the ruling coalition will prefer not to rebel after observing a low signal. Alternatively, if the dictator chooses such α as to make the ruling coalition indifferent between rebelling and not rebelling after observing a low signal, than the ruling coalition will prefer to rebel after observing a high signal.

Thus for the ruling coalition, only the actions $(\beta_L = 0, \beta_H > 0)$ and $(\beta_L > 0, \beta_H = 1)$ can be parts of an equilibrium. To obtain the equilibrium action profile, we solve for the indifference conditions.

In the case of $(\beta_L = 0, \beta_H > 0)$, we have

$$\beta_H^* = \frac{\mu}{\rho\left[\pi_{Hr}(1+\mu) - \pi_{Hc}\right]} \quad \text{and} \quad \alpha^* = \frac{\pi_{Hc}}{\pi_{Hc} + \pi_{Hr}\left(\frac{\epsilon}{1-\rho} - 1\right)}. \quad (3.5)$$

To verify that $\beta_L^* = 0$, it must be true that the ruling coalition prefers not to rebel after it observed a low signal,

$$\rho \leq \Pr(d|L)(1 - \epsilon) + 1 - \Pr(d|L). \quad (3.6)$$

After substituting α^* into

$$\Pr(d|L) = \frac{\pi_{Ld}\alpha^*}{\pi_{Ld}\alpha^* + \pi_{Lc}(1 - \alpha^*)},$$

inequality (3.6) can be reduced to

$$-\frac{(\pi_{Hr} - \pi_{Hc})(1 - \rho)[\rho - (1 - \epsilon)]}{\epsilon(\pi_{Hr} - \pi_{Hc}\pi_{Hr}) - (1 - \rho)(\pi_{Hr} - \pi_{Hc})} \leq 0,$$

which holds as long as $\rho \geq 1 - \epsilon$.

In the case of $(\beta_L > 0, \beta_H = 1)$, the indifference condition implies

$$\beta_L^{**} = \frac{\pi_{Hr} - \pi_{Hc} - (\frac{1}{\rho} - \pi_{Hr})\mu}{\pi_{Hr} - \pi_{Hc} - (1 - \pi_{Hr})\mu} \quad \text{and} \quad \alpha^{**} = \frac{1 - \pi_{Hc}}{\pi_{Hr} - \pi_{Hc} + (1 - \pi_{Hc})\left(\frac{\epsilon}{1-\rho}\right)}.$$

To verify that $\beta_H^{**} = 1$, it must be true that the ruling coalition prefers to rebel after it observed a high signal,

$$\rho \geq \Pr(d|H)(1 - \epsilon) + 1 - \Pr(d|H). \tag{3.7}$$

After substituting α^{**} into

$$\Pr(d|H) = \frac{\pi_{Hr}\alpha^{**}}{\pi_{Hr}\alpha^{**} + \pi_{Hc}(1 - \alpha^{**})},$$

inequality (3.7) can be reduced to

$$\frac{(\pi_{Hr} - \pi_{Hc})(1 - \rho)[\rho - (1 - \epsilon)]}{(\pi_{Hr} - \pi_{Hc})(1 - \rho) + \pi_{Hc}(1 - \pi_{Hr})\epsilon} \geq 0,$$

which holds as long as $\rho \geq 1 - \epsilon$.

Moreover, the expected payoff to *both* the dictator and the ruling coalition is greater in the equilibrium with $(\beta_L = 0, \beta_H > 0)$ than it is in the equilibrium with $(\beta_L > 0, \beta_H = 1)$. In the equilibrium with $(\beta_L = 0, \beta_H > 0)$, the expected payoff to the dictator is

$$\frac{b(\pi_{Hr} - \pi_{Hc})(1 + \mu)}{\pi_{Hr} - \pi_{Hc} + \pi_{Hr}\mu},$$

and it is

$$\frac{b(\pi_{Hr} - \pi_{Hc})(1 - \rho)(1 + \mu)}{\pi_{Hr} - \pi_{Hc} - \mu(1 - \pi_{Hr})}$$

in the equilibrium with $(\beta_L > 0, \beta_H = 1)$. The difference between the former and the latter is

$$(\pi_{Hr} - \pi_{Hc})(1 + \mu)(1 - \rho)\frac{\rho(\pi_{Hr} - \pi_{Hc}) - \mu(1 - \rho\pi_{Hr})}{[\pi_{Hr}(1 + \mu) - \pi_{Hc}][\pi_{Hr} - \pi_{Hc} - \mu(1 - \pi_{Hr})]},$$

which is positive as long as Assumption 3.1 is satisfied.

In the equilibrium with $(\beta_L = 0, \beta_H > 0)$, the expected payoff to the ruling coalition is

$$\frac{(\pi_{Hr} - \pi_{Hc})[\rho - (1 - \epsilon)] + \pi_{Hc}\epsilon\rho}{(\pi_{Hr} - \pi_{Hc})[\rho - (1 - \epsilon)] + \pi_{Hc}\epsilon},$$

and it is ρ in the equilibrium with $(\beta_L > 0, \beta_H = 1)$. The difference between the former and the latter is

$$\frac{(\pi_{Hr} - \pi_{Hc})(1 - \rho)[\rho - (1 - \epsilon)]}{(\pi_{Hr} - \pi_{Hc})(1 - \rho) + \pi_{Hr}\epsilon},$$

which is positive as long as $\rho \geq 1 - \epsilon$. Thus *both* the dictator and the ruling coalition prefer the equilibrium in which $(\beta_L = 0, \beta_H > 0)$ to the equilibrium in which $(\beta_L > 0, \beta_H = 1)$. This concludes all proofs associated with Proposition 1.

Proposition 3.2. *Recall that the probability of successful power-sharing is*

$$\Pr(\text{Successful Power-Sharing}) = (1 - \alpha^*)\left[\pi_{Hc}(1 - \beta_H^*) + (1 - \pi_{Hc})\right]$$
$$= (1 - \alpha^*)(1 - \pi_{Hc}\beta_H^*). \qquad (3.8)$$

We saw that under contested autocracy with $(\beta_L = 0, \beta_H > 0)$, both the probability that the dictator reneges (α^*) and the probability that the ruling coalition rebels after observing a high signal (β_H^*) increase as the balance of power (b) shifts in the dictator's favor. In turn, the probability of successful power-sharing is decreasing in the dictator's power.

The probability that the dictator successfully reneges is

$$\Pr(\text{Successful Reneging}) = \alpha^*\left[\pi_{Ld} + \pi_{Hr}(1 - \beta_H^*) + \pi_{Hr}\beta_H^*(1 - \rho)\right]$$
$$= \alpha^*(1 - \pi_{Hr}\rho\beta_H^*).$$

Substituting α^* and β_H^* from (3.5), we obtain

$$\Pr(\text{Successful Reneging}) = \frac{b\pi_{Hc}(\pi_{Hr} - \pi_{Hc})}{[\pi_{Hr}\epsilon - b(\pi_{Hr} - \pi_{Hc})][\pi_{Hr}(1 + \mu) - \pi_{Hc}]}.$$

Finally, differentiating with respect to b, we obtain

$$\frac{\partial \Pr(\text{Successful Reneging})}{\partial b} = \frac{\pi_{Hc}\pi_{Hr}(\pi_{Hr} - \pi_{Hc})\epsilon}{[\pi_{Hr}\epsilon - b(\pi_{Hr} - \pi_{Hc})]^2[\pi_{Hr}(1 + \mu) - \pi_{Hc}]} > 0.$$

Thus the probability that the dictator successfully reneges is increasing in his power.

Proposition 3.3. *By inspection of (3.5), we see that both α^* and β_H^* are decreasing in π_{Hr} and increasing in π_{Hc}. To see that α^* is increasing in π_{Hc}, differentiate α^* with respect to π_{Hc} to obtain*

$$\frac{\partial \alpha^*}{\partial \pi_{Hc}} = \frac{\pi_{Hr}b(\epsilon - b)}{[\pi_{Hr}(\epsilon - b) + \pi_{Hc}b]^2} > 0.$$

In turn, the probability of successful power-sharing in (3.8) is increasing in π_{Hr} and decreasing in π_{Hc}.

4

When and Why Institutions Contribute
to Authoritarian Stability

Commitment, Monitoring, and Collective Action Problems in Authoritarian Power-Sharing

> [We] failed to institutionalize and legalize inner-Party democracy...we drew up the relevant laws but they lacked due authority. This meant that conditions were present for the over-concentration of Party power in individuals and for the development of arbitrary individual rule and the personality cult in the Party.
>
> Communist Party of China, *Resolution on Party History (1949–81)*

> When an artful and bold man is placed at the head of an army or faction, it is often easy for him, by employing sometimes violence, sometimes false pretenses, to establish his dominions over a people a hundred times more numerous than his partisans. He allows no such open communication that his enemies can know, with certainty, their number and force. Even those, who are the instruments of his usurpation, may wish his fall; but their ignorance of each other's intentions keeps them in awe, and is the sole cause of his security.
>
> David Hume, *Of the Original Contract*

Xi Jinping, the presumptive successor to Hu Jintao as the "paramount" leader of China, will assume that post with an authority that may appear curiously circumscribed for a dictator.[1] He will be expected to serve no more than two five-year terms and be accountable to a set of institutions within the Communist Party of China that carefully balance two major political coalitions as well as regional and organizational interests within the Chinese political system (Li 2010). Members of these institutions – primarily the Standing Committee of the Politburo and the full Politburo – will themselves be similarly constrained by term limits and mandatory retirement-age provisions (Miller 2011).

Xi will inherit a political machinery engineered in the 1980s by Deng Xiaoping. Under Deng's leadership, the newly revised Constitution of the People's Republic of China prohibited certain officials from serving concurrently in more than one leadership post (Baum 1997, 349–51), adopted mandatory

---

[1] On Xi's succession to Hu, see, e.g., "China Anoints Its Next Leader," *The Wall Street Journal*, 9 October 2010.

Parts of this chapter draw on joint work with Carles Boix; see Boix and Svolik (2011).

retirement ages at various levels of the government hierarchy (Manion 1992; Miller 2008, 63), and limited tenure at top government posts to two consecutive five-year terms (Baum 1997, 349–51). At the same time, informal norms developed according to which analogous term limits and retirement-age provisions applied to members of key Party bodies. The Standing Committee of the Politburo, the Politburo, and the Central Committee began meeting regularly, following formal rules of consultation, division of labor, and consensual decision making (Miller 2008).

This is a political system that differs markedly from the one that Deng came to dominate after Mao Zedong's death. Toward the end of Mao's life, institutions of "collective leadership" within the Party and the government either were abandoned or, when they did survive, were staffed by Mao's courtiers and governed by his personal authority rather than formal rules.[2] Although Deng Xiaoping's personal authority also transcended the binding power of the institutional reforms that he initiated, they have effectively constrained subsequent generations of Chinese leadership. Deng's successor, Jiang Zemin, at first politically exploited mandatory retirement-age provisions by invoking them to retire opponents within the leadership in 1997. Yet the same term and age provisions eventually came to limit Jiang's own time in office when he was compelled to step down from his posts in the early 2000s (Huang 2008, 86). The tenure of Jiang's successor, Hu Jintao, as well as the selection of Hu's heir apparent, Xi Jinping, has in turn been fully governed by the set of rules introduced under Deng and implemented under Jiang (Miller 2011).

Why have institutions of collective leadership effectively constrained the last two generations of Chinese leaders? More generally, why would any dictator accept formal, institutional constraints on his authority? Are there benefits to such constraints and, if so, what are they? In this chapter, I argue that formal, deliberative and decision-making institutions in dictatorships facilitate authoritarian power-sharing. As highlighted in Chapter 3, authoritarian elites operate under distinctively toxic conditions. The combustible mixture of widespread secrecy, the absence of an independent authority that can enforce mutual agreements, and the ever-present potential for violence generate commitment problems that may undermine the stability of authoritarian rule.[3] The most pronounced of these is the dictator's temptation to renege on his promise to share with his allies the spoils from joint rule.

This chapter argues that the gruesome character of authoritarian politics may be mitigated by adopting institutions that alleviate this commitment problem in authoritarian power-sharing. More specifically, to overcome the dictator's commitment problem, his allies must be credibly capable of first detecting and then punishing the dictator's potential opportunism. Formal political institutions facilitate the first of these steps – that is, the monitoring of the dictator's

---

[2] See MacFarquhar (1974–1997), MacFarquhar (1997a), and MacFarquhar and Schoenhals (2006).

[3] See also Shih (2010), who argues that information paucity is one of the distinguishing features of authoritarian politics.

compliance. They do so through two distinct mechanisms: First, deliberative and decision-making institutions typically entail regular interaction between the dictator and his allies, which results in greater transparency among them. Second, because formal institutional rules – rather than informal norms or expectations – are less ambiguous and more broadly known, they facilitate the detection of the dictator's noncompliance with power-sharing. The former mechanism prevents misperceptions among the allies about the dictator's actions from escalating into unnecessary, regime-destabilizing confrontations; the latter reassures the allies that the dictator's potential attempts to usurp power will be readily detected. Formal political institutions thus enhance the stability of authoritarian power-sharing. In fact, this chapter shows that for a range of circumstances, power-sharing in dictatorships will succeed only when it is institutionalized.

However, the analysis in this chapter also clarifies the limits to the beneficial role of institutions. For authoritarian power-sharing to succeed, the dictator's potential opportunism must not only be detected but also credibly punished. As I emphasized throughout Chapter 3, the only effective deterrent against the dictator's opportunism is the allies' threat to replace him if he reneges on his promise to share power as agreed. Institutions will be ineffective or break down when the collective-action problem in replacing the dictator undermines this threat's credibility. The allies' collective-action problem is a strategic concern that I intentionally assumed away in Chapter 3. The model in this chapter shows that the intensity of the allies' collective-action problem is closely connected to the distribution of power between the dictator and his allies: the more even the distribution, the less severe is the collective-action problem in replacing the dictator and the more credible is the allies' threat to do so.

This chapter thus clarifies the complex interaction between collective-action, commitment, and monitoring problems in authoritarian power-sharing. Although institutions do have the potential to facilitate authoritarian power-sharing, only those dictatorships in which power is evenly distributed among the elites can take advantage of that potential. Institutions will be ineffective or break down if not backed by a credible threat of force.

This chapter's claims about the regime-stabilizing effects of formal, deliberative, and decision-making authoritarian institutions are empirically assessed in Section 4.4. While such institutions assume a multitude of forms across dictatorships, since at least the nineteenth century, they emerge most often as politburos, councils, or committees that are embedded within authoritarian parties and legislatures. Extant research typically assesses propositions about the stabilizing effects of these institutions by examining their effect on the survival of individual dictators (see, e.g., Gandhi and Przeworski 2006; Gandhi 2008). This is a flawed approach. As we saw in the previous chapter, a dictator may survive in office long and die peacefully not because he institutionalized power-sharing but precisely because he managed to rid himself of any dependence on his allies. The focus on the survival of individual dictators misses some of the most prominent cases of successful authoritarian power-sharing, like PRI–era Mexico, where presidents left office every six years because the Institutional Revolutionary Party not only facilitated contemporaneous power-sharing but also institutionalized leadership succession.

To overcome these limitations, this chapter instead examines the effects of parties and legislatures on the duration and nature of leadership transitions within authoritarian ruling-coalition spells. Ruling-coalition spells, which I introduced in Chapter 2, consist of the uninterrupted succession in office of politically affiliated authoritarian leaders. According to my arguments in this chapter, parties and legislatures should contribute to the durability of authoritarian ruling coalitions by preventing unnecessary, intraelite conflicts. Indeed, I find that the presence of either a legislature or a party results in significantly more durable ruling-coalition spells and fewer violent, nonconstitutional leadership transitions. These results are robust even after I use data on dictators' exits from office due to natural causes as a benchmark for diagnosing potential endogeneity in the adoption of parties and legislatures.

The arguments in this chapter thus depart from one prominent explanation for the presence of nominally democratic political institutions in dictatorships, according to which such institutions – especially legislatures – broaden the basis of the regime's support by *co-opting opposition* (Gandhi and Przeworski 2006; Gandhi 2008). By contrast, I argue that the primary function of these institutions in authoritarian governance is to reduce commitment and monitoring problems in *authoritarian power-sharing*, whether it is among those who already support the dictator or between the dictator and newly recruited supporters. In fact, as Chapter 2 and the conclusion to this chapter highlight, authoritarian legislatures rarely seat any political opposition. The key function of institutions like parties and legislatures in dictatorships is therefore distinctly authoritarian.

The next two sections elaborate on how institutions enhance the stability of authoritarian power-sharing and how the collective-action problem in replacing the dictator compromises their ability to do so. These arguments are formalized in Section 4.3 and empirically evaluated in Section 4.4. The conclusion explains why nominally democratic institutions in dictatorships serve distinctly authoritarian purposes. Detailed proofs of all technical results are in the appendix at the end of this chapter.

4.1 POLITICAL INSTITUTIONS AND AUTHORITARIAN POWER-SHARING

As emphasized throughout Chapter 3, dictators rarely come to office with enough resources to preclude challenges by those who are excluded from power. They therefore seek allies and promise to reward their support by sharing with them the spoils from joint rule. As discussed in Chapter 3, those spoils may be monetary, such as tax or natural resource revenue, but they also may take the form of a compromise over personnel appointments or policy direction. For instance, the Argentine military junta that came to power in 1976 agreed to rotate the country's presidency and equally divide the state apparatus among the three service branches of the military in what it referred to as the "power-arrangement" (Fontana 1987). Throughout this book, I refer to such agreements over the sharing of the spoils from joint rule as *authoritarian power-sharing*.

In dictatorships, power-sharing is complicated by a fundamental commitment problem: The dictator is tempted to betray his allies by defecting on his promise to share the spoils of joint rule. In 1995, for instance, the Qatari Emir Khalifah bin Hamad Al Thani was deposed after continuing suspicions that he was not sharing oil revenue with the rest of the Al Thani ruling family according to established rules, thus paralyzing the government's operation (Herb 1999, 116–26). The leader of the Shakespearean rebellion was the Emir's son, Hamad bin Khalifa. According to a lawsuit filed by the new Emir a year later, the profligate father misappropriated several billions of dollars from the "Ruling Family" account.[4]

Two distinguishing features of authoritarian politics compromise the success of power-sharing: (1) Dictatorships inherently lack an independent authority that could enforce agreements among the ruling elites and (2) in dictatorships, violence is the ultimate arbiter of political conflicts. Under these conditions, misperceptions of the dictator's actions may easily breed suspicions that spawn intraelite confrontations that needlessly bring down a dictator or even an entire regime. As discussed previously, the dictator's compliance is ultimately sustained by the allies' threat to replace him if he refuses to share power as agreed. This is a costly, crude, and thus, inefficient deterrent. It may have to be carried out on the mere suspicion of a dictator's defection, and when that suspicion is unfounded, it may trigger unnecessary regime-destabilizing confrontations.

Authoritarian regimes therefore benefit from establishing political institutions that alleviate monitoring problems in authoritarian power-sharing. Formal deliberative and decision-making institutions do so in two ways. First, the procedural aspects of institutionalized power-sharing increase the transparency among the authoritarian elites. Regular interaction within institutions like politburos, advisory councils, and legislatures typically involves deliberation over major policy changes and periodic reviews of government revenue and spending. A classic example of such transparency-enhancing institutional mechanisms are the Provisions of Oxford imposed on Henry III of England (Treharne 1986, 171). Bankrupted by several failed wars, Henry instigated a baronial rebellion after he pursued "excessively hideabout accounting routines" (Finer 1999, 907). Although these measures were short lived, the rebellion institutionalized the supervision of key government offices by a "Council of Fifteen,"

---

[4] The ex-Emir reportedly responded, "One cannot steal one's own money," to these accusations. See Kechichian (2008, 210–14); "Whose cash is it?," *The Economist*, 31 August 1996; and Mason, "Qatar to Pursue Case against Ex-Emir," *Financial Times*, 24 September 1996.

appointed jointly by the king and the barons, and provided for further parliamentary oversight of the Council's performance (Finer 1999, 907–8).

The second mechanism by which institutions alleviate monitoring problems in authoritarian power-sharing stems from their formal nature. Formal rules facilitate the detection of the dictator's noncompliance. Formal institutional rules about membership, jurisdiction, protocol, and decision making both embody a power-sharing compromise between the dictator and his allies and ensure that its violation is readily and widely observed. After Joseph Stalin's death in 1953, for instance, his ruling circle resurrected formal institutions of "collective leadership" out of fear that someone among them would attempt to replicate Stalin's usurpation of power. In contrast to its defunct status toward the end of Stalin's life (see, e.g., Gorlizki and Khlevniuk 2004), the new Presidium (as the Politburo was renamed in 1952) convened regularly after 1953 and adopted clear rules of membership, agenda setting, decision making, and protocol – thus making apparent any member's attempt to sidestep collective leadership.[5] Nikita Khrushchev's increasing unpredictability and unilateralism first united a majority of the Presidium's members in a failed attempt to unseat him – during the so-called anti-Party plot of 1957; a second attempt in 1964 led to his ultimate demise (Taubman 2004).

Therefore once formal, deliberative, and decision-making institutions are in place, two mechanisms alleviate commitment and monitoring problems inherent in authoritarian power-sharing: (1) The ease of monitoring reassures the allies that actual attempts by the dictator to usurp power will be caught before it is too late and (2) greater transparency among the ruling elites prevents misperceptions of the dictator's actions from escalating into regime-destabilizing confrontations.

The deliberative and decision-making institutions that perform these functions most typically take the form of committees, politburos, or councils that are embedded within authoritarian parties and legislatures. Thus according to Krauze (1997, 431), the National Revolutionary Party – which eventually became the Institutional Revolutionary Party that governed Mexico for seventy years – functioned between 1929 and 1938 as a "civilized conclave of generals who resolved their differences without drawing their revolvers." However, as Chapter 2 explained, because dictatorship is a residual category that contains all countries that fail to meet the criteria for democracy, we see extraordinary heterogeneity in authoritarian institutions. Hence even dictatorships that do not have regime parties or legislatures often maintain some other institutional body that serves to facilitate power-sharing among the elites. The Argentine,

---

[5] The Politburo of the Central Committee of the Communist Party of the Soviet Union was the main political decision-making body throughout the existence of that regime (Suny 1998, 128). Key decisions were made within other bodies such as the Council of Ministers (i.e., the removal of Beria in 1953), the State Defense Committee (i.e., during World War II), and the Central Committee (i.e., during the Revolution and in 1957), but only under extraordinary circumstances and often by membership that overlapped with the Politburo (Mawdsley and White 2000).

Brazilian, and Chilean military juntas, for instance, established highly specific formal rules of collective decision making.[6] In the case of the Argentine junta of 1976–1983, such rules – including the rotation of the presidency and the sharing of government posts among the multiple branches of the military – were explicitly motivated by the marginalization that the military experienced after bringing General Juan Carlos Onganía to power a decade earlier (Remmer 1989).

In other cases, institutions that facilitate authoritarian power-sharing build on traditional institutions, as in the case of various advisory councils in contemporary Arab monarchies (see, e.g., Herb 1999), or are sui generis, as in the case of the complex system of overlapping leadership institutions in postrevolutionary Iran. The latter includes the uniquely Iranian Council of Guardians and Assembly of Experts as well as the more common Parliament and Council of Ministers (see, e.g., Buchta 2000).

In some dictatorships, even elections – which are by definition restrictive and unfair – may serve this purpose. When power is widely dispersed, elections help to allocate resources to the most influential notables precisely because, under dictatorship, voters can be not only convinced but also bought and coerced.[7] This may have been the role of elections in the aristocratic republics of nineteenth-century Latin America (see, e.g., Safford 1985) and the city republics of Renaissance Italy. Only a small fraction of their populations could vote and, in the latter case, offices were frequently tied to guild membership, elected by lot, and rotated (Finer 1999, 963–1023). Similarly, elections in the single-party regimes of Kenya, Tanzania, Cameroon, and Ivory Coast served, according to Van de Walle (2007, 55), as "a mechanism for the accommodation and integration of a fairly narrow political elite" into broad multiethnic alliances.

As an illustration of the two mechanisms by which formal institutions alleviate commitment and monitoring problems in authoritarian power-sharing, consider again the institutional reforms initiated by Deng Xiaoping after Mao Zedong's death. After Deng emerged victorious from the struggle over the succession to Mao in 1980, he supervised an official appraisal of Mao's leadership. Adopted in 1981, the "Resolution on the Party History" condemned Mao's leadership for the "over-concentration of Party power in individuals," "the development of arbitrary individual rule," and the maintenance of a "personality cult" (MacFarquhar and Schoenhals 2006, 458). In the same vein, the revised 1982 Constitution of the People's Republic of China (PRC) declared that "no party member, whatever his position, is allowed to stand above the law or . . . make decisions on major issues on his own" (Baum 1997, 348). As a symbolic gesture of departure from Mao's leadership style, the simultaneously revised Party Constitution abolished the post of Party Chairman that Mao held, and Deng himself avoided any titular confirmation of his powers (MacFarquhar 1997b, 328).

---

[6] On these regimes, see Fontana (1987), Skidmore (1990), and Barros (2002), respectively.
[7] Blaydes (2010) advances a related argument about the role of elections in Mubarak's Egypt.

Consistent with the stated purpose of these reforms – that is, to prevent a return to the arbitrary, autocratic leadership that prevailed under Mao – key Party bodies began meeting with "metronomic regularity" (Miller 2008, 62), according to provisions of the new Party Constitution. The Politburo Standing Committee became the highest decision-making body and began meeting weekly (Miller 2004); and since 1987, the full Politburo has held regular monthly meetings (Miller 2008, 67). Formal procedures were established that required the General Secretary of the Party to report about the work of the Politburo Standing Committee to the full Politburo and similarly to report on the full Politburo's work to the Party Central Committee (Miller 2008, 67). Echoing our earlier discussion of the transparency-enhancing benefits of institutionalized interaction among authoritarian elites, observers of Chinese politics credit Deng's reforms with a number of regime-stabilizing effects: mitigating policy disputes (Huang 2008, 90), avoiding major crises (Miller 2008, 75), facilitating orderly leadership transitions (Nathan 2003, 7–8), and preventing the usurpation of power by any single leader or faction (Li 2010, 185).

Meanwhile the adoption of term limits and retirement-age provisions on the tenure of top leadership posts throughout the same period exemplifies how formal rules – as opposed to tacit norms or expectations – facilitate the monitoring of a dictator's commitment to sharing power. Prior to Deng Xiaoping's institutional reforms, there were no formal restrictions on lifelong tenure of political leaders. In fact, the expectation had been that, barring a political purge, leading officials would retire only when incapacitated by old age (Manion 1992; Baum 1997, 345–6). The 1982 PRC Constitution changed this by limiting the tenure of leading government posts, including the Presidency, Premiership, and Chairmanship of the National People's Congress, to two consecutive five-year terms (Baum 1997, 349–51).

At the same time, however, no formal term limits were adopted for leadership posts in the Party or the military. Although the 1982 Constitution did stipulate that leadership-Party cadres were "not entitled to lifelong tenure" (Manion 1992, 11; Miller 2008, 63), even Deng lacked the weight to institute any specific constraints on Party or military veterans with revolutionary credentials (Vogel 2011, 557). Instead, informal rules regulating term limits and mandatory retirement ages gradually developed for leading-Party posts. As a first step, Deng appealed to the revolutionary veterans, to which he belonged, to create room for a new generation of leaders, attempting to smooth their retirement from official posts by creating a new consultative body, the Central Advisory Commission (Baum 1997, 342–3; Vogel 2011, 556–7). Indeed, this generation of elites – including Deng – retired almost entirely from the highest Party posts by 1987. An informal norm barring the reappointment of Politburo members past the age of seventy emerged at the fifteenth Party Congress in 1997, when Jiang Zemin forced one of his competitors, Qiao Shi – who was seventy-five at the time and a member of the Politburo Standing Committee and Chairman of the National People's Congress – into retirement by invoking his advanced age (Dittmer 2002, 24–5; Nathan 2003, 8; Miller 2008, 70; Huang 2008, 89).

A test of the binding power of both formal term limits and informal retirement-age norms came at the time of Jiang Zemin's expected retirement as China's "paramount" leader. Since Jiang Zemin's tenure, political leadership of the PRC came to be associated with three posts: the General Secretary of the Communist Party, the Chairman of the Central Military Commission, and the President of the PRC. Only the last and most ceremonial of these, however, was subject to explicit, constitutionally mandated term limits. The informal nature of rules concerning retirement from leading Party or military posts opened the door for both speculation about their exact nature (Bo 2007, Chap. 1) and for maneuvering by Jiang, who in fact campaigned to retain the remaining two posts (Shirk 2002). Eventually, Jiang stepped down from the post of Party General Secretary in 2002 and from the Presidency in 2003, in accordance with both informal norms and the formal constitutional two-term limit, respectively.

However, Jiang did attempt to hold on to the Chairmanship of the Party and State Central Military Commissions for another term. When he retained those posts, Jiang claimed to be keeping them because of the "complicated international situation" and the "pressing demands of army-building" and to ensure "the smooth transition from the old to the new generation [of leaders]" (Mulvenon 2003b, 21; Mulvenon 2005, 3). Jiang also appealed to a precedent set by Deng Xiaoping, who held on to the same posts for several years after he retired from the Politburo (Vogel 2011, 588). Yet Jiang's reluctance to step down from all of his posts led to the immediate suspicion that he intended to use his Central Military Commission posts to exert continued political influence.[8] In fact, the *People's Daily* announcement of the leadership change that occurred at the sixteenth National Congress of the Chinese Communist Party in 2002 placed Jiang's photograph and resumé above the newly elected General Secretary Hu Jintao's, leaving the latter barely visible in subsequent media announcements.[9] Suspicions that Jiang may have been intent on exercising political influence from behind the scenes, questions about Hu's actual political authority, and signals of disagreements between the two leaders on key policy issues raised concerns about the potential instability that could attend a pronounced leadership struggle.[10] Following growing criticism from within the Party and the

---

[8] See, e.g., Eckholm, "Chinese Leader Gives up a Job but Not Power," *The New York Times*, 16 November 2002.

[9] See, e.g., Kahn, "Officially, Jiang Is History; in News, He's Still on Top," *The New York Times*, 17 November 2002.

[10] See, e.g., Kahn, "China's 2 Top Leaders Square Off in Contest to Run Policy," *The New York Times*, 2 September 2002; Eckholm, "China's Leader Won't Hold On, Anonymous Author Says," *The New York Times*, 5 September 2002; Kahn, "Analysts See Tension in China within the Top Leadership," *The New York Times*, 1 July 2003; and Kahn, "Former Leader Is Still a Power in China's Life," *The New York Times*, 16 July 2004.

military (Mulvenon 2003a,c; Huang 2008), Jiang eventually resigned from both Central Military Commissions by 2005, before the expiration of his term.[11] In his resignation letter, Jiang stated that he was stepping down because it served "the long-term peace and stability of the party and state" and ensured "the institutionalization, standardization, and proceduralization of the succession of new high-ranking party and state leaders."[12]

The contrast between the explicit term limit for government posts and the tacit norm about mandatory retirement ages in post-Mao China highlights the benefits of formal, institutionalized rules in authoritarian power-sharing. Because provisions about mandatory retirement ages were based on implicit expectations rather than formal rules, they allowed for speculation about their exact nature. The ambiguity typically associated with such informal norms not only creates incentives for maneuvering to circumvent them but also fosters suspicions that such attempts are taking place – even when they may not be. In turn, tacit, unwritten norms or expectations entail the risk of unnecessary, regime-destabilizing confrontations. By reducing the ambiguity about which actions constitute a violation of a power-sharing compromise, formal written rules avoid such inefficiencies in monitoring the dictator's commitment to sharing power.

4.2 THE ALLIES' COLLECTIVE-ACTION PROBLEM AND CREDIBLE POWER-SHARING

A notable feature of the institutionalization of "collective leadership" initiated by Deng Xiaoping is that it occurred only after Mao Zedong's death and, according to most observers, failed to effectively constrain Deng himself (see, e.g., Baum 1997, 342). In fact, formal institutions for "collective leadership" were put in place already under Mao but their political relevance quickly eroded. The Eighth Party Congress in 1956 established the Politburo Standing Committee as the highest institution of "collective leadership," charged the Party Secretariat and several "small leadership groups" with implementing the Politburo Standing Committee's decisions, and appointed members of institutions representative of the PRC's broader leadership (Miller 2008, 64–6). These institutions nevertheless failed to prevent Mao's arbitrary exercise of power, purges of recalcitrant Party members, and their own eventual decline into political irrelevance. After 1959, key Party bodies met only sporadically (Miller 2008, 62) and, following the launch of the Cultural Revolution in 1966, most became inconsequential until Mao's death a decade later (MacFarquhar and Schoenhals 2006, 296–301).

---

[11] See Kahn, "China Ex-President May Be Set to Yield Last Powerful Post," *The New York Times*, 7 September 2002; "Hu Takes Full Power in China as He Gains Control of Military," *The New York Times*, 20 September 2002.

[12] "China Publishes Jiang Zemin's Letter of Resignation," Xinhua News Agency, 19 September 2004, cited in Mulvenon (2005, 2).

Why have formal institutions of collective leadership successfully governed the tenures of Jiang Zemin and Hu Jintao but failed to constrain the personal authority of Mao Zedong and Deng Xiaoping? This chapter examines not only the potential of but also the limits to institutions as mechanisms that facilitate authoritarian power-sharing. Because the only deterrent against the dictator's temptation to renege on his agreement to share power with his allies is their threat to replace him, the credibility of that threat will condition the potential of institutions to alleviate commitment problems in authoritarian governance.

A key factor that potentially compromises the credibility of the allies' threat to replace the dictator is the collective-action problem entailed in staging a rebellion. As in Chapter 3, I use the term *rebellion* to denote the allies' collective attempt to replace the dictator. At the heart of the collective-action problem in staging a rebellion is the strategic uncertainty in that endeavor: A rebellion succeeds only if a sufficient number of allies participate in it; therefore, any ally's doubts about others' participation and the associated fear of the rebellion's failure may discourage him from joining it. In fact, most participants in leadership struggles are purely strategic: Their fear of joining the losing side outweighs any substantive preferences over who prevails. In turn, as Geddes (1999b, 131) put it, would-be rebels "keep their heads down and wait to see who wins."[13]

When modeling these strategic considerations in the next section, I therefore assume that allies have an approximate understanding but not common knowledge of their joint strength and, by extension, of the precise number of allies that must join the rebellion for it to succeed. As David Hume observed in the epigraph at the beginning of this chapter, one source of a dictator's security is the ignorance among those who may desire his downfall of one another's intentions, force, and number. This realistic assumption allows me to examine collective-action problems with an approach known as the *global-games methodology* (Carlsson and van Damme 1993; Morris and Shin 2003).[14] A key intuitive implication of the analysis in this chapter is that as the distribution of power between the dictator and his allies becomes more balanced, the collective-action problem of staging a rebellion becomes less severe. The equilibrium in which this relationship obtains is unique and therefore can be evaluated empirically. This finding thus justifies a simplifying step made in the preceding chapter, where I assumed that the likelihood of a successful rebellion is simply increasing in the allies' strength vis-à-vis the dictator.

Although this result may seem straightforward, its strategic analysis is far from that. The conventional formal study of analogous collective-action problems has been plagued by a multiplicity of equilibria and therefore fails to generate unambiguous, empirically testable predictions.[15] In fact, virtually all

---

[13] On a similar observation about military coups, see, e.g., Luttwak (1968, 59, 105–7).

[14] Edmond (2007) and Persson and Tabellini (2009) recently applied global games to collective action problems in regime and leadership change.

[15] On the multiplicity of equilibria in collective-action problems, see Chwe (2001), Medina (2007), and Shadmehr (2011).

existing research on authoritarian politics either ignores collective-action problems (see, e.g., Bueno de Mesquita et al. 2003; Acemoglu and Robinson 2005) or fails to connect their resolution to relevant political factors – such as the distribution of power between the dictator and his allies. For instance, a prominent literature proposes that the collective-action problem in replacing a dictator can be overcome by focal coordination on norms that encourage the allies' participation – in the spirit of "all for one and one for all" – and that institutions in fact help to cultivate such norms among the dictator's allies (North and Weingast 1989; Myerson 2008). This is unrealistic. Although such a norm-driven coordination of beliefs may be possible in principle, it occurs in only one among multiple equilibria and its success or failure is disconnected from the political setting in which the dictator and his allies interact. It seems unreasonable, for example, that a balance of power strongly favoring the dictator would not deter the allies from joining a rebellion. Such a balance of power, along with other intuitive factors, shapes the likelihood of a rebellion's success in the framework here. According to my arguments, political facts – as opposed to a focal coordination of beliefs – ultimately determine whether the allies overcome the collective-action problem in replacing the dictator.

This connection between the credibility of the allies' threat to replace the dictator, the balance of power between the dictator and his allies, and the collective-action problem of staging a rebellion helps us understand why only some dictatorships take advantage of the benefits of institutionalized power-sharing. Whereas institutions do have the potential to alleviate the commitment problem inherent in authoritarian governance, their capacity to do so is conditional on a balanced distribution of power between the dictator and his allies. To put it in the jargon of modern political science, the dictator's compliance with formal constraints on his power is self-enforcing only when backed by a credible threat of an allies' rebellion.

The emasculation of the Soviet Politburo by Joseph Stalin during his rise to power exemplifies the highly contingent role of formal institutions in authoritarian power-sharing. Once Stalin overpowered competing factions within the Soviet leadership by the end of the 1930s, the meetings of his ruling circle – which originally occurred within the formal institutional structure of the elected Politburo – degenerated into ad hoc informal meetings of select courtiers. The latter would be unilaterally and arbitrarily promoted or dismissed by Stalin and, depending on its fluid cardinality during this period, referred to as the ruling quintet, sextet, and eventually, a septet (Gorlizki and Khlevniuk 2004, 101–8). Stalin often called for meetings with the ruling group late at night in his dacha, rather than in the Kremlin, without a concrete agenda, supporting materials, or any respect for jurisdictional boundaries (Gorlizki and Khlevniuk 2004, 45–5). According to Milovan Djilas, the Yugoslav envoy to Moscow during this period, "Unofficially and in actual fact, a significant part of Soviet policy was shaped at these dinners.... It all resembled a patriarchal family with a crotchety head who made his kinsfolk apprehensive."[16] Even though

---

[16] Djilas (1962, 73–4), cited in Gorlizki and Khlevniuk (2004, 58–9).

the formal institution of the Politburo still existed, its potential to facilitate power-sharing became irrelevant because of the political predominance that Stalin eventually gained over the rest of the Soviet ruling elite.

Stalin's deteriorating health is one source of exogenous variation in the balance of power between Stalin and his inner circle that suggests that the dysfunction of the Politburo during this period was indeed the consequence of too much power in Stalin's hands. As Stalin's health deteriorated between 1950 and 1952 and he more frequently left Moscow, the remainder of the ruling group continued to meet without him. As the "Bureau of the Presidium of the Council of Ministers," the group formally held thirty-nine meetings in 1950, thirty-eight in 1951, and forty-two in 1952 (Gorlizki and Khlevniuk 2004, 106). In contrast to Stalin's Politburo, this group convened regularly and instituted a committee structure with clear membership rules, portfolios, procedures, and agendas. As this chapter explains, the markedly more even distribution of power within the Presidium allowed its members to establish institutional rules that would later serve as the foundation for the revived institutional "collective leadership" after Stalin's death.

Authoritarian institutions thus settle distributive or policy conflicts against the backdrop of the possibility of their crude, violent resolution.[17] This contingent nature of peaceful, institutionalized decision making helps us understand not only when and why institutions will have the potential to facilitate authoritarian power-sharing but also *which* institutions will be able to do so.

Consider the failed 1957 anti-Party plot against the Soviet leader Nikita Khrushchev: In June 1957, a majority within the highest decision-making body in the Soviet Union, the Presidium, attempted to unseat Khrushchev as First Secretary of the Communist Party.[18] Key participants were Stalinist hardliners who feared that Khrushchev's steps toward greater de-Stalinization – most notably his Secret Speech delivered at the twentieth Congress of the Communist Party – were in reality concealed attempts to marginalize them. In fact, the leaders of the plot – Vyacheslav Molotov, Georgy Malenkov, and Lazar Kaganovich – had been in political decline since Stalin's death. Molotov, the "ideological leader" of the conspiracy according to Khrushchev, had been recently forced to step down as Foreign Minister, a post in which he presided since 1939; Malenkov had lost the Premiership a few years earlier because of his closeness to the purged Lavrentiy Beria. Consistent with the collective-action model in this chapter, others joined the plot because of the promise of a reward, like Premier Nikolai Bulganin, who was promised Khrushchev's post, or after being convinced that the anti-Khrushchev group had a majority, as in the case of Secretary of the Central Committee Dimitri Shepilov. In fact, the

---

[17] See Acemoglu and Robinson (2005), Boix (2003), and (Przeworski 2011) on a similar contingent relationship between democracy and violent resolution of conflicts over the redistribution of wealth or holding office.

[18] This account is based on Chap. 3 in Breslauer (1982); Brown (2009, 245–54), Chap. 12 in Conquest (1967); Chap. 21 in Mićunović (1980); Suny (1998, 401–3); and Chap. 12 in Taubman (2004).

anti-Khrushchev group managed to form a seven-to-four majority of full voting Presidium members but nevertheless failed to force Khrushchev's resignation.

Khrushchev refused to resign after the vote within the Presidium unless the Central Committee, to which the Presidium was nominally accountable, confirmed the decision. Khrushchev was counting on support from the Central Committee, which stemmed from the administrative reforms that he had championed. During several months prior to the plot, Khrushchev had abolished several central ministries and transferred their policy-making authority to regional economic councils and Party organizations. Midlevel Party officials that headed them formed the majority of the Central Committee and thus had a natural reason to favor Khrushchev over his opponents. Khrushchev was further aided by Minister of Defense Georgy Zhukov and Head of the KGB and Kremlin security Ivan Serov, who transported and airlifted sympathetic Central Committee members to Moscow. Both owed their recent political ascendance to Khrushchev: Zhukov for being restored to national prominence after being demoted by Stalin and Serov for surviving his immediate superior Beria's downfall. As in the case of the anti-Khrushchev group, some joined for purely strategic reasons: Mikhail Suslov, a voting Presidium member, joined the pro-Khrushchev faction only after being convinced by another of Khrushchev's supporters, Anastas Mikoyan, that Khrushchev would eventually prevail. This indeed happened: Once the vote was moved to the Central Committee, Molotov and his rebel faction were defeated, 107 to 13.

The "anti-Party plot" ultimately failed because the anti-Khrushchev group failed to appreciate how significantly power had dissipated after Stalin's death away from the narrow membership of the Politburo toward the broader leadership within the Soviet Union – represented in part by the Central Committee. Thus according to Taubman (2004, 275), "under the rules of the game as played until then (the Presidium decides, the Central Committee rubber stamps), Khrushchev should have been finished." Stalin's death, however, left a vacuum that shifted the balance of power between the Party's top leadership and broader membership toward the latter. Therefore, although certainly self-serving, Khrushchev was not entirely misleading when he stated at the Central Committee plenum that "we members of the Presidium of the [Central Committee], we are servants of the Plenum, and the Plenum is our master" (Mawdsley and White 2000, 160). According to Suny's (1998, 402–3) summary of the post-Stalin shift in the distribution of power within the Soviet leadership, for instance, Khrushchev "was the chief oligarch, with his power limited by his colleagues in the party Presidium and ultimately sanctioned by the Central Committee." Suny's point is confirmed by how Khrushchev ultimately lost power in 1964, after his behavior became increasingly unilateral and unpredictable – in the hands of the same constituency that saved him in 1957.

Hence formal institutions under dictatorships and the particular rules about membership, jurisdiction, and decision making that govern their operation will only have the capacity to effectively settle disputes among authoritarian elites

TABLE 4.1. *Institutions, Balance of Power, and the Success of Authoritarian Power-Sharing*

	A Dictator's Power vis-à-vis Allies			
	Low	Medium	Large	Very Large
Need for allies:	Yes	Yes	Yes	No
Credible power-sharing:	With and without institutions	Only with institutions	Not feasible	Neither feasible nor necessary

when the outcomes they generate mirror those that would result under the alternative of their crude, violent resolution. As Khrushchev retorted to Bulganin's exasperated "But we are seven and you are four!" during the confrontation with the anti-Party group according to Crankshaw (1966, 249–50): "Certainly in arithmetic two and two make four. But politics are not arithmetic. They are something different."

Table 4.1 anticipates my key formal findings about how institutions and the balance of power among the authoritarian elites shape authoritarian power-sharing. We will see that, depending on the balance of power between the dictator and his allies, there will generally be four cases, distinguished by differences in the potential role of institutions and the feasibility of credible power-sharing. To streamline this presentation, I characterize the four cases by simplified labels that order the dictator's share of power vis-à-vis the allies; the thresholds that separate these four cases are characterized explicitly in Section 4.3. When the dictator controls either a very large or a large share of power, he either successfully survives in office without any allies or entirely lacks the ability to credibly commit to sharing power. In Chapter 3, I referred to the former case as "established autocracy" and explained why they are empirically rare. Established autocrats, like Joseph Stalin or Rafael Trujillo, acquired enough personal power over time to no longer need allies to survive in office – the credibility of power-sharing and the role of institutions is therefore irrelevant in their case. By contrast, when the dictator controls a large share of power, power-sharing is desirable but the dictator's own power prevents him from credibly committing to sharing it; the severity of the allies' collective-action problem undermines their threat to replace him. In this case, even institutions cannot alleviate that commitment problem. Like Ulysses, these dictators are better off giving up their own power if they want to survive in office in the long run.

However, barring such extreme imbalances of power among the elites, power-sharing is both possible and facilitated by institutions. In fact, for a range of balances of power between the dictator and the allies characterized as "medium" in Table 4.1, power-sharing will succeed only when institutionalized. This is when the capacity of institutions to simplify the monitoring of the dictator's actions is decisive for the success of power-sharing.

Finally, when power is distributed most evenly among the elites, power-sharing is feasible both with and without political institutions. Nevertheless, the model in the next section clarifies that, even in that case, institutions are not epiphenomenal – institutionalized power-sharing will result in more durable ruling coalitions and succeed under less favorable circumstances. This is because the transparency associated with regular, institutionalized interaction helps authoritarian elites to avoid unnecessary, regime-destabilizing conflicts that may emerge in the process of monitoring the dictator's commitment to power-sharing.

These findings explain why formal institutional rules have effectively constrained policy making and leadership succession under Jiang Zemin and Hu Jintao but not under Mao Zedong and Deng Xiaoping. The latter two leaders commanded personal authority grounded in revolutionary achievements and charismatic personalities that eclipsed any of their contemporaries. As evidenced by the Cultural Revolution, Mao in particular was capable of annihilating any opposition – whether individual or institutional – by exploiting his almost divine popular status (MacFarquhar and Schoenhals 2006). By contrast, Jiang and Hu commanded neither charisma nor revolutionary credentials; they instead owed their careers to bureaucratic and administrative skills. Both have been regarded as "firsts among equals" within two evenly balanced political coalitions in the Chinese leadership and, rather than dominating those coalitions, they depended on their support (Miller 2004; Huang 2008; Li 2010). The arguments in this chapter clarify why it is during their tenures that institutions of consensual, oligarchic decision making and effective, formal constraints on leading political posts took root. This transformation was made possible by the essentially even balance of power within the Chinese political elite left after the departure of Mao's and Deng's revolutionary generation.

4.3 A FORMAL MODEL

To investigate when and how institutions facilitate authoritarian power-sharing, I now reformulate the model from the preceding chapter as follows. As previously, the dictator recruits a ruling coalition of allies and offers them a power-sharing agreement according to which each member receives a share of benefits from joint rule. However, asymmetries of information between the dictator and the allies about the size of spoils to be shared will exacerbate the suspicion among the allies that the dictator is reneging on his commitment to share them as agreed – even when he may not be doing so at all.[19] Such defections may happen in two related but distinct ways. First, the dictator can simply refuse to share the benefits of joint rule as agreed – this is the defection that

---

[19] As in Chapter 3, I analytically focus on the dictator's potential defection on the power-sharing agreement as the key obstacle to successful authoritarian power-sharing. Although members of the ruling coalition may also attempt to strengthen their position at the dictator's expense, the latter controls the executive, which presents him with the greatest opportunity to renege on a power-sharing compromise.

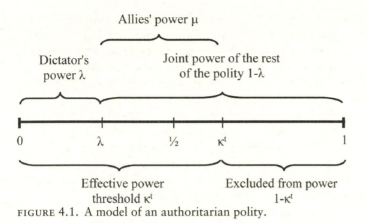

FIGURE 4.1. A model of an authoritarian polity.

I focused on in Chapter 3 and continue studying herein. However, dictators may also engage in a second, more subtle, type of defection: The secrecy that pervades authoritarian governance allows dictators to exploit their privileged access to information about the government and misrepresent the amount of available benefits to be shared. We will see that by reducing asymmetries of information between the dictator and his allies, institutions allow for more stable power-sharing and under less favorable circumstances than would be possible without them.

Consider an authoritarian polity in which power is controlled by a *dictator* and a continuum of *notables*. In substantive terms, I assume that the notables enjoy significant influence locally, but the power of any *single* notable is of little consequence at the national level.[20] The dictator controls a share λ of the total power within this polity while the notables control the rest, $1 - \lambda$.

To assume office at time $t = 0$, the dictator needs to form a *ruling coalition* that commands a κ^t fraction of total power, where $\kappa^0 \in [1/2, 1)$. We may call κ^t the *effective-power threshold*. When $\lambda \geq \kappa^0$, the dictator controls a sufficient amount of power to rule alone. In the terminology of Chapter 3, such a dictator is an established autocrat. However, when $\lambda < \kappa^0$, the dictator must recruit *allies* from among the notables to assume office. I focus on the politically interesting case when $\lambda < \kappa^0$ and the dictator must recruit a positive number of allies $\mu = \kappa^0 - \lambda > 0$ to form a ruling coalition at time $t = 0$.[21]

---

[20] The assumption that notables other than the dictator are atomless players on a continuum simplifies the analysis, but my results also hold in a setting where the number of allies is finite.

[21] The assumption that the dictator forms a coalition of size κ^0 is a simplifying one. The appendix to this chapter shows that forming a larger than minimum ruling coalition lowers the credibility of the rebellion and therefore cannot help the dictator share power. Thus the dictator cannot resolve the commitment problem in power-sharing by including more allies in the ruling coalition.

When the dictator recruits allies, he promises to share with them a β fraction of total *benefits* from joint rule, $0 < \beta < 1$.[22] As discussed in Chapter 3, these benefits may take the form of government revenue, bureaucratic appointments, or favorable policy choices. The allies may value these benefits because of pecuniary or ideological reasons or because they allow them to compensate their followers and cultivate their local political influence.

Total benefits may differ across periods as a result of exogenous conditions, such as administrative costs, economic performance, or political turmoil. To keep the analysis as simple as possible, suppose that total benefits are 1 with probability π (i.e., good times) and they are 0 with probability $1 - \pi$ (i.e., a crisis). Thus when the dictator keeps his promise, each ally receives the payoff β/μ with probability π and the payoff 0 with probability $1 - \pi$.

As long as $0 < \beta < 1$, power-sharing between the dictator and his allies is politically desirable: The dictator keeps a positive share of total benefits while maintaining μ allies. On the other hand, as long as a dictator keeps his promise to share a $\beta > 0$ fraction of total benefits with the allies, each ally receives a non-negative payoff in any period. I normalize the payoff to the notables excluded from the ruling coalition to 0.

4.3.1   Allies' Rebellion as a Collective-Action Problem

To understand when power-sharing between the dictator and his allies succeeds, I start by examining the credibility of the allies' threat to replace the dictator should the latter renege on his promise to compensate them for their support. As discussed previously, such a *rebellion* is the only punishment that the allies can use. Its credibility therefore determines the dictator's incentive to abide by the power-sharing agreement in the first place.

More specifically, I examine the allies' collective action problem in staging a rebellion. In a rebellion, each ally either *supports* the dictator or *rebels* against him by joining a *challenger*. As long as the dictator remains in power, each ally who supports him receives her share of benefits $b_I \geq 0$. If the dictator keeps his promise and shares β with the allies as agreed, then $b_I = \beta$. However, the dictator may also renege, in which case $b_I = 0$. If a rebellion is staged and succeeds, then the allies who joined the challenger will enjoy the share of benefits promised by the challenger, b_C. Meanwhile, the allies who supported the dictator will lose any benefits and receive the payoff 0. If a rebellion fails, an ally who joined the challenger will receive the payoff $-r$, where $r > 0$ represents the dictator's punishment of those who participated in a failed rebellion. Thus whereas rebelling entails the risk of a lower payoff in the case of failure, supporting the dictator is also risky because a rebellion may succeed.

A rebellion succeeds when the fraction of allies who join the challenger ϕ exceeds a threshold value ϕ^*. That is, a rebellion succeeds when $\phi > \phi^*$ and

---

[22] Thus both κ^0 and β can be viewed as the outcome of bargaining at the time of ruling coalition formation.

	$\phi \le \phi^*$	$\phi > \phi^*$
Support	b_I	0
Rebel	$-r$	b_C

FIGURE 4.2. Payoffs to ally i, given the proportion of allies that rebel ϕ.

fails otherwise, where $\phi \in [0, 1]$. Figure 4.2 summarizes this dependence of an ally's payoff on her own action as well as the proportion of other allies who choose to rebel.

What determines the threshold ϕ^*? Recall that at time $t = 0$, the dictator recruits the minimum number of allies to form a coalition of size κ^0, which is $\mu = \kappa^0 - \lambda$. Suppose that the regime's strength changes to κ^t in any subsequent period $t = 1, 2, \ldots$, because of exogenous shifts in power between those within and outside of the ruling coalition. If $\kappa^t < \lambda$, then $\phi^* > 1$ and the dictator survives in office without any allies. By contrast, if $\kappa^t > \kappa^0$, then $\phi^* = 0$ and the dictator definitely loses his office. And if $\lambda \le \kappa^t \le \kappa^0$, then the proportion of allies required for a successful rebellion must be greater than

$$\phi^* = \frac{\kappa^0 - \kappa^t}{\kappa^0 - \lambda}. \tag{4.1}$$

Equation (4.1) suggests that we may consider κ^t a measure of the *regime's current strength* vis-à-vis those excluded from power. When κ^t is large, a smaller fraction of allies must rebel for the rebellion to succeed. A *large* κ^t thus corresponds to a regime that is currently *weak*. Accordingly, the threshold ϕ^* in (4.1) is decreasing in κ^t.

Meanwhile, we may think of λ as a measure of the *balance of power within the ruling coalition*. Equation (4.1) implies that the threshold ϕ^* is increasing in λ. In other words, weak dictators are more vulnerable to a rebellion because a smaller proportion of allies can rebel successfully against them.

I assume that all aspects of this setting except the regime's current strength κ^t are common knowledge. More precisely, each ally privately observes an imperfect signal k_i of κ^t and, in turn, each ally makes a private inference about the proportion of allies whose support the dictator needs to stay in power at time t. The signal k_i is distributed uniformly on the interval $[\kappa^t - \varepsilon, \kappa^t + \varepsilon]$, and the realizations of k_i are independent across allies. We may think of $\varepsilon > 0$ as "small" and thus view each ally's signal k_i as containing a small idiosyncratic noise. This informational imperfection arises because the regime's strength depends not only on the power held by those within the ruling coalition but also on the power held by those excluded from it. Allies may learn about any shifts in power between the two groups via separate private channels, and each ally may assess the regime's strength differently because of differences in individuals' positions or networks. For expositional simplicity, I assume that κ^t has a uniform prior density on the interval $[0, 1]$.[23]

[23] These simplifying distributional assumptions are inconsequential as long as the support of κ^t contains the interval $[\lambda, \kappa^0]$ and $\varepsilon > 0$ is small. The present results would be qualitatively

Suppose a challenger offers $b_C > b_I$ to any ally that joins him in a rebellion against the dictator. Should an ally join the rebellion? To answer this question, consider first a simpler, alternative setting in which the regime's current strength κ^t is public information and thus common knowledge among the allies. If $\kappa^t < \lambda$, the dictator does not need any allies to survive in office. Hence a rebellion would fail even if all allies abandoned the dictator. Alternatively, if $\kappa^t > \kappa^0$, then a rebellion definitely succeeds. Thus for any ally, rebelling strictly dominates supporting the dictator when $\kappa^t > \kappa^0$ and supporting the dictator strictly dominates rebelling when $\kappa^t < \lambda$.

However, when the regime's current strength κ^t is in the interval $[\lambda, \kappa^0]$, this model resembles a multiperson stag hunt. That is, supporting the dictator is an ally's optimal choice whenever at most ϕ^* allies rebel, and rebelling is her optimal choice as long as more than ϕ^* allies rebel. Thus whether a rebellion succeeds is unrelated to key political factors in this setting: the benefit from supporting the dictator b_I, the benefit from successfully rebelling and joining the challenger b_C, the cost of a failed rebellion r, or the dictator's power λ. Instead, a rebellion's success depends only on what each ally believes about the intentions of other allies.[24]

This indeterminacy as well as the lack of connection to political factors disappears in the present setting where each ally observes an imperfect signal k_i of the regime's current strength κ^t. Given our assumptions about the distribution of k_i, each ally has an unbiased estimate of κ^t. More precisely, after ally i observes the signal k_i, she believes that κ^t is distributed uniformly on the interval $[k_i - \varepsilon, k_i + \varepsilon]$, and her expectation of κ^t is k_i. However, she does not know the signals $k_{\sim i}$ that other allies observed; in turn, the true value of κ^t is not common knowledge. In other words, each ally is not only uncertain about the regime's strength but also about other allies' perception of the regime's strength.

Suppose, therefore, that each ally follows a threshold strategy according to which she rebels when her signal k_i is above some threshold k^* and supports the dictator otherwise. An ally who observes the signal $k_i = k^*$ must be indifferent between supporting and rebelling against the dictator. Ally i's expected payoff from supporting the dictator is

$$\Pr(\phi \leq \phi^* | k_i = k^*)b_I + [1 - \Pr(\phi \leq \phi^* | k_i = k^*)]0 = \Pr(\phi \leq \phi^* | k_i = k^*)b_I,$$

whereas her expected payoff from rebelling is

$$\Pr(\phi \leq \phi^* | k_i = k^*)(-r) + [1 - \Pr(\phi \leq \phi^* | k_i = k^*)]b_C$$
$$= b_C - \Pr(\phi \leq \phi^* | k_i = k^*)[b_C + r].$$

---

identical if I instead assumed that κ^t is distributed normally, as is common in the global games literature (see, e.g., Morris and Shin 2003).

[24] In an equilibrium in mixed strategies, the success of a rebellion depends on b_I, b_C, r, and λ, but it does so in an empirically implausible way. For instance, the likelihood of a successful rebellion is increasing in the dictator's power vis-à-vis the allies.

Then an ally who observes the signal $k_i = k^*$ is indifferent between supporting and rebelling against the dictator if

$$\Pr(\phi \le \phi^* | k_i = k^*) = \frac{b_C}{b_C + b_I + r}. \tag{4.2}$$

What is the probability that a rebellion will fail, $\Pr(\phi \le \phi^*)$? Given the threshold strategy around k^*, the proportion of allies ϕ who rebel corresponds to the proportion of allies with the signal $k_i > k^*$. Because the signal k_i is distributed uniformly on the interval $[\kappa^t - \varepsilon, \kappa^t + \varepsilon]$, this proportion is

$$\phi = \frac{\kappa^t + \varepsilon - k^*}{2\varepsilon}.$$

A threshold signal k^* thus implies the existence of a threshold regime strength κ^* such that a rebellion fails if $\kappa^t \le \kappa^*$ and succeeds if $\kappa^t > \kappa^*$. In turn, when the regime's strength is κ^*, the rebellion barely fails,

$$\phi^*(\kappa^*) = \frac{\kappa^* + \varepsilon - k^*}{2\varepsilon} \quad \text{or, equivalently,} \quad \kappa^* = k^* + 2\phi^*(\kappa^*)\varepsilon - \varepsilon. \tag{4.3}$$

In equilibrium, therefore,

$$\Pr(\phi \le \phi^*(\kappa^*) | k_i = k^*) = \Pr(\kappa^* \le k^* + 2\phi^*(\kappa^*)\varepsilon - \varepsilon)$$
$$= \frac{k^* + 2\phi^*(\kappa^*)\varepsilon - \varepsilon - (k^* - \varepsilon)}{2\varepsilon} = \phi^*(\kappa^*).$$

In other words, an ally with the threshold signal $k_i = k^*$ believes that the proportion of allies who will rebel is distributed uniformly,

$$\Pr(\phi \le \phi^*(\kappa^*) | k_i = k^*) = \phi^*(\kappa^*). \tag{4.4}$$

Substituting $\phi^*(\kappa^*)$ from (4.1) and $\Pr(\phi \le \phi^*(\kappa^*) | k_i = k^*)$ from (4.2) into (4.4), we can solve for the threshold regime strength,

$$\kappa^* = \frac{\lambda b_C + \kappa^0(b_I + r)}{b_C + b_I + r}. \tag{4.5}$$

After substituting (4.1) and (4.5) into (4.3), we see that the threshold signal is

$$k^* = \kappa^* - 2\phi^*\varepsilon + \varepsilon = \frac{(\lambda - \varepsilon)b_C + (\kappa^0 + \varepsilon)(b_I + r)}{b_C + b_I + r}. \tag{4.6}$$

The equilibrium thresholds on regime strength κ^* (4.5) and allies' signal k^* (4.6) characterize a unique equilibrium and imply a simple and intuitive relationship between the likelihood of a successful rebellion and the key political factors in our setting. Recall that a high value of κ^t corresponds to a regime that is vulnerable because only a smaller fraction of allies must rebel for the rebellion to succeed. In turn, the threshold strategy around k^* asks an ally to rebel when her private information indicates that the regime is weaker than some threshold κ^*. A balance of power λ that favors the dictator vis-à-vis the allies, a large payoff to the allies b_I, a small offer from the challenger b_C, and a high cost of a failed rebellion r all raise the thresholds κ^* and k^*, thereby lowering the probability that a rebellion will succeed. Stated differently, the dictator knows that a rebellion is more likely to succeed when he is weak, when he pays his allies poorly, when a challenger offers them more, or when the punishment for those who participate in a failed rebellion is lenient.[25]

Proposition 4.1. *In a unique Bayesian Nash equilibrium, an allies' rebellion fails if $\kappa^t \leq \kappa^*$ and succeeds if $\kappa^t > \kappa^*$, and each ally supports the dictator if $k_i \leq k^*$ and rebels if $k_i > k^*$,*

$$\kappa^* = \frac{\lambda b_C + \kappa^0(b_I + r)}{b_C + b_I + r} \quad and \quad k^* = \frac{(\lambda - \varepsilon)b_C + (\kappa^0 + \varepsilon)(b_I + r)}{b_C + b_I + r}.$$

4.3.2 Authoritarian Power-Sharing without Institutions

So far, this chapter has established how the credibility of the threat of a rebellion depends on key factors in our political setting: the balance of power between the dictator and the allies, the allies' payoff from supporting the dictator and defecting to the challenger, and the punishment of those who participate in a failed rebellion. I now examine how the credibility of this threat affects power-sharing between the dictator and the allies.

The timing of actions in this extensive game is as follows. In period $t = 0$, the dictator and the allies form a power-sharing agreement according to which the dictator pays $\mu = \kappa^0 - \lambda$ allies a β share of total benefits from joint rule in each period. The timing of actions in any period $t \geq 1$ is as follows. First, nature determines the size of total benefits (which is 1 with probability π and 0 otherwise). The dictator then privately observes the size of these benefits, reports it (and possibly lies) to the allies, and compensates each ally with $b_I = \beta/\mu$. Next, the allies observe the dictator's report and their compensation but *not* the size of total benefits. Finally, each ally observes a signal of the regime's strength and either supports or rebels against the dictator. If a rebellion succeeds, the game ends and a new power-sharing agreement forms between the former challenger and his allies. On the other hand, if the rebellion fails, the power-sharing agreement remains in place but the rebellious allies are replaced by new ones from among the notables previously excluded from the ruling coalition.

I study a Markov perfect equilibrium in which the allies condition their actions in any period $t \geq 1$ only on the dictator's announcement of total benefits in that period; the compensation that the allies receive; and, if a rebellion is staged, the regime's strength.[26] Recall that a rebellion is the only punishment

---

[25] The appendix to this chapter contains proofs of these comparative statics as well as a discussion of equilibrium uniqueness.

[26] In contrast to strategies that would condition on the past history of play in a richer way, this strategy is the least demanding on coordination by the allies: It only asks the allies to consider

with which the allies can threaten the dictator. To compel the dictator to share power as agreed, the threat of rebellion must accomplish two objectives: (1) it must discourage the dictator from paying the allies less than the promised fraction β of benefits and (2) the same threat must also deter the dictator from lying about the size of benefits.

To deter the dictator from both types of defection – that is, not sharing benefits and lying about their size – the allies may threaten to rebel in any period in which they receive any payoff other than $b_I = \beta/\mu$. Importantly, when I say that *allies rebel* I require only that once the allies receive a payoff other than $b_I = \beta/\mu$, each ally considers the regime's strength (based on her signal k_i) and decides whether to rebel. Given this threat, if the dictator defects, he optimally does so by paying allies 0.[27] In turn, the allies cannot distinguish between the two types of defection because both hurt them equally ($b_I = 0$).

Consider, therefore, when the threat of a rebellion in periods when $b_I = \beta/\mu$ deters the dictator from lying about the size of benefits. The dictator can benefit from lying only during normal times and, according to Proposition 4.1, the probability that a rebellion succeeds when each ally receives the payoff $b_I = 0$ during normal times is $\rho^N = 1 - (\lambda b_C + \kappa^0 r)/(b_C + r)$. Then the threat of a rebellion will deter the dictator from lying if

$$1 - \beta + \delta V \geq (1 - \rho^N)(1 + \delta V), \tag{4.7}$$

where $\delta \in (0, 1)$ is a discount factor and V is the dictator's expected discounted payoff when the incentive constraint in (4.7) is satisfied,

$$V = \pi(1 - \beta + \delta V) + (1 - \pi)(1 - \rho^C)\delta V = \frac{\pi(1 - \beta)}{1 - \delta[1 - \rho^C(1 - \pi)]}. \tag{4.8}$$

This expression for V recognizes that when the incentive constraint in (4.7) is satisfied, rebellions occur only during crises. In that case, $b_I = b_C = 0$ and the probability that a rebellion succeeds is $\rho^C = 1 - \kappa^0$, with $\rho^C < \rho^N$. Because both types of defection yield the same benefit β to the dictator, the threat of a rebellion according to (4.7) will also discourage the dictator from refusing to share benefits as agreed.

Solving (4.7) for δ, we see that the dictator will comply with the power-sharing agreement as long as:

$$\delta \geq \frac{\beta - \rho^N}{(\beta - \rho^N)(1 - \pi)(1 - \rho^C) + \beta\pi(1 - \rho^N)}. \tag{4.9}$$

the regime's strength in the period in which a suspected defection occurred and not in any previous period, in which the membership of the ruling coalition may have differed.

[27] Alternatively, no ally has incentive to consider the regime's strength when a rebellion is not in place, as long as others do not. Thus the dictator's and allies' actions are best responses in each period, both during a rebellion and when a rebellion is not in place.

4.3.3   Authoritarian Power-Sharing with Institutions

The above analysis highlights the limits to authoritarian power-sharing when the threat of an allies' rebellion is the sole deterrent against the dictator's opportunism. Although the threat of a rebellion may compel the dictator to share benefits as agreed, it is a crude deterrent: Even when the dictator complies with the power-sharing agreement, power-sharing will collapse in any crisis period if a rebellion succeeds (which happens with probability $(1 - \pi)\rho^C$).

Both the dictator and the allies therefore would prefer to eliminate such unnecessary rebellions by establishing institutional mechanisms that would let allies verify the actual size of benefits from joint rule. Such institutional mechanisms may include periodic reviews of government spending and revenue or the consultation of major policies by a council composed of allies or their representatives. To simplify the analysis, I assume that institutions completely reveal the size of benefits to the allies in any period.[28]

Once power-sharing is institutionalized, the threat of an allies' rebellion will serve to deter the dictator from both lying about the size of benefits to be shared and the refusal to share benefits as agreed – both are now observable to the allies. The dictator will comply with the power-sharing agreement as long as inequality (4.7) is satisfied. Crucially, when power-sharing is institutionalized, a rebellion no longer needs to be staged every time the dictator claims there is a crisis in order to deter him from lying about the size of benefits. Therefore the dictator's expected discounted payoff is instead

$$V = \pi(1 - \beta) + \delta V = \frac{\pi(1 - \beta)}{1 - \delta}. \tag{4.10}$$

Solving (4.7) for δ, we see that the dictator complies with an institutionalized power-sharing agreement when

$$\delta \geq \frac{\beta - \rho^N}{\beta - \rho^N + \pi(1 - \beta)\rho^N}. \tag{4.11}$$

I denote the threshold discount factors under power-sharing with and without institutions by δ^I from (4.11) and $\delta^{\sim I}$ from (4.9). Comparing them, we see that $\delta^I < \delta^{\sim I}$. This result is intuitive: When power-sharing is institutionalized, the allies no longer need to stage a rebellion every time the dictator claims there is a crisis. Institutions allow the allies to verify the dictator's claims and preclude such wasteful rebellions. In turn, the expected payoff from power-sharing is greater when it is institutionalized, which reduces the dictator's temptation to renege on it.

Proposition 4.2. *In a Markov Perfect equilibrium, power-sharing is feasible under a greater range of discount factors when it is institutionalized, $\delta^I < \delta^{\sim I}$.*

---

[28] The intuition in the more realistic case – when institutions reveal the size of benefits via an imperfect but correlated signal – is a straightforward extension of this argument.

By clarifying the consequences of institutionalized power-sharing for authoritarian stability as well as the circumstances under which it is feasible, this analysis helps us understand when and why dictators adopt institutions. Institutionalized power-sharing leads to more stable ruling coalitions because it avoids unnecessary rebellions and allows for power-sharing when it otherwise would not be possible because it yields a greater expected payoff to the dictator. However, the dictator's promise to share power as agreed is credible only when the allies' threat of a rebellion succeeds with a sufficiently high probability.

The implications of these findings are sharpest when we consider how a change in a key factor in our political setting – the distribution of power between the dictator and the allies λ – affects the feasibility and desirability of institutionalized power-sharing. When $\lambda < \kappa^0$, three scenarios arise for a sufficiently high discount factor δ as the likelihood of a successful rebellion declines with an increase in the dictator's power vis-à-vis the allies: (1) when the dictator is weak, the threat of a rebellion is sufficiently credible to allow for power-sharing both with *and* without institutions – these are the cases when $\delta^I < \delta^{\sim I} \leq \delta$; (2) as the dictator's power grows past a threshold $\lambda^{\sim I}$ at which $\delta = \delta^{\sim I}$, power-sharing becomes feasible only when it is institutionalized, $\delta^I \leq \delta < \delta^I$; and (3) once the dictator's power grows past a threshold λ^I at which $\delta = \delta^I$, power-sharing is no longer feasible – with or without institutions. Finally, when $\lambda \geq \kappa^0$, the dictator controls enough power to rule alone and therefore does not need institutions to facilitate power-sharing.

To illustrate these results, consider the following numerical example. Suppose $\kappa^0 = 2/3$, $\lambda = 1/3$, $\beta = 4/5$, $r = 2$, $\pi = 0.6$, and $\varepsilon = 0.1$. Then $\mu = 1/3$ and, if the dictator defects during normal times, $b_I = 0$ and $b_C = 2.4$. In equilibrium, ally i rebels if his signal k_i is greater than the threshold signal $k^* = 0.48$, and the rebellion succeeds if the regime is weaker than the threshold $\kappa^* = 0.49$ (i.e., $\kappa^t > 0.49$).

Figure 4.3 plots the effect the dictator's power λ vis-à-vis the allies on threshold discount factors δ^I and $\delta^{\sim I}$ for $\lambda < \kappa^0$. For a discount factor $\delta = 0.85$, $\lambda^{\sim I} = 0.21$ and $\lambda^I = 0.49$. That is, power-sharing is feasible both with and without institutions as long as $\lambda \leq 0.21$; institutions are indispensable for the success of power-sharing when $0.21 < \lambda \leq 0.49$; and power-sharing is not feasible – with or without institutions – when $0.49 < \lambda \leq 2/3$. Once $\lambda > 2/3$, the dictator does not need allies to survive in office – the contribution of institutions to the credibility of power-sharing is therefore no longer relevant.

To summarize, this theoretical analysis shows that the success of authoritarian power-sharing depends on the credibility of the allies' threat of a rebellion and the presence of institutions that eliminate asymmetries of information between the dictator and his allies. The threat of an allies' rebellion is credible when the power of the dictator vis-à-vis the allies is small and when the cost of a failed rebellion is low. When institutions eliminate asymmetries of information about the size of benefits from joint rule, they lead to more stable ruling coalitions and expand the conditions under which power-sharing is feasible. Yet even institutionalized power-sharing agreements may collapse when the

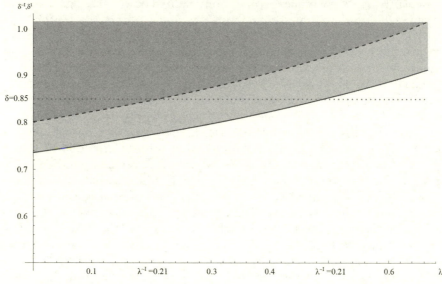

FIGURE 4.3. Effect of the dictator's power vis-à-vis the allies λ on threshold discount factors δ^I (solid line) and $\delta^{\sim I}$ (dashed line) for $\lambda < \kappa^0$. The dotted line plots a hypothetical discount factor $\delta = 0.85$.

distribution of power within the ruling coalition shifts in the dictator's favor and thus lowers the credibility of the allies' threat of a rebellion.

4.4 POWER-SHARING INSTITUTIONS AND AUTHORITARIAN STABILITY

According to the theoretical analysis in this chapter, formal deliberative and decision-making institutions in dictatorships alleviate commitment and monitoring problems in authoritarian power-sharing, thereby enhancing the stability of dictatorships. I now empirically evaluate two key implications of that analysis: Authoritarian regimes that institutionalize power-sharing should (1) avoid unnecessary intraelite conflicts and therefore (2) be more durable.

Unfortunately, information on the presence and functioning of high-level bodies like politburos, advisory councils, and legislative committees that I claim perform the regime-stabilizing functions is not available in the form of comprehensive large-N data. Yet as I pointed out earlier, most of these institutions are embedded within authoritarian parties and legislatures. We therefore can use the data on the political organization of dictatorships introduced in Chapter 2 to conduct an indirect test of this chapter's key empirical claims.

I assess the first hypothesis about the stabilizing role of parties and legislatures by examining the durability of authoritarian ruling coalition spells. Recall from Chapter 2 that a ruling coalition spell consists of the uninterrupted

TABLE 4.2. *Legislatures and the Survival of Authoritarian Ruling Coalitions, 1946–2008*

Legislature	Duration of All Ruling Coalition Spells			Duration of Multileader Ruling Coalition Spells		
	Median	Mean	N	Median	Mean	N
No	6.91	11.69	60	8.75	18.52	29
	(3.91,8.21)	(7.06,16.32)		(6.91,14.45)	(9.94,27.10)	
Yes	16.07	25.87	231	39.64	41.17	100
	(12.02,20.58)	(22.04,29.66)		(32.47,46.01)	(35.04,47.29)	
Log-rank test	24.83***			22.85***		
Wilcoxon test	24.21***			29.95***		

Note: The unit of observation is an authoritarian ruling coalition; 95% confidence intervals are in parentheses. Longest ruling coalition durations are right-censored; means therefore are underestimated.

succession in office of politically affiliated authoritarian leaders. Table 4.2 presents the mean and median survival times of ruling coalition spells for dictatorships with and without a legislature. Below each quantity, I list the corresponding 95 percent confidence interval.[29] To ensure that this analysis is not skewed by ruling coalitions that consist of only a single leader – such ruling coalitions may be inherently unstable and, in fact, comprise about one-half of all cases – I also present results that exclude such singletons.

Table 4.2 shows that ruling coalitions in dictatorships with legislatures indeed survive much longer than those in dictatorships without a legislature. There is no overlap between the 95 percent confidence intervals, whether we consider all ruling coalition spells or only those with multiple leaders. These findings are further corroborated by tests for the equality of survivor functions, which compare the overall similarity between survivor functions rather than only summary statistics (like the mean or the median). Table 4.2 reports the χ^2 statistics from two common tests for the equality of survivor functions, the log-rank and the Wilcoxon, both of which confirm that dictatorships with a legislature indeed have longer-lived ruling coalition spells.

An analogous analysis of the association between the presence of authoritarian parties and the survival of ruling coalition spells is presented in Chapter 6. There, I focus on the presence of "authoritarian regime parties," which I define as those that either have the dictator as a member or are endorsed by him. Chapter 6 shows that ruling coalitions in dictatorships with regime parties survive longer than those without, and outlines additional theoretical arguments that account for this observation.

[29] The presence of a legislature may vary throughout the duration of a ruling coalition. I present estimates based on the presence of a legislature at the end of a ruling coalition's existence. To account for the presence of right-censoring in ruling coalition data, I estimate the quantities in Table 4.2 using the Kaplan–Meier estimator; see Klein and Moeschberger (2003, Chap. 4).

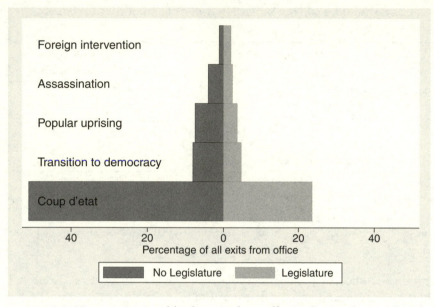

FIGURE 4.4. Nonconstitutional-leader exits from office in dictatorships with and without legislatures, 1946–2008. *Note:* Exits of interim leaders are not included. Unambiguous determination of exit was not possible for 13 leaders.

The second empirical prediction from this chapter's theoretical analysis is that formal institutions preclude avoidable, intraelite conflicts in authoritarian power-sharing. We therefore should expect that dictators with parties and legislatures will be less likely to lose office by nonconstitutional means, especially by a coup d'état. To assess this hypothesis, I use the data on leadership change in dictatorships introduced in Chapter 2.

Figure 4.4 contrasts nonconstitutional exits from office in dictatorships with and without a legislature. The percentage values along the horizontal axis refer to each category's share of all exits, conditional on having a legislature. As we saw in previous chapters, coups are the most frequent mode of nonconstitutional leader exit from office. Importantly, however, the relative frequency of coups – as well as the frequency of most of the remaining nonconstitutional exits – differs greatly between dictatorships with and without a legislature. In dictatorships without a legislature, leaders are more than twice as likely to be removed in a coup, a transition to democracy, a popular uprising, or an assassination than leaders in dictatorships with a legislature. Similar patterns obtain when we compare nonconstitutional entries to office or when we contrast these outcomes in dictatorships with and without parties.

Nevertheless, these differences in the nature of leadership transitions between dictatorships with and without parties and a legislature could be the result of the varying circumstances under which we observe these regimes instead of the institutions that are the focus of this analysis. I therefore examine the effect of legislatures and parties on the likelihood of three prominent modes of leader exit from office – coups, popular uprisings, and natural deaths – while controlling for the effect of other covariates that may plausibly affect these outcomes.

I focus on the first two outcomes because they are the most frequent forms of nonconstitutional leader exit and therefore should be good indicators of failed power-sharing – the first direct and the second indirect. In the latter case, the failure of power-sharing may enable a successful popular uprising.[30] I examine the last of the three types of leader exits from office – natural exits – in order to control for potential, unobserved endogeneity in the presence of parties and legislatures across dictatorships: There may be unobserved factors beyond the covariates included in the estimation herein that affect whether dictators adopt legislatures and parties. Because of their nonpolitical nature, exits from office due to natural causes should not be affected by any factors other than the age of a leader. Hence any positive association between legislatures or parties and long-surviving leaders might indicate that such leaders tend to adopt these institutions for reasons that we control for in the present analysis. If that is the case, then we must be careful when interpreting our estimation results.

Beyond the presence of parties and legislatures, I control for a range of covariates that may potentially affect the occurrence of coups and uprisings. Among economic factors, poverty and economic recessions may raise the risk of these outcomes; I therefore control for *GDP per capita* and *GDP growth*. Similarly, significant natural-resource wealth may intensify conflicts in power-sharing over control of those resources and thereby the risk of both coups and popular uprisings. I account for natural-resource wealth with the dummy variable *fuel and ore exports* that takes the value 1 if a country's annual fuel or ores and metal exports amount to more than 10 percent of its merchandise exports and 0 otherwise. These data are from Maddison (2008) and the World Bank (2008).

I further control for a dictatorship's ethnic and religious composition because the potential for ethnic or religious strife may complicate power-sharing and intensify the conflict between the ruling coalition and those excluded from power. The data on ethnic and linguistic *fractionalization* are from La Porta et al. (1999). Most *communist* regimes received material and institutional support from either Moscow or Beijing, which may account for their resilience to coups and uprisings; I therefore include a dummy variable for all communist leaders. On the other hand, dictatorships governed by the military may face a higher risk of coups for reasons unique to either the institution of the military or because of their direct access to the tools of violence; I therefore distinguish between *civilian* and *military* dictatorships. The latter two covariates are based on data on the political organization of dictatorships presented in Chapter 2.

---

[30] Transitions to democracy happen more frequently than popular uprisings but may be qualitatively distinct from other crises of authoritarian power-sharing because of the unique circumstances that accompany regime change.

TABLE 4.3. *Legislatures, Parties, and the Survival of Authoritarian Leaders, 1946–2008*

	Natural Causes		Coups		Uprisings	
Legislature	0.456*		0.298***		0.087***	
	(0.198)		(0.068)		(0.059)	
Party		0.574		0.674*		0.367*
		(0.251)		(0.141)		(0.213)
Log GDP per	1.413	1.400	0.714***	0.758*	0.756	0.696
capita	(0.310)	(0.296)	(0.105)	(0.111)	(0.295)	(0.256)
Growth	1.016	1.014	1.010	1.006	1.009	1.004
	(0.027)	(0.027)	(0.017)	(0.015)	(0.043)	(0.040)
Fuel and ore	1.977	2.251*	1.601	1.805**	0.859	1.529
exports	(1.015)	(1.102)	(0.488)	(0.541)	(0.749)	(1.294)
Ethnic	1.010	1.012*	0.994	0.997	0.998	0.996
fractionalization	(0.007)	(0.006)	(0.003)	(0.003)	(0.010)	(0.009)
Military	0.869	1.007	3.182***	4.115***	1.106	2.161
(vs. Civilian)	(0.323)	(0.355)	(0.843)	(0.954)	(0.685)	(0.171)
Communist[a]	2.236	2.147	0.165*	0.155*		
	(1.751)	(1.689)	(0.167)	(0.157)		
Cold War	0.238***	0.224***	0.411***	0.398***	1.232	1.009
	(0.131)	(0.123)	(0.141)	(0.136)	(0.787)	(0.616)
Age	1.061***	1.060***	1.028***	1.020*	1.039	1.052**
	(0.017)	(0.017)	(0.011)	(0.010)	(0.028)	(0.027)
Log-likelihood	−158.856	−166.236	−556.325	−609.954	−64.365	−75.365
Leaders	309	408	390	408	390	408
Leader-years	2,900	2,997	2,903	3,000	2,903	3,000
Exits	41	43	116	122	16	17

Note: Cox survival model, coefficients are expressed as hazard ratios; Breslow method for ties. Standard errors in parentheses. Significance levels *10%, **5%, ***1%.
[a] Not included in the model for uprisings because it is a perfect predictor.

Finally, to control for any potential temporal effect of the Cold War struggle between the United States and the Soviet Union on the likelihood of coups or uprisings, I include a dummy variable for the *Cold War*, which takes the value 1 between 1945 and 1990 and 0 otherwise. To maintain their exogeneity with respect to the outcomes studied, all time-varying covariates are lagged by one year.

Table 4.3 presents the results of a competing risk analysis based on the semiparametric Cox survival model. A competing risks approach allows me to examine the possibly different effect of each covariate on the three types of leader exit from office.[31] The estimated coefficients are presented in the

---

[31] On competing risk models, see Chap. 10 in Box-Steffensmeier and Jones (2004) and Crowder (2001).

form of a hazard ratio: A coefficient smaller than 1 implies that a covariate reduces the relative risk of the associated type of exit from office. I estimate two specifications per mode of exit, separately examining the effect of legislatures and parties on the risk of coups, popular uprisings, and exits from office due to natural causes.

Consider first the association between parties or legislatures and exits from office due to natural causes. As indicated above, I use this nonpolitical outcome as a check on any unobserved endogeneity in the presence of parties and legislatures across dictatorships. The key factor associated with exits due to natural causes should be the age of a leader, which in fact is the case. However, note that the presence of a legislature is associated with longer leader tenures that end in an exit from office due to natural causes – even if at a low level of statistical significance. This suggests that the adoption of legislatures across dictatorships may be endogenous to expected tenure duration.

Now consider how the presence of parties and legislatures affects the likelihood of coups and popular uprisings. Consistent with my theoretical claims, the existence of either a legislature or a party significantly reduces the likelihood of these two most frequent forms of nonconstitutional exits from office. The presence of a legislature reduces the hazard of a coup by about 70 percent and almost entirely eliminates the risk of a popular uprising. Similarly, the presence of a party reduces the hazard of coups and uprisings by about 32 and 63 percent, respectively. These results are robust to the exclusion of any controls that reduce the size of the sample and to alternative estimation techniques.[32]

Finally, coefficient estimates on the remaining, control covariates are very sensible. Among those with a high level of statistical significance, a high GDP per capita reduces the risk of coups, whereas natural-resource wealth and military (as opposed to civilian) rule increase this risk. The risk of coups was much higher during the Cold War, as was the frequency of long-serving dictators who died in office. Superpower intervention in client states during the Cold War in the Third World is the most likely cause of the former, whereas support for favored dictators in Soviet and American zones of influence may account for the latter.

Thus we see strong, systematic empirical association between authoritarian parties or legislatures and the stability of dictatorships. Regimes that govern with these institutions have more durable ruling coalitions and avoid violent nonconstitutional leadership transitions. Consistent with the theoretical analysis in this chapter, parties and legislatures reduce the risk of coups – the empirical counterpart to allies' rebellions in my theoretical model. However, we also see that they reduce the likelihood of popular uprisings, possibly because once they are less likely to collapse from within, regimes that institutionalize power-sharing are more likely to withstand challenges from the masses.

---

[32] Parametric methods for the analysis of survival data yield qualitatively identical results.

Nevertheless, these results come with three caveats. First, the data on parties and legislatures used herein provide only a crude measure of the high-level, deliberative, and decision-making bodies within these institutions that I argued facilitate authoritarian power-sharing. Second, I used exits due to natural causes in order to diagnose potential endogeneity in the adoption of parties and legislatures by long-lived dictators. We saw some evidence that legislatures, although not parties, appear to be adopted by leaders who, on average, stay in office longer and exit due to natural causes. Third, the formal analysis in the previous section suggests that established autocrats – those who, over time, have acquired enough personal power to rid themselves of the need for allies – should also avoid a violent fate and alone constitute long-lived "ruling coalitions." In the above empirical analysis, I only partially account for such cases by separately presenting results for multileader ruling coalitions, which should exclude most established autocrats.[33] Jointly, these caveats suggest that these empirical results should be interpreted with care and on their own they provide indirect, tentative support for the theoretical arguments advanced in this chapter.

4.5 CONCLUSION: THE DISTINCTLY AUTHORITARIAN PURPOSE OF NOMINALLY DEMOCRATIC INSTITUTIONS IN DICTATORSHIPS

The vast majority of dictatorships maintain political institutions that at least in name may conceal their true authoritarian nature. Perhaps surprisingly, throughout the period 1946–2008, more than 80 percent of all dictatorships maintained a legislature and at least 46 percent allowed for more than one political party to be seated in the legislature. In most cases, this implies that these dictatorships also held elections.

Yet in most dictatorships, parties, legislatures, and elections do not perform the same political functions as their democratic counterparts. Authoritarian legislatures, for instance, are hardly representative of their supposed constituencies. As Figures 2.4 and 2.6 in Chapter 2 reveal, 17 percent of authoritarian legislatures are either unelected or appointed; 37 percent permit only a single party or candidate per legislative seat; and, in a further 13 percent, the largest and almost always regime-sanctioned, governing political party controls more than 75 percent of legislative seats. Authoritarian legislatures thus are far from representative of the multitude of interests among their regimes' populations and only rarely seat any genuine political opposition. Most often, they are a gathering of the "Who's Who" in a regime's echelons of power.

Throughout this book, I argue that the nominal resemblance between some authoritarian and democratic institutions is misleading. This chapter explains how high-level, deliberative, and decision-making bodies within parties and

---

[33] Additionally, my arguments in Chapter 3 explain why established autocracies should be empirically rare – hence the imperfect accounting for their presence should not significantly skew my estimation results.

legislatures facilitate power-sharing among a regime's elite. Regular interaction between the dictator and his allies within parties and legislatures reduces the potential for misperceptions that may breed suspicion among the ruling coalition that the dictator is reneging on their agreement to share power. Meanwhile, elections – a quintessentially democratic institution – help to allocate power to the most politically relevant notables and arbitrate conflicts among them. The dictator's compliance with the formal rules that these institutions entail constitutes an unambiguous signal of his commitment to sharing power. This latter aspect explains why authoritarian power-sharing benefits from formal institutionalization even if the transparency-increasing benefits of joint, regular interaction in principle could obtain without the actual formal institution of the Chinese Politburo, the Chilean Junta de Gobierno, or the Saudi Allegiance Commission.

A better understanding of the mechanisms by which formal institutions contribute to the success of power-sharing in turn helps explain why some dictatorships establish and maintain nominally democratic institutions like parties, legislatures, and even elections. These institutions stabilize power-sharing among authoritarian elites, thereby performing functions that are distinctly authoritarian. As the empirical analysis in this chapter suggests, by being less likely destabilized from within, regimes that institutionalize power-sharing may even be more successful at confronting mass challenges. Dictators' resolution of the latter type of challenge – what I refer to as the problem of authoritarian control – is the focus of the next two chapters.

4.6 APPENDIX: PROOFS

This appendix contains proofs of those technical results that do not follow directly from the discussion in Section 4.3.

The uniqueness of the equilibrium in Proposition 4.1.

Carlsson and van Damme (1993, 995–6, 1003–5) and Morris and Shin (2003, 65–71) summarize and discuss the conditions for a unique equilibrium in a global game. Morris and Shin (2003, 65–67) prove that an equilibrium of a global game is unique (by surviving iterated elimination of strictly dominated strategies) if it satisfies the following five properties: (1) action monotonicity, (2) state monotonicity, (3) strict Laplacian state monotonicity, (4) limit dominance, and (5) continuity.

In the present context, (1) action monotonicity requires that the incentive of an ally to rebel is nondecreasing in the number of other allies who plan to rebel (ϕ); (2) state monotonicity requires that the incentive of an ally to rebel is nonincreasing in the strength of the regime (κ^t); (3) strict Laplacian state monotonicity requires that there is a unique regime strength (κ^*) that satisfies the indifference condition (4.2) for an ally who observes the signal $k_i = k^*$; (4) limit dominance requires that there are high and low levels of κ^t

(and, by extension, of k_i) such that an ally strictly prefers to rebel and support the dictator, respectively, regardless of other allies' actions; and (5) continuity requires that the allies' expected payoff from rebelling is continuous in k_i and $\Pr(\phi > \phi^*)$.

The present setting satisfies these conditions; thus the equilibrium character-ized by Proposition 4.1 is unique. The main technical difference from Morris and Shin (2003) is the bounded support of the probability distribution of k_i, which is unbounded in Morris and Shin (2003). Morris and Shin (2003, 65, footnote 3), explain that their proofs extend to the case of bounded support; see also Carlsson and van Damme (1993, 1003–5).

Comparative static results from Proposition 4.1.

The relevant partial derivatives of κ^* are

$$\frac{\partial \kappa^*}{\partial \lambda} = \frac{b_C}{b_C + b_I + r} > 0,$$

$$\frac{\partial \kappa^*}{\partial b_I} = \frac{\partial \kappa^*}{\partial r} = \frac{b_C(\kappa^0 - \lambda)}{(b_C + b_I + r)^2} > 0,$$

and

$$\frac{\partial \kappa^*}{\partial b_C} = -\frac{(b_I + r)(\kappa^0 - \lambda)}{(b_C + b_I + r)^2} < 0.$$

The relevant partial derivatives of k^* are

$$\frac{\partial k^*}{\partial \lambda} = \frac{b_C}{b_C + b_I + r} > 0,$$

$$\frac{\partial k^*}{\partial b_I} = \frac{\partial k^*}{\partial r} = \frac{b_C(2\varepsilon + \kappa^0 - \lambda)}{(b_C + b_I + r)^2} > 0,$$

and

$$\frac{\partial k^*}{\partial b_C} = -\frac{(b_I + r)(2\varepsilon + \kappa^0 - \lambda)}{(b_C + b_I + r)^2} < 0.$$

Forming a larger than minimum ruling coalition κ^0.

An extension of the ruling coalition beyond κ^0 has two consequences in the present model of a rebellion. First, as the number of allies increases, a larger fraction must rebel to depose the incumbent dictator. Second, each ally now obtains a smaller benefit because he shares total benefits β with a larger num-ber of allies. The present model of a rebellion implies that the former effect dominates the latter. That is, forming a larger than minimum ruling coalition lowers the credibility of the rebellion and therefore cannot help the dictator share power.

Suppose that an incumbent and a challenger can choose a larger than minimum ruling coalition $\kappa' \geq \kappa^0$ (holding κ' the same for the incumbent and the challenger). This has two implications. First, as κ' increases, a larger fraction of allies must rebel to depose the incumbent,

$$\phi^* = \frac{\kappa' - \kappa^t}{\kappa' - \lambda} \quad \text{and} \quad \frac{\partial \phi^*}{\partial \kappa'} = \frac{\kappa' - \lambda}{(\kappa' - \lambda)^2} > 0.$$

But second, holding the fraction of total benefits from joint rule β that an incumbent and a challenger share with the allies equal, each ally obtains a smaller benefit $b_C = \frac{\beta}{\mu} = \frac{\beta}{\kappa' - \lambda}$ as κ' increases.

The former effect dominates the latter. After substituting the updated ϕ^* and b_C into the expression for ρ, we obtain

$$\rho = 1 - \frac{\beta\lambda + \kappa'(\kappa' - \lambda)r}{\beta + (\kappa' - \lambda)r} = \frac{\beta(1 - \lambda) + (1 - \kappa')(\kappa' - \lambda)r}{\beta + (\kappa' - \lambda)r}.$$

Differentiating ρ with respect to κ', we obtain

$$\frac{\partial \rho}{\partial \kappa'} = -\frac{(\kappa' - \lambda)r[2\beta + (\kappa' - \lambda)r]}{[\beta + (\kappa' - \lambda)r]^2} < 0.$$

Thus forming a larger than minimum ruling coalition reduces the probability that a rebellion succeeds and cannot help an incumbent to strengthen the credibility of his promise to share benefits as agreed. (Constraint (4.7) is more difficult to satisfy as the probability that a rebellion succeeds declines.)

This result also implies that forming a minimum-size ruling coalition κ^0 is challenge-proof at the formation stage. If we think of the formation of the initial ruling coalition as a bidding process in which two candidates for the dictator propose the size of the ruling coalition to the notables (again, holding β that the incumbent and the challenger share with the allies equal), then the candidate who offers to form a minimum winning coalition κ^0 will not be beatable. A minimum winning coalition gives the allies the greatest influence over the leader because it maximizes the likelihood that a rebellion succeeds if staged, and it gives each ally the largest payoff because she only shares β with the smallest necessary number of allies.

PART II

THE PROBLEM OF AUTHORITARIAN CONTROL

5

Moral Hazard in Authoritarian Repression and the Origins of Military Dictatorships

> The soldan of Egypt, or the emperor of Rome, might drive his harmless subjects, like brute beasts, against their sentiments and inclination: but he must, at least, have led his *mamelukes*, or *praetorian bands*, like men, by their opinion.
>
> David Hume, *Of the First Principles of Government*

> [Those] emperors who came to power... by corrupting the soldiers... depended solely upon two very uncertain and unstable things: the will and the Fortune of him who granted them the state.
>
> Niccolò Machiavelli, *The Prince*

> Our principle is that the Party commands the gun, and the gun must never be allowed to command the Party.
>
> Mao Zedong, *Problems of War and Strategy*

The removal or installation of governments by soldiers results in the establishment of a prominent type of authoritarian regime: the military dictatorship. According to the data on institutions and leadership change in dictatorships introduced in Chapter 2, the military was directly or indirectly involved in about 30 percent of all authoritarian governments between 1946 and 2008. Yet what is striking is not only the frequency but also the distribution of military interventions in politics: They tend to recur within the same countries. Thus between 1946 and 2008, soldiers participated in the removal or installation of roughly two of every three Latin American leaders. Meanwhile, the Communist dictatorships of Eastern Europe maintained firm political control over their armed forces throughout most of their existence.

Why do men with guns obey men without guns in some countries but not others?[1] As I outlined in Chapter 1, any dictatorship must resolve two political conflicts: the problem of authoritarian power-sharing and the problem of authoritarian control. This is the first of two chapters that focus on the latter. At the heart of the problem of authoritarian control is the conflict between a

---

[1] I am borrowing this phrase from Holmes (2003, 24) and Przeworski (2007, 495).

small authoritarian elite in power and the much larger population excluded from power. Dictatorships resolve this problem in two principal ways: by repression and by co-optation. In this chapter, I argue that the origins of military intervention in politics – and, by implication, of military dictatorships – lie in dictatorships' reliance on repression. This is because authoritarian repression entails a fundamental moral hazard: The very resources that enable the regime's repressive agents to suppress its opposition also empower them to act against the regime itself.

Consider Uruguay under Juan María Bordaberry, who assumed the presidency in 1972. Facing an increasingly polarized society, militant labor unions, and a continuing leftist insurgency by the Tupamaro Movement of National Liberation, Bordaberry expanded the central role that the Uruguayan military assumed in the suppression of domestic opposition under his predecessor, Jorge Pacheco Areco. Although democratically elected, Pacheco began to rule by emergency decrees in 1968, used emergency military conscription to suppress labor strikes in 1969, and put the military directly in charge of fighting the Tupamaros in 1971 (Gillespie 1991, Chap. 3; Wright 2001, 155–6). Bordaberry, who came to office after elections wrought with unprecedented violence and accusations of fraud (Weinstein 1975, 125–7), soon lost the support of a majority in the National Assembly and continued militarizing internal repression by expanding the army's autonomy, immunity, and jurisdiction in the fight against leftist "subversives."

The Uruguayan military soon capitalized on its newly acquired political strength: The generals began to publicly diagnose Uruguay's political ills, press for its preferred solutions, and veto Bordaberry's policies and appointments. By the end of 1973, Bordaberry was a figurehead president of a military dictatorship that disbanded the National Assembly, banned all political parties, and in 1976, forced Bordaberry's resignation, preferring to govern through a more compliant figurehead (Gillespie 1991, 54–7).

Contrast Bordaberry's policies and fate to those of the former Tunisian President Zine El Abidine Ben Ali, who fled into exile in January 2011 amid widespread popular protests against his government.[2] Ben Ali, like his predecessor Habib Bourguiba, relied for repression on internal security forces rather than the military (Ware 1985, 37). Both presidents deliberately kept the Tunisian military small, underequipped, and out of politics, fearing that a politically indispensable military might turn against them (Nelson 1986, Chap. 5). When mass protests erupted in December 2010, Ben Ali ordered the army to assist the overwhelmed police and internal security services in suppressing the protesters. Seeing the magnitude of the protests and lacking a vested interest in the regime's survival, the army chief of staff General Rachid Ammar refused the order, thereby sealing Ben Ali's fate.[3]

---

[2] See, e.g., "A Dictator Deposed," *The Economist online*, 15 January 2011; "Ali Baba Gone, but What about the 40 Thieves?," *The Economist*, 22 January 2011.

[3] See, e.g., "Tunisia's Upheaval: No One Is Really in Charge," *The Economist*, 29 January 2011.

Ben Ali's and Bordaberry's fates illustrate a key dilemma in authoritarian repression: If dictators exclude soldiers from repression, they become vulnerable to threats from the masses. However, if they heavily rely on their militaries for repression, they expose themselves to challenges from within their repressive apparatus. Thus when deciding how much to rely on repression, dictators make a trade-off between their exposure to external threats from the masses excluded from power and their vulnerability to internal threats from their mamelukes and praetorian bands.

This intuition anticipates two questions that I address in this chapter in order to explain the origins of military dictatorships. The first is: Why do some dictatorships rely heavily on their militaries for repression? The answer to this question helps us to understand why soldiers in some countries acquire the leverage to intervene in politics. I argue that this occurs when an underlying, politywide conflict results in threats to the regime that take the form of *mass, organized, and potentially violent opposition*. Under these circumstances, the military is the only force capable of defeating such threats. The military's advantage lies in its size, labor-intensive nature, and proficiency in the deployment of large-scale violence. Although the military is the repressor of last resort in most dictatorships, regimes that frequently face mass, organized, and violent opposition must integrate their militaries within their repressive apparatus by granting them corresponding material and institutional resources. It is these resources – especially the autonomy over personnel decisions and legal impunity for internal repression – combined with their political pivotalness that empower militaries to intervene in politics.

Hence in regimes that rely on brute force, those who dispense it wield leverage that they can exploit. However, political indispensability and the attendant resources alone do not explain why militaries overtly intervene in politics. Their existing political leverage should allow soldiers to extract any institutional or political concessions from the government, thus precluding the need to replace leaders or actually govern. A politically pivotal military should be an *éminence grise* behind the throne.

This argument points to the second question addressed in this chapter: When and why does bargaining over institutional or policy concessions between a government and the military break down and result in overt military intervention? The answer to this question lies in the different political resources of the two actors. The military would like to exploit its pivotal political role by demanding greater institutional autonomy, resources, and influence over policy from the regime. Yet its only bargaining chip is the crude threat to intervene. This threat is tenuous for two reasons: First, the government understands that the military – like the government – would like to avoid overt intervention; and second, the government anticipates that the military may exaggerate its willingness to intervene. Thus when the government devises and implements policies, it has an incentive to question the military's resolve to intervene. Military interventions occur when, in this push-and-shove play for influence between the military and the government, the latter oversteps and "rocks the boat" too much.

The theoretical model developed in Section 5.3 integrates the answers to these two questions and yields two central insights. First, as I suggested earlier, the moral hazard entailed in authoritarian repression compels dictators to trade off between their exposure to external, mass threats from those excluded from power and their vulnerability to internal threats from the regime's repressive agents. Ultimately, however, the specter of a successful regime overthrow limits any dictator's leeway in choosing between these two vulnerabilities. This leads to the second insight: As the magnitude of mass threats grows, three regimes of interaction between the government and the military may emerge – *perfect political control, brinkmanship*, and *military tutelage*. As we move across these regimes, the military's autonomy and resources expand while the government's ability to implement its most preferred policies diminishes. Crucially, however, overt military interventions occur only under the brinkmanship regime. Thus I explain why the military remains docile in some dictatorships, why it overtly intervenes in others, and why it influences politics from behind the scenes elsewhere.[4] Theoretical extensions of this logic explain why military interventions occur in new democracies and account for the increased susceptibility of military dictatorships to interventions by other soldiers.

The analysis in this chapter implies that the empirical association between the severity of threats from those excluded from power and the likelihood of overt military interventions will be nonmonotonic – that is, first increasing and then decreasing in the magnitude of mass threats. I find strong empirical support for this prediction when I proxy for the intensity of the latent conflict between the authoritarian elite in power and the masses by economic inequality. Societywide inequality is one factor in particular that systematically favors a dictatorship's use of the military in repression. In economically unequal dictatorships, poor peasants or workers may threaten to expropriate or replace the rich, ruling elite in power. These threats typically take the form of labor strikes, land invasions, and guerilla attacks. To measure military intervention in politics, I use data on the nature of the entry or exit of authoritarian leaders during the period 1946–2008 that was introduced in Chapter 2. Consistently with the arguments in this chapter, I find that the likelihood of military intervention in politics is first increasing and then decreasing in the level of a country's economic inequality. By conceptually connecting the intensity of the moral hazard in authoritarian repression to structural conditions that tend to persist over the long haul – like societywide economic inequality – this chapter accounts for the empirically observed recurrence of military interventions within the same set of countries.

The next two sections explain what the moral hazard in authoritarian repression is and how it affects bargaining between an authoritarian government and the military over the former's policies or the latter's institutional autonomy.

---

[4] This distinction has been studied in the historical and case-study literature on military interventions in politics but without a clear statement of its determinants (see Finer 1962; Nordlinger 1977; Perlmutter 1977).

I then develop a game-theoretic model of bargaining that takes place in the shadow of military intervention. Extensions of this model help us understand why military interventions frequently occur in new democracies, as well as why military dictatorships are susceptible to repeated military interventions. I evaluate my claims by examining data on economic inequality and military interventions in Section 5.4.

5.1 THE MORAL HAZARD PROBLEM IN AUTHORITARIAN REPRESSION

Most dictatorships do not rely on their militaries for repression. In fact, everyday repression in virtually all dictatorships is handled not by soldiers but rather by the police and specialized internal security agencies. However, when opposition to a regime is mass based, organized, and potentially violent, the military is the only force capable of defeating it. As the Uruguayan Tupamaros and the Tunisian uprising illustrate, the police and internal security services simply do not have enough personnel, equipment, or training to combat armed guerrillas or suppress an uprising of several tens of thousands of protesters.

Soldiers, therefore, are any dictator's repressive agent of last resort. Crucially, soldiers understand when they play a pivotal political role, and they exploit it by demanding institutional and policy concessions from the government. Dictatorships that frequently face or anticipate mass, organized, and violent opposition endow their militaries with corresponding material resources and institutional autonomy, and they create a legal framework that allows the military to participate in internal repression.

The primary cost of heavy reliance on repression, however, is not budgetary but rather political: The more indispensable soldiers become in the suppression of internal opposition, the greater their capacity to turn against the regime. In turn, politically pivotal militaries can and do demand privileges and immunities that go beyond what is necessary for suppressing the regime's opposition. As David Hume (1748, 16) observed in the epigraph at the beginning of this chapter, a ruler cannot use the threat of violence to ensure the obedience of those who are in charge of dispensing it – instead, "mamelukes and praetorians" must be led by their interests.

Thus we frequently observe that in return for the military's complicity in the suppression of internal opposition, the government concedes to it greater institutional autonomy, resources, and a say in policy. Classic examples of such concessions are the donativa and privileges that Roman emperors gave the praetorian guards and the army in return for their support against rivals and the Senate (see, e.g., Campbell 1994, Chap. 7). A modern counterpart is the autonomous sources of revenue that militaries enjoyed in some dictatorships, such as the military-run enterprises in Egypt (Cook 2007, 19) and Indonesia (Crouch 1978) or the military's monopoly over smuggling in Paraguay (Miranda 1990) and import licenses in Syria (Droz-Vincent 2007, 202).

More frequently, however, the military's political indispensability enables it to both demand and obtain greater institutional autonomy, in the form of self-rule over personnel, budgetary and procurement decisions – as well as legal limits on the prosecution of military personnel (Pion-Berlin 1992). Once the Uruguayan military acquired a central role in internal repression and Bordaberry lost his party's support in the National Assembly, the military was in a position to impose its policy and institutional preferences on the administration. The military rejected Bordaberry's choice of a new defense minister in 1972 and demanded the creation of a National Security Council that institutionalized its role in government in 1973. When the National Assembly refused to lift the immunity of a senator suspected of links to insurgents in the same year, the military insisted that Bordaberry dissolve the Assembly and replace it with an appointed Council of State (Weinstein 1975, 130–5; Rouquié 1987, 248–57).

The example of Uruguay is unusual in terms of the speed at which the Uruguayan military's eventual interference in politics followed its initial involvement in internal repression.[5] In most cases, actual interventions are preceded by the military's rise to a pivotal political role at more distant historical junctures than in the case of Uruguay. Consider, for instance, Cuba at the beginning of the twentieth century: The army became indispensable in suppressing internal disorder because of the limited capacity of the newly independent Cuban state after the withdrawal of U.S. forces. Rather than national defense, the primary mission of the Cuban military became "the suppression of revolutions, rural uprisings, and riots" (Pérez 1976, 46). Additionally, due to provisions in the Platt Amendment of 1901 that effectively conditioned Cuban sovereignty on the successful protection of American economic interests on the island, the military's role extended to the suppression of radical activity, especially labor agitation and strikes (Pérez 1976, 61, 102).

The central role played by the Cuban army in the maintenance of domestic stability was soon mirrored by a growth in its political prominence. Pérez (1976, Chap. 5) documents how, by the time of Gerardo Machado's election in 1925, presidential candidates had to seek the army's support. Machado rewarded the army's loyalty with a larger budget, an expansion of peacetime personnel, and exemption from the jurisdiction of civilian courts. Facing growing legislative opposition and internal disorder during his second term, Machado began substituting compromise with the opposition by repression. The army was put in charge of censorship, and military authorization was required for the public assembly of three or more persons. By mid-1933, according to Pérez (1976, 64), the army became "the single most important underpinning of the beleaguered Machado government." Machado's reliance on the army proved fatal when he lost the support of the U.S. administration after internal unrest in Cuba increasingly threatened American economic interests. The Cuban

---

[5] In 1958, the Latin Americanist John J. Johnson concluded that by the end of World War I, the Uruguayan armed forces "had been so reduced in size and prestige that they no longer decisively influenced political development.... In no other republic of Latin America ... have the armed forces been more apolitical in the past quarter century" (Johnson 1958, 51); see also Rouquié (1987, 234).

military, forced to choose between the specter of U.S. intervention and supporting Machado's dictatorship, forced Machado's resignation.

The Cuban military thus acquired political influence due to a combination of favorable structural conditions: the lack of a strong state; the presence of a mass, violent opposition; and a critical political juncture – Machado's decision to substitute compromise with growing opposition with repression by the military. After the fall of Machado, the Cuban military no longer promoted the interests of politicians in exchange for benefits; instead, it exploited its pivotal role to directly promote its own institutional and political interests (Pérez 1976, 104). The Cuban military's political ascendance under the Machadato allowed a group of disgruntled lower officers to stage a "sergeants' revolt" immediately after Machado's downfall and propelled one of its leaders, Colonel Fulgencio Batista, into political prominence. By 1934, Batista was in a position to orchestrate the impeachment of a president who dared to veto legislation that he proposed (Pérez 1976, 108–9); to promote his own presidential candidacy in 1940; and to return to office in a coup d'état in 1952 (Pérez 1995, Chap. 10).

Once soldiers attain a politically privileged position, they naturally attempt to preserve it.[6] Thus in El Salvador, according to Stanley (1996, 6–7), "the military earned the concession to govern the country . . . in exchange for its willingness to use violence against class enemies of the country's small but powerful economic elite." Once it acquired this privileged position in the 1930s, the military perpetuated it by exaggerating – and sometimes manufacturing – threats from the opposition. The Salvadoran state eventually succeeded in subduing the military in the 1980s, but only after the military's failure to defeat the leftist FMLN insurgency became apparent (Stanley 1996, 220). Thus, many dictatorships – as well as democracies – simply inherit a politically pivotal military from their predecessors, as Cuba did after the Machadato.

The subordination of politically pivotal militaries therefore may be feasible only at rare historical junctures that create a window of opportunity to do so. The vast social and political transformation brought about by the Russian Revolution and the ensuing Civil War helped the Bolsheviks institutionalize measures that would facilitate political control over an army still dominated by imperial officers (Von Hagen 1990); the Civil War allowed for a similar transformation in China (Teiwes 1987); and the Mexican Revolution allowed for the subjugation and incorporation of the Mexican military within a party that would later become the PRI (Rouquié 1987, 202–7).

Democratic transitions provide such windows of opportunity only occasionally, typically when the preceding dictatorship leaves the military discredited and therefore unable to resist the withdrawal of its existing privileges and immunities. This was the case in Argentina, after the military junta's debacle in the Falklands War (Rock 1987, Chap. 9). Frequently, however, the military is able to preserve its autonomy during democratic transitions or to even claim

---

[6] Desch (1999), for instance, argued that internal threats against militaries lead to their intervention in politics.

to serve as the guardian of democracy. In Turkey, the 1961 constitution – written under the military's supervision after the 1960 coup d'état, led by General Cemal Gürsel – established a National Security Council that actually formalized the military's historically prominent political role (see, e.g., Hale 1994). In the two decades that followed, according to Zürcher (2004, 245), the Council "gradually extended its influence over government policy and became a powerful watchdog, sometimes replacing the cabinet as the center of real power and decision-making."

The challenges involved in reigning in politically entrenched militaries in the absence of such large-scale political transformations are illustrated by the early years of the Iraqi Baath regime. The Iraqi army had been the primary agent of internal repression since Iraq's independence in 1932 (Makiya 1998, 21, 35) and, since General Qasim's overthrow of the monarchy in 1958, every regime "depended on support from the army or a critical portion of it" (Marr 1975, 125). The Baath Party's first challenge, even before it came to power, was that "in a political system that thrived on physical force, [it] simply lacked the necessary means to overwhelm [its] opponents" (Karsh 2002, 29). The 1968 July Revolution – as the coup d'état that brought the Baath Party to power came to be known – succeeded only because of the defection of key military officers from President Abd al-Rahman Aref's regime. The Baath Party enlisted the Head of Military Intelligence (i.e., Colonel Abd al-Razzaq Nayif), the Commander of the Republican Guard (i.e., Colonel Ibrahim Abd al-Rahman Da'ud), the Commander of the Republican Guard's armored brigade (i.e., Colonel Sa'dun Ghaydan), and the Commander of the Baghdad Garrison (i.e., Hammad Shihab). Whereas the latter two were Baath sympathizers, the former two exacted a high price for their betrayal: Nayif demanded Prime Ministership and Da'ud demanded the Ministry of Defense (Karsh 2002, 29–30).

Immediately after assuming power, however, the new Baathist regime faced a second challenge: If it wanted to survive, it had to rid itself of its dependence on the military. As a Party political report outlined in 1974, from the earliest days, the Party had to "consolidate its leadership of the armed forces . . . to immunize them against the deviations which the [Qasim] and Arif regimes and their military aristocrats had committed in the army's name."[7] Between 1958 and 1968, Iraq experienced more than ten attempted or successful military coups, soldiers occupied more than one-half of leading policy-making positions, and three presidents and most prime ministers were former military officers (Marr 1975, 125–6). Moreover, two years after the Iraqi Baath Party assumed power, the military wing of its Syrian cousin purged the Party's civilian membership after an intraparty coup d'état lead by Minister of Defense Hafez al-Asad (Van Dam 1979, Chap. 5; Hinnebusch 1990, Chap. 5) – precisely the type of praetorianism that the Baath's leadership feared.

The Baath Party at first considered outright disbanding the army and replacing it with a party militia (Makiya 1998, 31). However, because the Baath Party acquired power in a system in which "naked force has constituted the

---

[7] ABSP Report 103, cited in Makiya (1998, 26).

sole agent of political change" for so long (Karsh 2002, 3), it had to move gradually. As summarized by an internal Party report, in 1968 the Party did not yet

have the machinery to replace the state system, as did for example the Chinese Revolution . . . [it] could not simply dismantle the existing system and build a new one as, for instance, the Russian [R]evolution had done.[8]

The Baath Party therefore, first, unexpectedly arrested and exiled the two non-Baathist elite defectors from Aref's regime, then moved against those Party members whose careers originated in the army (Karsh 2002, 47–52; Makiya 1998, 25), and finally embarked on subjugating the institutional structure of the Iraqi army to the Party's control (Farouk-Sluglett and Sluglett 1987, 120–2).[9] In the course of these steps, the army's "historically central function of internal suppression was being taken over by other institutions" (Makiya 1998, 35), primarily by internal security services that were overwhelmingly staffed by individuals from Tikrit (Batatu 1978, Chap. 58) – President Ahmed Hassan al-Bakr's and then–Vice President Saddam Hussein's place of origin. By the second half of the 1970s, according to Makiya (1998, 25), the Iraqi military had "metamorphosed into a creature of the Baath party" and was no longer a political force (Makiya 1998, 31).

Nevertheless, even dictatorships that do not face mass, organized, and violent threats must deter those who are excluded from power from challenging the regime. In the absence of those structural conditions, however, mass threats to the ruling elite are rare. Instead, most threats come either from defectors within the political elite itself or from tight-knit networks of ideological dissenters. Such challenges are small enough that they do not require systematic reliance on the military and can be countered successfully by intelligence-gathering security services and the police.

Therefore in these regimes, the military does not acquire a politically pivotal role. In turn, it cannot resist the institutionalization of the regime's effective political control. In Bourguiba's and Ben Ali's Tunisia, for instance, military personnel were not allowed any political association, including membership in the regime-sanctioned Socialist Destourian Party (renamed Constitutional Democratic Rally Party under Ben Ali), and both leaders maintained exclusive power to promote military officers (Ware 1985). When members of the Tunisian military planned to participate in the ruling party's congress in 1979, Bourguiba refused to attend and dismissed the defense minister (Nelson 1986, 290).

An extensive literature examines such measures and argues that they are key to effective political control over politically entrenched militaries.

---

[8] ABSP Report 110, cited in Makiya (1998, 41).
[9] Nayif was forced into exile after being ambushed at the presidential palace by Saddam Hussein, while Da'ud was lured into Jordan and ordered to stay there (Karsh 2002, 32–4). The former was later assassinated in London. Saddam Hussein recounted these events during interviews after his capture by U.S. forces, although he claimed that "God killed Nayif" (U.S. Department of Justice 2009, 5).

Coup-proofing measures, as they are sometimes called, include the creation of parallel armed forces, multiple security agencies, and the exploitation of religious and ethnic loyalties (see, e.g., Quinlivan 1999). Thus in Baathist Iraq, for instance, the "pedagogical value of the Baath Party's militia was to counterbalance the army" (Makiya 1998, 31); the preferential treatment of Alawis under the al-Asads reinforced the Syrian military's loyalty to the political leadership (Van Dam 1979, Chap. 9); the rotation of commanders in Qaddafi's Libya kept the officers in line (Schumacher 1986/1987, 338); the Arab Socialist Union served as "a civilian counter to the military" in Nasser's Egypt (Waterbury 1983, 316); and the attachment of political commissars to Soviet military units ensured "that the army does not itself become an independent force, and break away from the Soviet regime."[10]

The arguments in this chapter, however, imply that effective control of the military is a political problem before it is an organizational or a managerial one. While the right institutional measures may facilitate the political control of militaries under favorable conditions, the underlying reason why some regimes subordinate soldiers to political control is that they do not depend on them for repression.

Hence the Communist Party successfully subordinated Soviet armed forces throughout its existence because the latter never became pivotal in domestic repression. When Khrushchev accused General Georgy Zhukov – the Defense Minister, Politburo member, World War II hero, and key ally in his rise to power – of Bonapartism, the latter was summarily stripped of all political posts without any opposition from the Soviet military (Colton 1979, Chap. 8). By contrast, when Honduran President Ramón Villeda Morales attempted to limit the military's role in internal affairs by creating a civil guard that would be directly accountable to him, the military swiftly removed him. The Honduran military had acquired a pivotal political role when it brought Villeda Morales to power after an electoral stalemate in 1954 and, in exchange, obtained complete autonomy over its budget, promotions, and key leadership positions (Bowman 2002, Chap. 5). Thus, coup-proofing measures are effective only when they are put in place *before* the military's political ascendance.

Nevertheless, even dictatorships that do not rely on their militaries for repression must suppress threats from the opposition and, in turn, face the moral hazard that the reliance on any repressive agent entails. Nikita Khrushchev's depiction of Joseph Stalin's fear of betrayal by his chief of secret police, Lavrentiy Beria, provides a summary of the risks entailed in endowing even nonmilitary agents with the capacity for repression:

Stalin realized that if Beria could eliminate anyone at whom Stalin pointed his finger, then Beria could also eliminate someone of his own choosing.... Stalin feared that he would be the first person Beria might choose. (Taubman 2004, 220)

---

[10] The quote is from a decree signed by Trotsky in his capacity as War Commissar during the Russian Civil War (Benvenuti 1988, 22).

Stalin's heirs were aware of this danger when they orchestrated Beria's arrest and execution in 1953 (Knight 1995, Chap. 9).

Crucially, however, when the heads of internal security services do betray their masters and succeed in replacing them, that action is not a military intervention – and the outcome is not a military dictatorship. The recently deposed Tunisian President Ben Ali served as his predecessor Habib Bourguiba's security chief and rose to prominence after suppressing the 1984 bread riots.[11] He ousted Bourguiba not in a military but rather a medical coup – by declaring Bourguiba incapacitated according to the Tunisian constitution (Ware 1988, 591–2). Similarly, Saddam Hussein rose to the Iraqi presidency as the head of the Baath Party's internal security apparatus. In a carefully orchestrated event in 1979, President Ahmed Hassan al-Bakr asked to be relieved from his duties because of failing health and transferred the presidency to Saddam Hussein, "the man best qualified to assume the leadership" (Karsh 2002; Makiya 1998). In both cases, key agents of internal repression became powerful political rivals; however, because neither regime relied on its military for repression, their ascent did not bring about a military dictatorship.

A large literature identifies the origins of military interventions in politics more narrowly in the military's institutional or political interests (Janowitz 1964; O'Donnell 1973; Nordlinger 1977); professionalization (Stepan 1988) or the lack thereof (Huntington 1957; Perlmutter 1977; Geddes 2009); the erosion of a political culture (Finer 1962); the political or professional ambitions of individual officers (Decalo 1990); and the operational aspects of interventions (Luttwak 1968; Perlmutter 1977; Farcau 1994).[12] Importantly and by contrast, I argue that the underlying reason why militaries intervene in politics goes back to their indispensability in authoritarian repression.[13] Once they become indispensable in repression, they acquire a politically pivotal role and, in turn, garner greater autonomy and resources. Only then are soldiers in a position to intervene in politics should their institutional interests, political preferences, or personal ambitions be threatened.[14]

---

[11] Bourguiba appointed Ben Ali as Minister of National Security in 1985, Minister of the Interior in 1986, and Prime Minister and General Secretary of the Destourian Socialist Party in 1987 (Reich 1990, 79–80).

[12] See Feaver (1999) for a review.

[13] Acemoglu et al. (2008) also relate the emergence of military dictatorships to moral hazard problems in authoritarian repression and economic inequality. However, their formulation of the moral hazard problem between a dictator and the military differs from the present one and predicts an increasing rather than curvilinear relationship between economic inequality and military interventions.

[14] In their focus on politywide political rather than organizational or situational factors, the arguments here are thus much closer to Huntington's later work. In *Political Order in Changing Societies*, for instance, Huntington (1968, 194) wrote that "the most important causes of military intervention in politics are not military but political and reflect not the social and organizational characteristics of the military establishment but the political and institutional structure of society."

5.2 BARGAINING IN THE SHADOW OF MILITARY INTERVENTION

Any explanation for the emergence of military dictatorships must not only offer reasons for how and why the military becomes politically indispensable but also account for why the military actually intervenes in politics. I argue that this occurs when bargaining between a government and a politically pivotal military over the government's policies or the military's autonomy breaks down. The form and the likely outcome of this bargaining – as well as the propensity for its breakdown – depend on the magnitude of mass threats to the regime and the corresponding degree of the military's political pivotalness.

In the model that I develop, in Section 5.3, I treat the emergence of mass threats, the subsequent allocation of the military's resources by an authoritarian government, and the bargaining between the government and the military as three sequential choices under a single authoritarian regime. This is simply an analytical convenience. As I discussed earlier, the transition from the emergence of a mass threat under a dictatorship to the military's political ascendance to actual conflict between the two that may escalate into an overt military intervention often takes years or even decades. The latter may even occur after the dictatorship that initially created a political pivotal military transitions to democracy. I show that depending on the level of the military's political pivotalness, three qualitatively distinct patterns of interaction between an authoritarian government and the military may emerge.

The first is *perfect political control*, which obtains when mass threats to the regime are small. In this case, dictators either do not need to use their militaries for internal repression or they are consciously accepting some degree of vulnerability to threats from the masses in exchange for maintaining political control over their militaries. The latter is a trade-off that Tunisian presidents Habib Bourguiba and Zine El Abidine Ben Ali appear to have found acceptable. The few instances when deployment of the Tunisian military against internal opposition was deemed necessary – during a nationwide strike in 1978 and the bread riots of 1984 and 2008 – were isolated and followed by the soldiers' immediate return to the barracks. The risk entailed in this strategy proved fatal when the 2010–11 protests overwhelmed Ben Ali's internal security services and deposed him.

At the other extreme – when mass threats from those excluded from power are greatest – dictators have no choice but to concede expansive resources to their militaries. In this case, the military's ability to intervene successfully is so credible that it does not need to be carried out in order to compel the government to yield both resources and policy concessions to the military. These governments are under effective *military tutelage*, which is the second pattern of interaction that the model in this chapter identifies. This was the position of Cuban governments after the fall of Machado in 1933. When in 1936, President Miguel Mariano Gómez – the first after the Machadato who did not owe his post to an overt military intervention – criticized the bloated military budget and vetoed a bill that expanded the army's role in rural education, the bill's sponsor and army chief of staff Fulgencio Batista asked the Congress to impeach the president. The imminent prospect of a surefire coup compelled the Cuban Congress to comply with Batista's demand and the new president, Federico Laredo Brú, served as a "pliant accomplice to military rule for the remainder of the 1930s" (Pérez 1976, 108–11).

I find that genuine bargaining between governments and their militaries occurs when the magnitude of mass threats is between these two extremes. In this case, the military's resources are large enough that it is tempted to use the threat of intervention to extract concessions from the government, yet the threat alone is not sufficient to deter the government from questioning the military's resolve to intervene. Because this interaction between the government and the military entails the conscious manipulation of the risk of an overt military intervention – an outcome that both parties prefer to avoid – I call it *brinkmanship bargaining*.[15]

When the government and the military engage in brinkmanship bargaining, both sides face a dilemma: Whereas the soldiers would like to use their guns to extract concessions from the government by threatening intervention, the government knows that the miliary prefers to obtain any concessions without actually having to openly intervene. From the military's point of view, overt intervention in politics is costly. It is costly not only because it may fail – resulting in the imprisonment or death of the participants – but also because successful interventions highlight political differences within the armed forces and often necessitate purges of officers who are opposed to intervention (see Finer 1962; Huntington 1957; Nordlinger 1977; Stepan 1988; Geddes 1999b). Such purges undermine the military's cohesion and chain of command as the display of the right political loyalties becomes more important than professional accomplishments. Military interventions thus frequently trigger abortive coups by dissatisfied junior factions within the armed forces. After the 1960 Turkish coup d'état, General Gürsel's faction within the Turkish military retired 235 of 260 generals and some 5,000 colonels and majors, fearing their opposition to Gürsel's policies. Such fears were warranted: Gürsel faced two failed abortive coups (Zürcher 2004, 241–4).

The government's bargaining dilemma, on the other hand, stems from its position rather than its power. Unlike the military, the government actually designs and implements policy. But like the military, it prefers to avoid an overt intervention because it wants to stay in office. When in 1972, Bordaberry attempted to assert his presidential authority by appointing a defense minister opposed by the Uruguayan military, he backed down after a six-day stalemate. During that short period, his inability to survive in office without the military's support became obvious (Klieman 1980, 152).

---

[15] On brinkmanship as a bargaining strategy that uses threats "that leave something to chance," see Schelling (1960, 187–206).

The distinctive features of brinkmanship bargaining stem from both the government's and the military's preference for avoiding the latter's overt intervention. The military cannot credibly "draw a line in the sand" and claim that it will intervene if that line is crossed; the government cannot credibly feign complete ignorance of the military's capacity to use force. In turn, both resort to brinkmanship and bargain by "rocking the boat," to borrow Schelling's (1960, 196) metaphor: The military has an incentive to exaggerate its demands, while the government has an incentive to test the military's resolve to intervene by defying those demands. Military dictatorships emerge when this push and shove for influence between the regime's repressive agent and its presumed master escalates into an overt military intervention.

The model in the next section additionally clarifies why incentives for brinkmanship bargaining intensify in military dictatorships and new democracies. Just like civilian dictators, military dictators confront the moral hazard in authoritarian repression and must placate their supporters within the military proper with institutional and policy concessions. Thus the Egyptian president Gamal Abdel Nasser, who came to power soon after the Free Officers brought down the Egyptian monarchy in 1952 (Waterbury 1983, Chap. 14), was suspicious of his own military because "he was able to seize power using his alliances within it, and there was no logical reason why others still in uniform could not do the same"(Waterbury 1983, 336). Nasser came to rely on Field Marshal Abd al-Hakim Amir to maintain his support within the military proper. In return, Amir demanded "a free hand in building his own clientele within the military." He "successfully kept control of the promotion process within the officers corps and was able, in addition, to place his people in upper-level management in the growing public sector as well as the diplomatic corps and the ranks of provincial governors" (Waterbury 1983, 336).

In military dictatorships, brinkmanship is more likely to escalate into an intervention because the military is no longer restrained by a concern over its institutional integrity. The institutional cost of the military's politicization was sunk in the form of politically motivated purges after the initial intervention that brought the military to power. As a result, when officer factions in the government differ over policy preferences with one another or with other officers in the military, all parties are less restrained when "rocking the boat" as they bargain.[16] Bitter disputes emerged within the Argentine military junta almost immediately after it seized power in 1976 over the control of the presidency, the Ministry of Economics, as well as the degree of the regime's openness and the timing of an eventual return to civilian rule (Fontana 1987). In 1981, these confrontations resulted in the ouster of President Roberto Viola by the head of the army, Leopoldo Galtieri (Rock 1987, 375). The brinkmanship-bargaining framework developed in this chapter thus helps us to understand why military

---

[16] Barros (2002, Chap. 2), Fontana (1987, Chap. 2), and Skidmore (1990) describe such differences within the Chilean, Argentine, and Brazilian military dictatorships, respectively.

coups frequently instigate further coups (Nordlinger 1977; Londregan and Poole 1990; Geddes 2005; Debs 2009).[17]

The present framework also explains why incentives for brinkmanship bargaining are more pronounced in new democracies. Unlike dictators, elected governments can take advantage of their popular support to discourage their militaries from intervening. Perhaps counterintuitively, this actually exacerbates a government's incentive to test the military's resolve when bargaining over its institutional privileges or the government's policies. More specifically, an elected government will be tempted to assert its formal authority precisely because the military will be concerned about any adverse popular reaction to an intervention.[18] Military interventions in new democracies occur when in this "tug of war" over the military's political influence the government underestimates the military's resolve and forces its hand.

This is what Pakistani Prime Minister Nawaz Sharif did during his last term in office. In 1998, the Pakistani Army Chief of Staff General Jehangir Karamat suggested that the government create a National Security Council that would permanently institutionalize the army's role in policy making. That role, according to the general, included management of the economy and combating internal political instability.[19] Enjoying widespread popularity after a landslide electoral victory in 1997, Sharif forced the general to resign in a public confrontation over the issue (Nawaz 2008, 497–502). However, when in 1999, after his popularity waned, Sharif attempted to dismiss Karamat's successor Pervez Musharraf in another public confrontation – this time over Pakistan's defeat in the Kargil War with India – he was deposed by the army.[20] The moral hazard in authoritarian repression therefore not only helps us to understand the repressive choices and the resulting vulnerabilities of dictatorships but also sheds light on the vulnerabilities of new democracies that inherit politically entrenched militaries.[21]

---

[17] In a competing explanation, Debs (2009) argues that military dictators lose power sooner and more violently than civilian ones because their expertise in the use of violence undermines their ability to credibly share power in the long run. Meanwhile, Rivero (2011) argues that the instability of military dictatorships is the result of factional balancing within armed forces.

[18] According to Nordlinger (1977, 94–5), for instance, "the overthrow of legitimate governments will spark mass protests, general strikes, riots, sporadic violence, and possibly armed resistance.... Soldiers thus rarely overthrow legitimate governments because they do not want to bring on, or deal with, the disorderly and violent behavioral expressions of popular censure."

[19] See "Pak Army Chief Tells Sharif to Create a Security Council," *The Times of India*, 7 October 1998; "Backdoor Junta," *The Times of India*, 8 October 1998; and "Pakistani Premier Prevails in Clash with General," *The New York Times*, 20 October 1998.

[20] See Nawaz (2008, 524–9), "A Soldier's Soldier, Not a Political General," *The New York Times*, 13 October 1999; and "Countdown to Pakistan's Coup: A Duel of Nerves in the Air," *The New York Times*, 17 October 1999.

[21] This is consistent with Cheibub (2007), who explains that the underlying reason why military coups occur more frequently in presidential than parliamentary democracies is that the former tend to emerge in countries with politically entrenched militaries.

TABLE 5.1. *Moral Hazard in Authoritarian Repression and Military Intervention in Politics*

	Regime of Interaction		
	Perfect Political Control	Brinkmanship Bargaining	Military Tutelage
Mass Threats	Low	Medium	High
Military's Political Indispensability	Low	Medium	High
Likelihood of Military Intervention	Low	High	Low

Table 5.1 summarizes the anticipated relationship between the magnitude of mass threats to the regime, the military's political indispensability, the nature of interaction between the government and the military, and the likelihood of military intervention in politics.

5.3 A FORMAL MODEL

Consider a *government* that faces a mass *threat* of magnitude $R > 0$ from those excluded from power. The government does not perfectly observe the threat's magnitude R but knows that it is distributed uniformly on the interval $[\underline{R}, \overline{R}]$, with the expected magnitude of $\hat{R} = (\underline{R} + \overline{R})/2$. This uncertainty reflects the government's difficulty in precisely estimating the magnitude of threats that depend on the success of mass collective action or guerilla activity.[22]

To counter the mass threat, the government endows the *military* with *resources* of size $r \in [0, \infty)$.[23] At the end of the game, a military with resources r defeats a mass threat of magnitude R with probability $\phi(R, r) = r/(r + R)$. Intuitively, the probability $\phi(R, r)$ is decreasing in the magnitude of the threat R and increasing in the military's resources r; the odds of a success and a failure are even if the threat's magnitude equals the military's resources, $\phi(R, r) = 1/2$ if $r = R$; the threat R succeeds with certainty if the government leaves the military without any resources, $\phi(R, 0) = 0$; and the probability that the military defeats the threat approaches 1 as its resources grow, $\lim_{r \to \infty} \phi(R, r) = 1$.[24]

In return for the military's support against domestic threats, the government agrees to accommodate the military's institutional and policy preferences on various issues as they emerge. The government can adopt one of two *policies* $p = \{p_G, p_M\}$. The government would ideally adopt policy p_G, whereas the military prefers policy p_M. To model the bargaining between the two as new policy issues emerge, suppose that depending on the *state* of the world $\theta = \{C, N\}$, the military is either willing to compromise ($\theta = C$) about an issue or

---

[22] See, e.g., Kuran (1991); the choice of the uniform probability distribution and a concrete functional form for $\phi(R, r)$ are simplifications that can easily be generalized.

[23] An extension to the case with a budget constraint $\overline{r} > 0$ is straightforward. If the optimal level of resources according to Proposition 5.1 violates the budget constraint, the government endows the military with resources $r^* = \overline{r}$.

[24] Hirshleifer (1989) discusses alternative functional forms appropriate for $\phi(R, r)$.

not ($\theta = N$). State C occurs with probability $\pi = Pr(\theta = C) \in (0, 1)$ and π may vary across issue areas. For instance, the government may believe that the military is more likely to compromise about economic policy (a high π) than about its institutional autonomy (a low π).[25]

Crucially, only the military observes the state of the world θ. Only the military knows whether it is willing to compromise on an issue; the government does not. The military may attempt to communicate its position to the government by sending a *message* $\mu = \{c, n\}$. The military reports the state θ truthfully when it sends the message $\mu = c$ whenever $\theta = C$ and $\mu = n$ whenever $\theta = N$; the military exaggerates its inability to compromise when it reports $\mu = n$ when $\theta = C$.[26] Hence when the government receives the military's message, it understands that the military is tempted to exaggerate its inability to compromise in order to pressure the government to adopt the military's favorite policy p_M.

After it receives the military's message μ, the government adopts one of the two policies $p = \{p_G, p_M\}$. The military's message $\mu = n$ is in effect a demand that the government accommodate the military's preferences by adopting its favorite policy p_M; the message $\mu = c$ implies that the military is willing to compromise and accept the government's favorite policy p_G. I will say that the government *concedes* to the military if it adopts policy p_M after hearing from the military that is not willing to compromise, $\mu = n$, and that the government *defies* the military if it adopts policy p_G after receiving the message $\mu = n$. Intuitively, the government has no incentive to adopt a policy other than p_G after receiving the message $\mu = c$ because p_G is its preferred policy and the military is willing to compromise.

Finally, after the government adopts a policy, the military either *acquiesces* to the policy or *intervenes*. The latter is a threat that the military uses to compel the government to adopt the military's preferred policy p_M. An intervention succeeds with probability $\rho(r)$ and typically takes the form of a coup d'état that replaces the civilian government with a military government. The probability of a coup's success $\rho(r)$ is an increasing, concave, and differentiable function of the military's resources r, $\rho'(r) > 0$, $\rho''(r) < 0$. I assume that the coup fails if the military lacks any resources, $\rho(0) = 0$, and the probability that the coup succeeds approaches 1 as the military's resources grow, $\lim_{r \to \infty} \rho(r) = 1$. By letting both the probability $\rho(r)$ of a successful coup and the probability $\phi(R, r)$ that the military defeats the mass threat increase in r, we are capturing the fact that the same resources that empower the military to suppress regime opposition also enable it to extract concessions from the government.

---

[25] This general formulation places no restriction on the particular content of these policies or the nature of the government's and the military's disagreement over them. Thus this model is general enough to account for the empirical variation in militaries' revealed policy preferences (Remmer 1989). For instance, unlike most Latin American militaries, the Peruvian military under Velasco was to the left of Belaúnde's administration on social and economic issues (Klaren 1999, Chap. 11).

[26] We can ignore the possibility that the military would report $m = c$ when $\theta = N$; such a message could only hurt the military.

The payoffs to the government and the military depend on the state θ; the policy p that the government adopts; the resources r spent on repression; the outcome of the coup if the military intervenes; and on whether the mass threat is defeated at the end of the game. If the threat is defeated, the government's payoffs are g and 1 when the adopted policy is p_G and p_M, respectively, and the military acquiesces or intervenes but the coup fails. By letting $g > 1$, we are capturing the government's preference for adopting policy p_G regardless of the state θ. The government's payoff when the military intervenes and the coup succeeds – in which case the military removes the current government – is normalized to 0. The worst outcome for the government obtains when the threat R succeeds, in which case its payoff is $-R$, reflecting the concern that large threats may not only remove the government from power but also bring about a correspondingly costly regime change. To account for the budgetary cost of resources that could be put into alternative uses but are spent on repression, we subtract the $C(r)$ from each payoff, where $C(r)$ is an increasing and differentiable cost function.

The military, on the other hand, obtains the payoff m when the government adopts its preferred policy p_M. If the government instead adopts policy p_G and the military acquiesces, its payoff depends on the state θ and its message m. If the military is willing to compromise ($\theta = C$) and communicates it truthfully ($\mu = c$), the military obtains the normalized payoff 1. However, if the military exaggerates its resolve by pretending to be unwilling to compromise ($\theta = C$ but $\mu = c$) yet backs down after the government calls its bluff by adopting policy p_G, the military obtains the payoff $1 - \epsilon$, where $\epsilon > 0$ is a small but positive reputational cost of backing down. Meanwhile, if the government adopts policy p_G in state $\theta = N$ and the military acquiesces, the latter obtains the payoff 0. The assumption $0 < \epsilon < 1 < m$ thus reflects the military's preference for adopting its favorite policy p_M.

As I discussed earlier, intervention is costly for the military both because it may fail and because its overt involvement in politics may undermine its cohesion. Whereas the former cost materializes only if a coup fails, the latter cost is borne by the military regardless of the success of a coup. I denote this latter cost by c, where $0 < c < m$. If the military intervenes, a successful coup ensures that its preferred policy is adopted and the military receives the payoff $m - c$. By contrast, if the military intervenes but the coup fails, it receives the payoff $-c$. Hence the military's preferences entail both its policy preferences and its institutional interests (Geddes 1999b, 125–9). The two considerations conflict when the military actually carries out the threat of a coup.[27]

I now examine a perfect Bayesian equilibrium of this extensive game with imperfect information. The timing of actions is as follows. First, the government chooses the military's resources r. The military (but not the government)

---

[27] Unlike for the government, we do not need to differentiate between the military's payoffs depending on the success of the mass threat R because the military's actions do not affect whether the mass threat succeeds or fails (i.e., the military does not choose its resources r).

then learns the state θ and communicates it by sending a (possibly untruthful) message μ to the government. The government then either concedes to the military or defies it by choosing a policy p. Next, the military observes the policy p and either acquiesces or intervenes. If the military intervenes, the coup either succeeds or fails with probability $\rho(r)$. Finally, the threat R realizes and the military defeats it with probability $\phi(R, r)$. I proceed by backward induction; proofs of all technical results that do not follow directly from the text are in Appendix I.

Consider first how the military's willingness to intervene depends on the probability $\rho(r)$ that an intervention succeeds. The military's expected payoff from intervening is

$$\rho(r)(m - c) + [1 - \rho(r)](-c) = \rho(r)m - c, \qquad (5.1)$$

whereas the military's payoff from acquiescing to policy p_G in state N is 0. The military therefore acquiesces and the government defies it even if the military reports $\mu = n$ for any $\rho(r) \leq c/m$. In this range of values of $\rho(r)$, the likelihood of a successful intervention by the military is so low – relative to the cost of a coup and the military's preference for its favorite policy – that the military would not want to intervene even if the government always defied its demands. In turn, the government adopts its favorite policy p_G regardless of the military's message. Thus when $\rho(r) \leq c/m$, the government maintains *perfect political control* over the military.

On the other hand, the likelihood of a successful intervention may be so high that the military will intervene unless the government *always* adopts its favorite policy p_M. This will be the case if the military prefers to intervene unless the government adopts its favorite policy p_M even if the state is C,

$$\rho(r)m - c > 1 \text{ or, equivalently, when } \rho(r) > \frac{1 + c}{m}.$$

In this scenario, the military always claims to be unable to compromise and the government complies with that demand by adopting the military's favorite policy p_M. We may say that when $\rho(r) > (1 + c)/m$, the government operates under a *military tutelage*.

Thus we see that the government and the military will genuinely bargain over policy concessions only when $c/m < \rho(r) \leq (1 + c)/m$. For these parameter values, the likelihood of a successful intervention is large enough so the military is willing to intervene when the government defies its demands on an issue on which it cannot compromise, but it is not so large that the military would intervene unless the government always adopted its favorite policy.

Consider therefore what happens when the military uses the threat of intervention to extract policy concessions from the government when $c/m < \rho(r) \leq (1 + c)/m$. The government's imperfect knowledge of the military's willingness to compromise θ, as well as the shared interest of both actors to avoid an intervention, creates opportunities for *brinkmanship*: The military is tempted to exaggerate its resolve by misrepresenting its willingness to compromise and the government, in turn, faces an incentive to test the military's resolve to intervene. If the government were to believe the military's report $\mu = n$, the military would always want to claim that it is unable to compromise. In equilibrium therefore, the military cannot credibly commit to report the state θ truthfully.

I now show that by engaging in brinkmanship, the military succeeds in *partially* communicating its unwillingness to compromise to the government. The military does so by exaggerating only occasionally – that is, with a positive probability. Brinkmanship bargaining thus entails the use of mixed strategies.[28]

Denote by α the probability with which the military exaggerates its unwillingness to compromise by reporting $\mu = n$ if $\theta = C$, and denote by β the probability with which the government defies the military's demand by adopting policy p_G if it receives the message $\mu = n$.[29] Proceeding by backward induction, consider first the government's strategy β. In a mixed strategy equilibrium, the government defies the military's demands with probability β^* that makes the military indifferent between reporting the state θ truthfully and exaggerating. When the military reports the state θ truthfully, its expected payoff is

$$\pi + (1 - \pi)\big(\beta[\rho(r)m - c] + (1 - \beta)m\big),$$

where the expected payoff that follows the term $(1 - \pi)$ accounts for a positive probability of the military's intervention when the government defies its demands on an issue on which it cannot compromise.

On the other hand, the military's expected payoff when it exaggerates the state θ is

$$\pi[\beta(1 - \epsilon) + (1 - \beta)m] + (1 - \pi)\big(\beta[\rho(r)m - c] + (1 - \beta)m\big),$$

where the expected payoff that follows π reflects the military's reputational cost of having to back down from the threat of intervention when its bluff is called by the government.

The military is indifferent between reporting the state θ truthfully and exaggerating whenever

$$\beta^* = \frac{m - 1}{m + \epsilon - 1}.$$

Intuitively, β^* is increasing in the intensity of the military's preference for its favorite policy and decreasing in its reputational concerns. When the military cares a lot about its favorite policy, the government defies the military's demands with greater probability because it knows this is when the military

[28] When $c/m < \rho(r) \leq (1 + c)/m$, this game also has an implausible equilibrium in which the military always exaggerates its inability to compromise and, anticipating that, the government always defies it. Similar implausible equilibria exist in many extensive games with imperfect information, as well as in the model in Chapter 3.

[29] Because the government prefers policy p_G to p_M, it will always adopt p_G whenever the military is willing to compromise, $\mu = c$. And since the military prefers policy p_M to p_G, it never wants to claim that it is willing to compromise ($\mu = c$) when it is not ($\theta = N$).

is most tempted to exaggerate its unwillingness to compromise. The opposite holds for the military's reputational concerns.

Now consider the military's equilibrium strategy α^*. In a mixed strategy equilibrium, the military exaggerates its unwillingness to compromise with probability α^* that makes the government indifferent between conceding to the military's policy demand and defying it. The government's payoff from conceding is $1 - C(r)$, whereas its expected payoff from defying the military's demand when $\mu = n$ is

$$Pr(\theta = N|\mu = n)[1 - \rho(r)]g + [1 - Pr(\theta = N|\mu = n)]g - C(r).$$

Above, the term on the left accounts for military intervention in case the military is unwilling to compromise; the right-hand term corresponds to the military backing down after its bluff was called; and $Pr(\theta = N|\mu = n)$ denotes the government's belief that the military is indeed unwilling to compromise when it says so. This belief is consistent with the military's strategy α according to Bayes' rule when

$$Pr(\theta = N|\mu = n) = \frac{1 - \pi}{1 - \pi + \pi\alpha}.$$

In equilibrium, the military exaggerates its unwillingness to compromise with the probability

$$\alpha^* = \left(\frac{1 - \pi}{\pi}\right)\frac{1 - [1 - \rho(r)]g}{g - 1}. \tag{5.2}$$

Observe that α^* is increasing in $\rho(r)$ and decreasing in π and g. Intuitively, the military exaggerates its resolve more often as the probability of a successful coup increases because it knows that this is when the government is less prone to defy it. On the other hand, the military exaggerates less often when the government cares more about its favorite policy and when the government believes that the military is willing to compromise on an issue.[30] In both instances, the military anticipates that the government will be more tempted to defy it.

To focus on realistic political scenarios, we may exclude large values of g according to which the government would be so attracted to its preferred policy that it would defy the military's demand even if the latter never exaggerated its unwillingness to compromise. In that case, defiance would automatically result in intervention. Such implausible behavior by the government is precluded as long as $\alpha^* > 0$ or, equivalently, as long as $g < 1/[1 - \rho(r)]$. Because $\rho(r)$ is at least c/m under brinkmanship, the effective upper bound on the government's payoff from its favorite policy is $\overline{g} = m/(m - c)$.

Thus we see that when $c/m < \rho(r) \leq (1 + c)/m$, both the government and the military engage in brinkmanship bargaining. Both take risky actions – the

---

[30] The latter may be interpreted as saying that the military exaggerates more when bargaining over issues that the government anticipates the military will not be willing to compromise about (e.g., issues concerning the military's institutional autonomy).

military by exaggerating its unwillingness to compromise with the probability α^* and the government by defying the military's demands with the probability β^* – that may result in a military intervention, an outcome that both prefer to avoid.

With appropriate modifications, our results about perfect political control, brinkmanship bargaining, and military tutelage extend to two prominent types of military interventions, as follows.

Military Interventions in Military Dictatorships. As discussed in Section 5.2, the military's institutional cost of intervention c is essentially sunk after the initial intervention that brings the military to power. Thus c is lower in military dictatorships than in civilians dictatorship, as are the thresholds c/m and $(1 + c)/m$. Perfect political control therefore should be rare in military dictatorships.

Military Interventions in Democracies. Unlike dictators, an elected government can exploit its popular support in its confrontation with the military. For any optimal r (which I derive below), the probability of a successful military intervention $\rho(r)$ therefore will be smaller in democracies than dictatorships. This difference shifts some democracies that otherwise would be above the thresholds c/m and $(1 + c)/m$ below them and since α^* is increasing in $\rho(r)$, exacerbates the military's incentive to exaggerate its unwillingness to compromise under brinkmanship.

Finally, consider the government's initial choice of the military's resources r. Our discussion implies that the military's capacity to intervene differs sharply across two scenarios. When $\rho(r) \leq c/m$, the military does not have sufficient resources to stage a successful coup and the government maintains perfect political control over the military. This scenario obtains when the level of the military's resources r that maximizes the government's expected payoff over the probability that the mass threat succeeds

$$\phi(\hat{R}, r)g - [1 - \phi(\hat{R}, r)]\hat{R} - C(r), \tag{5.3}$$

also satisfies the condition $\rho(r) \leq c/m$. Recall that in (5.3), $\phi(\hat{R}, r)$ is the probability of defeating the mass threat, $\hat{R} = (\underline{R} + \overline{R})/2$ is the expected magnitude of the mass threat, and $-\hat{R}$ is the government's payoff if the mass threat succeeds.

The level of the military's resources r that maximizes (5.3) solves the first-order condition

$$C'(r) = (g + \hat{R})\phi'(\hat{R}, r) \tag{5.4}$$

and is increasing in the expected magnitude of the mass threat $\hat{R}$. The optimal level of the military's resources therefore will satisfy the condition $\rho(r) \leq c/m$ for threats with a small expected magnitude $\hat{R}$. We may denote it by r_1^* and denote the threshold value of $\hat{R}$ that delimits such small threats by $\hat{R}_1$.[31] Thus for $\hat{R} \leq \hat{R}_1$, the government can devote the optimal level of resources

---

[31] For most functional forms for $\rho(r)$ and $C(r)$, r_1^* and $\hat{R}_1$ can be characterized only implicitly.

to defeating the mass threat without endowing the military with the capacity to intervene in politics – that is, the government maintains perfect political control over the military.

For mass threats of a larger magnitude, however, the government anticipates that the use of the military for repression may lead to its subsequent intervention in politics; this is the second scenario. Formally, an increase in the military's resources and autonomy r raises the probability of defeating the mass threat $\phi(R,r)$ but also the likelihood $\rho(r)$ that a coup succeeds if staged. When the mass threat R implies an optimal level of resources in (5.4) such that $\rho(r) > c/m$, the government will weigh the risk of being overthrown by the mass threat against the risk of intervention by the military.

More specifically, the government will accept some vulnerability to the mass threat R in exchange for the ability to maintain some control over the military. When $c/m < \rho(r) \leq (1+c)/m$, the government and the military engage in brinkmanship and the military intervenes with a positive probability. The government obtains the expected payoff

$$\pi\left(\alpha^*[\beta^*g + (1-\beta^*)] + (1-\alpha^*)g\right)$$
$$+ (1-\pi)\left(\beta^*\left(\rho(r) + [1-\rho(r)]g\right) + (1-\beta^*)\right) - C(r)$$

or, equivalently,

$$g[1 - (1-\pi)\rho(r)] - C(r) = G - C(r). \tag{5.5}$$

Intuitively, the government obtains a smaller expected payoff when it is more likely that the military is unwilling to compromise (i.e., a low π) – this is precisely when brinkmanship may result in the government's downfall. The government therefore will compare the expected payoff under the largest r consistent with perfect control over the military in (5.3) against its expected payoff under brinkmanship. For a range of values of $\hat{R}$, $\hat{R}_1 < \hat{R} \leq \hat{R}_2$, the government prefers the former alternative: By adopting r_2^* that solves $\rho(r) = c/m$, the government accepts some vulnerability to the mass threat R in exchange for maintaining perfect control over the military.

However, for large values of $\hat{R}$, the government can no longer afford to keep the military's resources low enough to maintain perfect control over it. When $\hat{R} > \hat{R}_2$, the government endows the military with the optimal resources r consistent with brinkmanship, $c/m < \rho(r) \leq (1+c)/m$. That is, the government either endows the military with the level of resources r_3^*, which maximizes

$$\phi(\hat{R},r)G - [1 - \phi(\hat{R},r)]\hat{R} - C(r), \tag{5.6}$$

or, if $\rho(r_3^*) > (1+c)/m$, with the largest amount of resources r that satisfies the constraint $\rho(r) \leq (1+c)/m$. In the latter case, the government chooses r_4^*, which solves $\rho(r_4^*) = (1+c)/m$ and thus stops short of subjecting itself to military tutelage.

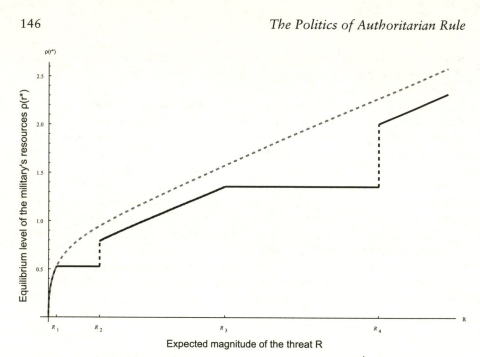

FIGURE 5.1. Effect of the expected magnitude of the mass threat $\hat{R}$ on the equilibrium choice of the military's resources r^*.

Finally, for extreme values of $\hat{R} > \hat{R}_4$, the specter of the mass threat forces the government to accept military tutelage. In this case, the military's level of resources maximizes

$$\phi(\hat{R}, r) - [1 - \phi(\hat{R}, r)]\hat{R} - C(r). \tag{5.7}$$

Proposition 5.1 summarizes this equilibrium behavior.

Proposition 5.1 (Military Intervention in Politics). *In a perfect Bayesian equilibrium, three regimes of political control over the military obtain:*

(1) *If $0 < \hat{R} \le \hat{R}_2$, **perfect political control:** $p = p_G$ and r^* solves (5.4) if $0 < \hat{R} \le \hat{R}_1$ or r^* solves $\rho(r^*) = c/m$ if $\hat{R}_1 < \hat{R} \le \hat{R}_2$.*
(2) *If $\hat{R}_2 < \hat{R} \le \hat{R}_4$, **brinkmanship:** $\alpha^* = \left(\frac{1-\pi}{\pi}\right)\frac{1-[1-\rho(r)]g}{g-1}$, $\beta^* = \frac{m-1}{m+\epsilon-1}$, and r^* maximizes (5.6) if $\hat{R}_2 < \hat{R} \le \hat{R}_3$ or r^* solves $\rho(r) = (1+c)/m$ if $\hat{R}_3 < \hat{R} \le \hat{R}_4$.*
(3) *If $\hat{\underline{R}} > \hat{R}_4$, **military tutelage:** $p = p_M$ and r^* maximizes (5.7).*

Figure 5.1 portrays the relationship between the government's equilibrium choice of the military's resources r^* and the expected magnitude of the threat $\hat{R}$. I let $g = 1.5$, $m = 3$, $c = 1$, $\epsilon = 1$, $\pi = 3/4$, and $C(r) = 0.8r$, and I assume that a military coup succeeds with the probability $\rho(r) = \frac{1}{1+e^{-r}} - \frac{e^{-r}}{2}$. At these parameter values, $\hat{R}_1 = 0.31$, $\hat{R}_2 = 1.93$, $\hat{R}_3 = 6.62$, and $\hat{R}_4 = 12.38$.

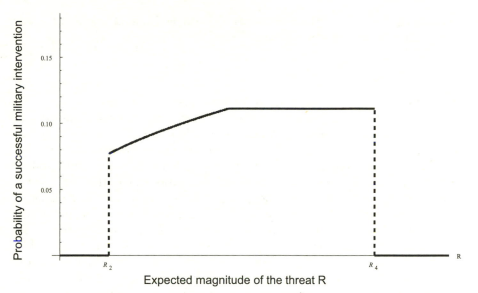

FIGURE 5.2. Effect of the magnitude of the mass threat $\hat{R}$ on the equilibrium probability of a successful military intervention.

We see that the equilibrium choice of the military's resources r^* is weakly increasing in the expected value of the threat $\hat{R}$. The dashed gray line plots the resources that the government would optimally endow the military with if it were able to maintain perfect control over the military regardless of its level of resources. We see that for mass threats of a small expected magnitude, $\hat{R} \leq \hat{R}_1$, the government can endow the military with such resources. For mass threats of a larger magnitude, $\hat{R}_1 < \hat{R} \leq \hat{R}_2$, the government accepts some vulnerability to the mass threat in exchange for the ability to maintain perfect control over the military. For medium values of $\hat{R}$, $\hat{R}_2 < \hat{R} \leq \hat{R}_4$, the government exposes itself to the risk of military intervention by engaging in brinkmanship with the military, and, when $\hat{R}_3 < \hat{R} \leq \hat{R}_4$, the government accepts increasing exposure to the mass threat to avoid military tutelage. Finally, large threats, $\hat{R} > \hat{R}_4$, force the government to accept military tutelage.

Continuing with the parameter values used previously, Figure 5.2 plots the relationship between the equilibrium probability of a successful military intervention and the expected magnitude of the mass threat $\hat{R}$. We see that military interventions do not occur at either small or large magnitudes of the mass threat. In the former case, $0 < \hat{R} \leq \hat{R}_2$, the government maintains perfect political control over the military; in the latter case, $\hat{R} > \hat{R}_4$, the government operates under the military's tutelage. Military interventions occur at medium levels of the mass threat, $\hat{R}_2 < \hat{R} \leq \hat{R}_4$, when the government and the military engage in brinkmanship. In equilibrium, the probability of a successful military intervention is $(1 - \pi)\beta^*\rho(r^*)$ and it is increasing in the mass threat for $\hat{R}_2 < \hat{R} \leq \hat{R}_3$ and constant for $\hat{R}_3 < \hat{R} \leq \hat{R}_4$. The next section evaluates this prediction about the relationship between the magnitude of the threat $\hat{R}$ and the likelihood of successful military interventions.

5.4 EMPIRICAL ANALYSIS

The model in this chapter integrates within a single framework two political mechanisms that account for the emergence of military dictatorships: (1) the moral hazard in authoritarian repression and (2) the resulting bargaining between the government and the military over concessions to the latter. This analysis predicts that the magnitude of mass threats to authoritarian regimes will have a systematic yet nonobvious relationship to the likelihood of actual military interventions: Although the military's autonomy and resources will expand as we move from perfect political control to brinkmanship bargaining to military tutelage, overt military interventions will occur only under brinkmanship bargaining – that is, when regimes face medium levels of mass threats. The likelihood of an overt military intervention in politics therefore should have a nonmonotonic relationship to the magnitude of the threat posed by those excluded from power and the autonomy and resources accordingly conceded to the military: Military interventions should be first increasing and then decreasing in the magnitude of mass threats to the regime.

I evaluate these arguments by focusing on one prominent, structural source of mass threats that favor the employment of the military in repression – economic inequality. In highly unequal dictatorships, a major threat to a rich ruling elite's hold on power comes from poor peasants or workers who desire a more even distribution of wealth and political power (Boix 2003; Acemoglu and Robinson 2005). As Acemoglu and Robinson (2005, 36) put it, "everything else equal, greater inter-group inequality makes revolution more attractive for the citizens." Indeed, economically unequal dictatorships frequently confront social unrest, labor strikes, land invasions, and guerilla attacks (Drake 1996; Wright 2001).[32] The military's size thus makes it both well suited and often the only force capable of repressing such threats. Meanwhile, historical and case-study research on Latin America and Southern Europe provides rich accounts of how the threat of social unrest leads to an alliance between the military and a landed elite or the bourgeoisie (O'Donnell 1973; Stepan 1988; Loveman 1993; Drake 1996; Paige 1997).

Of course, a high level of politywide economic inequality is not the only or even the main factor that privileges the use of the military in domestic repression. Weak state authority, the discovery of natural resources, civil wars, and recent independence are alternative structural conditions that may precipitate the military's political ascendence. In Latin America during the nineteenth and

---

[32] Cross-national research finds that economic inequality is related to the tendency toward and – conditional on the level of state capacity and repression – the occurrence of mass political violence (Muller and Seligson 1987; Goodwin 2001; MacCulloch 2005). See Shadmehr (2011) for a theoretical model.

early twentieth centuries, for instance, regionally based strongmen depended on irregular military forces to maintain or usurp power, often in an alliance with local landowners and merchants (Bethell 1985, 371–81; Rouquié 1987, Chap. 2). In dictatorships that are rich in natural resources, control over them becomes a precondition for assuming and remaining in power. A loyal military is thus a necessary deterrent against competitors who otherwise may attempt to gain control over them.[33] And a common symptom of many African coups d'état has been ethnic rivalries within the armed forces, a vestige of ethnically based recruitment into precolonial, indigenous military units that served as mercenary forces of colonial repression (Horowitz 1985, 527–8). In the following analysis, I attempt to control for these factors. However, I focus primarily on economic inequality because, although still limited, the data on this factor are more comprehensively available for a cross section of dictatorships.

To evaluate my theoretical claims, I use two different measures of military intervention: the participation of the military in the *entry* and *exit* of leaders. My original data on these measures of military intervention cover leadership change in all authoritarian regimes throughout the period 1946–2002. The data consist of 738 leaders from 139 countries, with between 1 and 47 annual observations per leader and between 1 and 24 leaders per country. The military intervened in the entry of 291 and in the exit of 224 of the 738 authoritarian leaders. I find strong support for the nonmonotonic relationship between economic inequality and military intervention predicted by the arguments in this chapter. Notably, this association holds regardless of the measure of military intervention used.

The two outcomes that I consider – that is, military intervention in the entry and exit of leaders – capture key aspects of military intervention in authoritarian politics. The most frequent form of leadership change in authoritarian regimes is the coup d'état: It accounts for about 28 percent of all leader entries and exits overall and for more than 60 percent of leader entries and exits when we exclude constitutional leader changes, such as elections, natural deaths, and hereditary successions. Militaries have staged about 86 percent of the coups that installed new leaders, and 59 percent of military leaders come into office via a coup. Yet as these frequencies imply, military interventions often occur in forms other than a coup, and many leadership transitions in dictatorships do

---

[33] In Equatorial Guinea, for instance, the discovery of large oil reserves in 1996 was followed by two failed coups against President Obiang Nguema in 2004 and 2009. The stated intent of the first mercenary-lead coup was to replace Nguema by an exiled opposition politician Severo Moto and to renegotiate existing oil contracts to the benefit of the coup plotters. Nguema responded with an increase in repression and defense expenditures. See "The Fog and Dogs of War," *The Economist*, 20 March 2004; "Intrigue in Equatorial Guinea," *The Economist*, 24 February 2009; "Oil Makes Friends of Us All," *The Economist*, 17 July 2009; and Ghazvinian (2008). On the relationships between natural resources, political conflict, and regime stability, see Collier and Hoeffler (1998), Karl (1997), Humphreys (2005), Morrison (2009), Ross (2004), and Snyder and Bhavnani (2005); for skeptical views, see Fearon (2005) and Bates (2008).

not involve the military.[34] The two measures of military intervention used here therefore correspond to distinct ways in which the military may intervene and together provide a comprehensive measure of military intervention in authoritarian politics. To summarize the worldwide pattern of military interventions throughout the period 1946–2002, I plot the average annual frequency of military interventions in leader entry or exit by country in Figure 5.3.

To test my arguments rigorously, I also use two distinct measures of economic inequality: the Gini coefficient and the Theil statistic. The data on Gini coefficients come from Babones (2008); this is a standardized version of the frequently used data by Deininger and Squire (1996) and UNU-WIDER (2008). The Theil statistic is an alternative, entropy measure of inequality collected by the University of Texas Inequality Project (UTIP–UNIDO 2008). Although the two inequality measures are not directly comparable, both increase with the level of a country's inequality. For dictatorships, the Gini coefficient ranges from 16 (i.e., Bulgaria in 1968) to 68 (i.e., Sierra Leone in 1989), whereas the Theil statistic is between 20 (i.e., Czechoslovakia in 1988) and 64 (i.e., Paraguay in 1991). According to both measures, Communist regimes are the most economically equal of dictatorships; both measures list oil-rich Middle Eastern monarchies as well as South American and sub-Saharan African countries as the most unequal of dictatorships. The correlation coefficient of the two inequality measures is 0.76.

Although both measures of economic inequality represent the most extensive coverage available, missingness severely affects the data on dictatorships: Either measure is available for at most 34 percent of the 5,393 country-years in these data. To examine as representative a sample as possible, I work with two modifications of these data: (1) I use Babones's (2008) polynomial intra- and extrapolations of the Gini coefficient and (2) to expand coverage of the Theil data, I perform a multiple imputation of missing values. This second approach is a statistically superior one: Estimates based on multiple-imputed data account for the uncertainty associated with missing values (Rubin 1987; King et al. 2001). When performing multiple imputations, I use statistical routines developed by Honaker and King (2009), which are appropriate for cross-sectional time-series data and lead to sensible imputed values.[35]

As a preliminary test of the predicted, nonmonotonic relationship between military intervention and inequality, consider the frequency of the two measures of military intervention at different levels of economic inequality. These relationships are summarized in Table 5.2. The five inequality intervals correspond to the quintiles of each measure. With one exception, we see that the frequency of military interventions is first increasing and then decreasing in inequality, as my theoretical model predicts. This pattern holds across the two

---

[34] For instance, the military may support a mass uprising or a faction in a civil war that results in a type of exit or entry of an authoritarian leader that is not a coup.

[35] I properly impute forty datasets. Given the current rate of missingness, the relative efficiency (Rubin 1987, 114) of this number of imputations exceeds 99 percent. Further details about the multiple imputation procedure are in Appendix II.

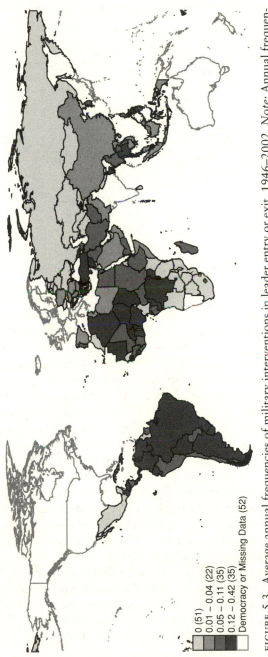

FIGURE 5.3. Average annual frequencies of military interventions in leader entry or exit, 1946–2002. *Note:* Annual frequencies, number of countries in each category in parentheses.

0 (51)
0.01 – 0.04 (22)
0.05 – 0.11 (35)
0.12 – 0.42 (35)
Democracy or Missing Data (52)

TABLE 5.2. *Military Intervention in Dictatorships by Level of Economic Inequality*

Form of Military Intervention	Inequality (Gini)				
	Below 34.89	35.51–42.47	42.49–47.01	47.08–53.44	Above 53.61
Leader Entry	15%	45%	49%	50%	31%
Leader Exit	10%	35%	39%	40%	27%

Form of Mililary Intervention	Inequality (Theil)				
	Below 39.74	39.74–42.89	42.89–45.37	45.37–48.28	Above 48.28
Leader Entry	33%	38%	37%	36%	32%
Leader Exit	29%	36%	37%	37%	38%

Note: Inequality intervals correspond to the quintiles of each measure. The unit of observation is a leader-year.
Data sources: Babones (2008); UTIP-UNIDO (2008).

distinct measures of military intervention and for both measures of economic inequality.

I now investigate the relationship between economic inequality and military intervention in dictatorships statistically, accounting for covariate effects and estimation concerns specific to cross-sectional time-series data on dictatorships. The previous theoretical discussion as well as existing research suggest that several factors other than economic inequality may be associated with military intervention in authoritarian politics. Among economic factors, poverty and economic recessions may facilitate military intervention (see, e.g., Londregan and Poole 1990). Thus, I control for *GDP per capita* and *GDP growth*. On the other hand, a dictatorship's integration in the world economy may deter military intervention; I therefore control for *trade openness*. In dictatorships that are rich in natural resources, conflict over control of those resources may increase the likelihood of military intervention (see, e.g., Humphreys 2005). I measure natural-resource wealth with the dummy variable, *fuel and ore exports*, which takes the value 1 if a country's annual fuel or ores and metal exports amount to more than 10 percent of its merchandise exports and 0 otherwise. These data are from Eichengreen and Leblang (2008), Maddison (2008), and the World Bank (2008).

To account for the possibility that the military enjoys a privileged political position in dictatorships that have recently fought a war, I create two dummy variables, *interstate war* and *civil war*, which take the value 1 if a country has fought or intervened in the corresponding war during any of the past three years and 0 otherwise. These variables are based on the Correlates of War data (Sarkees 2000b).

I also control for a dictatorship's ethnic and religious composition, given that the potential for ethnic or religious strife may affect the likelihood of military intervention. I therefore include a measure of ethnic and linguistic *fractionalization* as a control variable; these data are from La Porta et al. (1999).

Furthermore, international factors, such as the Cold War struggle between the United States and the Soviet Union or the prevalence of democracy in the world, may independently affect the likelihood of military intervention in dictatorships. Accordingly, I include a dummy variable for the *Cold War*, which takes the value 1 between the years 1945 and 1990 and 0 otherwise, as well as a covariate that measures the proportion of democracies among a dictatorship's *neighbors* in any given year. I created these data by combining regime-type data with the contiguity data in the Correlates of War (2006).

To avoid conflating military intervention in authoritarian politics in general with the political instability that may be particular to military dictatorships, I control for whether the previous or current authoritarian leader came from the *military*. The extension of the model in Section 5.3 implies that military dictatorships are especially vulnerable to intervention by other factions within the military. In fact, Geddes (1999b), Gandhi (2008, Chap. 6), and Debs (2009) found that leaders of military dictatorships are less likely to survive in office than leaders of civilian dictatorships. Therefore, in models for leader entry, I control for whether the *preceding* leader's primary position prior to taking office was in the military. In models for leader exit, I control for whether the *current* leader's primary position prior to taking office was in the military. About 31 percent of all leaders, or those in 1,667 of the 5,393 country-years covered by the data, held a primarily military position prior to taking office.

Finally, to account for potential serial correlation in military interventions, I include the log of *time* since the last military intervention within a country. That is, I control for the possibility that coups may breed further coups (Londregan and Poole 1990). I lag each covariate by one year to maintain their exogeneity with respect to military intervention. To facilitate exposition, I suppress time subscripts for all covariates.

The two measures of military intervention that I employ – that is, intervention in the entry and exit of authoritarian leaders – are dichotomous outcomes: In any country-year, either a military intervention occurred or did not. I therefore estimate a logistic regression model for each measure. However, the standard logistic model assumes that after accounting for covariates, observations on any two authoritarian leaders are independent. This is unlikely to be the case in the present setting because we may reasonably expect that even after accounting for available covariates, outcomes for leaders from the same country will be correlated. For instance, based on our qualitative knowledge of PRI–era Mexico, we may anticipate that factors specific to Mexico, which cannot be readily included as covariates, reduce the chances that any Mexican leader will be removed by the military. On the other hand, country-specific unobserved factors may affect the likelihood of military intervention in Myanmar in the opposite direction.

To avoid any estimation bias resulting from such unobserved country-specific heterogeneity, I estimate a country-level, random-intercept logistic regression model of military intervention y_{it},

$$Pr(y_{it} = 1|z_{it}, \mathbf{x}_{it}) = logit^{-1}(\beta_1 z_{it} + \beta_2 z_{it}^2 + \mathbf{x}_{it}'\boldsymbol{\gamma} + \zeta_{j[it]}),$$

$$\text{for } i = 1, \ldots, n, \text{ and } t = 1, \ldots, T,$$

where z_{it} denotes economic inequality and $\mathbf{x}_{it}$ is a vector of controls. In a random-intercept logistic regression model, intercepts are allowed to vary across groups of observations according to a probability distribution.[36] In the present context, I assume that leaders from the same country will share a common random effect $\zeta_{j[it]}$ that is distributed normally with a mean of zero and variance σ_ζ^2, which I will estimate. Thus $\zeta_{j[it]} \sim N(\zeta, \sigma_\zeta^2)$, where I denote leaders by i, time periods by t, and countries by j. A positive ζ_j implies that leaders from country j are more likely to experience military intervention. In turn, random effects ζ_j capture the combined effect of unobserved or omitted country-level factors.[37]

Estimation results based on the random-intercept logistic regression model are presented in Table 5.3. I approximate the predicted, nonmonotonic relationship between military intervention and economic inequality via a quadratic term for inequality. Accordingly, the likelihood of military intervention is first increasing and then decreasing in economic inequality when the coefficient β_1 associated with the linear term is positive and the coefficient β_2 associated with the quadratic term is negative. Indeed, this is the case for both forms of military intervention, as predicted. Importantly, the nonmonotonic association between economic inequality and military intervention is statistically significant in all specifications. Furthermore, a likelihood-ratio test indicates that including the quadratic term for economic inequality significantly improves the fit of two of the four specifications and provides a comparable fit in the remaining two.[38] Thus we see strong support for the predicted, nonmonotonic association between economic inequality and military intervention in dictatorships.

To illuminate the substantive implications of these results, the estimated effect of economic inequality on military intervention is plotted in Figure 5.4. These plots are based on the Gini data; corresponding plots based on the Theil statistic are almost identical. Recall that the likelihood of military intervention depends on both the covariates and the unobserved country-level random effects $\zeta_{j[it]}$, the size of which is not directly estimated. However, we can treat the random effects as parameters and estimate their size using empirical Bayes

---

[36] See Rabe-Hesketh and Skrondal (2008), Gelman and Hill (2006), and Cameron and Trivedi (2005) for a discussion of multilevel models.

[37] A fixed-effects model is not suitable here because several of the country-level covariates do not vary over time, and several countries either contribute only a few observations or do not experience a military intervention. These covariates and countries are dropped by a fixed-effects estimation; see Beck and Katz (2001) and Cameron and Trivedi (2005, 701–2).

[38] I follow Li et al. (1991) when computing likelihood-ratio tests for multiple imputed data.

TABLE 5.3. *Impact of Economic Inequality on Military Intervention in Dictatorships*

| | Form of Military Intervention | | | |
| | Leader Entry | | Leader Exit | |
Inequality Measure	Gini	Theil	Gini	Theil
Inequality	0.460**	0.462*	0.331**	0.330*
	(0.018)	(0.278)	(0.025)	(0.225)
Inequality²	−0.005**	−0.005*	−0.003**	−0.004*
	(0.002)	(0.003)	(0.002)	(0.003)
Log of GDP per capita	−0.075	−0.140	0.068	−0.428**
	(0.315)	(0.272)	(0.237)	(0.195)
GDP growth	0.012	0.013	−0.016	0.007
	(0.035)	(0.024)	(0.015)	(0.014)
Log of Trade of Openness	0.005	0.014	−0.068	−0.089
	(0.139)	(0.090)	(0.083)	(0.065)
Fuel and Ore Exports	−0.632*	0.040	−0.139	0.183
	(0.370)	(0.445)	(0.271)	(0.285)
Cold War	−1.203*	0.557	0.494	0.615**
	(0.632)	(0.419)	(0.435)	(0.324)
Democratic Neighbors	−1.539**	−0.488	−0.431	0.182
	(0.599)	(0.622)	(0.514)	(0.454)
Ethnic Fractionalization	−1.196	−0.016**	−0.848	−0.009*
	(0.984)	(0.008)	(0.600)	(0.006)
Interstate War	−1.146**	−0.574	−1.809*	−1.451*
	(0.550)	(0.788)	(1.076)	(0.742)
Civil War	0.054	0.374	−0.009	−0.146
	(0.489)	(0.412)	(0.155)	(0.307)
Military Leader	0.066	0.646**	0.054	−0.088
	(0.415)	(0.321)	(0.375)	(0.230)
Log of Time	−0.339***	−0.402**	−0.008	−0.138
	(0.120)	(0.158)	(0.155)	(0.121)
Intercept	−7.002	−9.777	−11.670***	−7.581
	(4.740)	(7.229)	(4.162)	(5.267)
S.d. of the random effect, σ_ζ^a	1.253***	1.400***	0.980***	0.804***
LR test of quadratic fit, χ_1^2	4.18**	1.79	4.08**	2.07
Log-likelihood	−176.98	−231.181	−426.918	−537.668
Observations	307	409	2,436	3,292
Leaders	307	409	350	471
Countries	71	95	74	101

[a] Standard deviation of the country-level, random effect; significance levels are based on the $\frac{1}{2}\chi_0^2 + \frac{1}{2}\chi_1^2$ likelihood-ratio test statistic.

Note: Estimation results for a country-level, random-intercept logistic regression model. Unit of observation is a leader in the models for entry and a leader-year in the models for exit. Robust standard errors (clustered by country) are in parentheses. Significance levels *10%, **5%, ***1%, one-sided hypothesis tests for *Inequality* and *Inequality²*.

Data Sources: See text. All covariates are lagged by one year.

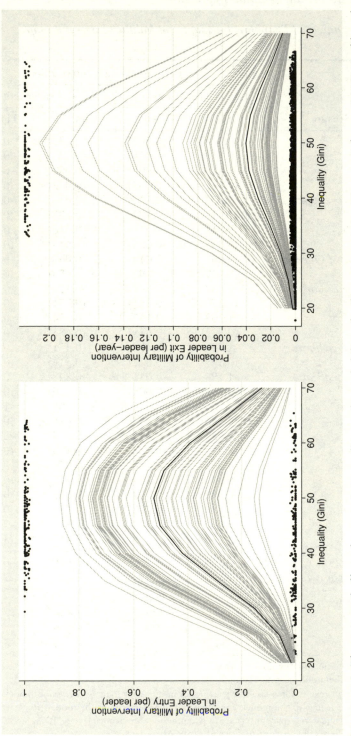

FIGURE 5.4. The estimated effect of economic inequality on the probability of military intervention. *Source:* Babones (2008), Svolik and Akcinaroglu (2006).

methods (Gelman and Hill 2006; Rabe-Hesketh and Skrondal 2008). Accordingly, the gray lines in Figure 5.4 trace the estimated relationship between military intervention and economic inequality for each country in the data, conditional on the size of its random effect; the remaining covariates are held at their sample medians.[39] The black line corresponds to a country with the median random effect. Thus, for instance, we see that for the median country, an increase in the Gini coefficient from 25 (e.g., Bulgaria in the 1980s) to 40 (e.g., Morocco in the 1980s) raises the likelihood of military intervention in leader entry eightfold, from 0.05 to 0.40. This likelihood peaks at 0.50 when the Gini coefficient is around 50 and declines thereafter. But note that the effect of inequality on military intervention may be much larger or smaller depending on values of the country-specific random effects, as this plot indicates. We see a similar effect of economic inequality on military intervention in leader exit, although the extent of the unobserved, country-level heterogeneity in this model is larger.

Additionally, we may use the estimated random effects as a diagnostic of model fit. More specifically, we can use our qualitative knowledge of the data to try to identify the unobserved country-level factors that may explain those random effects that depart the furthest from the population mean. In all of the specifications in Table 5.3, Mexico ranks near the bottom of the distribution of the predicted random effects, whereas Greece ranks near the top. That is, given their levels of economic inequality and other covariate values, these two countries experienced too little and too much military intervention, respectively. The unique institutional features of Mexican politics during the hegemony of the Institutional Revolutionary Party (Magaloni 2006; Greene 2007) and the legacy of the Greek civil war (Gerolymatos 2009) figure prominently in the political history of the two countries and therefore may be just such country-level factors that account for their deviations. This close match between the estimated random effect size and our qualitative country-specific knowledge provides an informal indication that the present, random-intercept specification fits the data well.

The estimated effects of the remaining covariates on the likelihood of military intervention are as expected for a majority of covariates and specifications. However, only a few of these covariates are significant at conventional levels of statistical significance across all four specifications. A positive coefficient implies an increase in the likelihood of the associated form of military intervention. Thus, for instance, we see that the likelihood of military intervention in leader entry decreases in the *time* since the last military intervention within a country. Yet contrary to findings in the existing large-N research on coups d'état (Londregan and Poole 1990), a decrease in *GDP per capita* or

[39] These medians correspond to a country during the *Cold War* with the annual *GDP per capita* of $1,542, *GDP growth* of 1.67 percent, the log of *trade openness* of −0.84, an index of ethnolinguistic *fractionalization* of 0.35, 20 percent democratic neighbors, that had its last military intervention thirty-seven years ago, is not a major *fuel exporter*, and is not engaged in an *interstate* or *civil war*.

GDP growth does not consistently raise the likelihood of military interventions. Importantly, however, previous studies did not account for the possible effect of economic inequality on the likelihood of military interventions. My results suggest that in terms of both direction of the effect and statistical significance, economic inequality is a more robust predictor of military intervention in authoritarian politics than economic recessions or low levels of economic development.

Finally, the estimation results presented here are robust to alternative estimation methods. Estimates based on the standard, pooled logistic model are identical in their qualitative implications, with coefficient estimates statistically significant at even higher levels. Nevertheless, a likelihood-ratio test of the estimated random effect variance suggests that between-country unobserved heterogeneity is large enough to warrant the random-intercept approach in all four models. We may further assess whether a more complex, random-coefficient model is appropriate. That is, we may model the effect of country-level unobserved factors on the likelihood of military intervention via both a random effect on the intercept as well as a separate, random effect on the coefficients associated with inequality and resource wealth. Estimates based on this model confirm the nonmonotonic effect of inequality on the likelihood of military intervention. However, a likelihood-ratio test of the estimated variance of the random coefficients suggests that this more complex model does not improve the fit of the random-intercept model that I have examined.[40]

To summarize, the empirical analysis in this section provides strong support for the theoretical arguments in this chapter. Both the descriptive statistics and estimation results support the predicted nonmonotonic association between economic inequality and military intervention in dictatorships. I examine original, detailed data that distinguish between military interventions in the entry and exit of leaders. Furthermore, I use two different measures of economic inequality: the Gini coefficient and the Theil statistic. To account for the limited availability of cross-national data on inequality in dictatorships, I perform a multiple imputation of missing values. I also estimated a country-level, random-intercept logistic regression model to control for the effect of unobserved or omitted country-level factors, and I obtain similar results using alternative specifications. In sum, the results of this empirical analysis support my theoretical claims and are robust to different measures of economic inequality, unobserved country-level heterogeneity, and a range of statistical specifications and estimation methods, and they hold for two distinct forms of military intervention.

---

[40] The present results are also robust to alternative specifications and measures of military intervention. I obtain qualitatively identical results when using Geddes's (1999b), Cheibub and Gandhi's (2005), and Banks's (2001) coding of military dictatorships as a measure of military intervention. Similarly, estimation results do not change significantly when I consider only military interventions against civilian leaders, or when I estimate the models for leader exit using only the last observed year per leader.

5.5 CONCLUSION: THE POLITICAL PRICE OF AUTHORITARIAN REPRESSION

The Ugandan dictator General Idi Amin Dada established one of the most brutal modern dictatorships after he came to power in a military coup d'état in 1971 (Jackson and Rosberg 1982, 252–5). During the second half of the 1960s, Amin's loyal following within the military became essential to his predecessor Milton Obote's struggle against, first, opposition in the Ugandan Parliament, then the country's ceremonial president Edward Mutesa, then an attempt at a regional secession in Baganda, and ultimately defecting factions from within Obote's own Uganda People's Congress Party (Mutibwa 1992, Chap. 5). Obote rewarded the military's support by increasing its size, affording it training opportunities outside of Africa, and promoting Colonel Idi Amin to Major-General and Army Chief of Staff (Mutibwa 1992, 37, 64). A few years later, Idi Amin deposed by then-dictator Obote when his plans to remove the general from the leadership of the Ugandan armed forces became apparent (Mutibwa 1992, 73).

Yet according to Decalo (1990, 10), General Idi Amin was "literally nothing and nobody" without "his uniform and the power it conferred." Decalo's focus on Amin's uniform alone is misplaced. According to the arguments in this chapter, Amin's and other soldiers' underlying power stems not from their guns or uniforms but rather from the pivotal political position that they acquire in some dictatorships.

As summarized by Mutibwa (1992, 64), by the time Obote defeated his rivals and established a one-party dictatorship:

> ... the government needed the army for its survival and its security more than the army needed the government.... By giving [Amin] the power that went beyond his ability to provide military support ... Obote let a genie out of the bottle ... it was a genie which grew so much that by about 1969 it was much too big to be forced back: Amin had acquired a political as well as military base, which he would use without qualms and with sophistication.

Amin's political ascendance exemplifies the moral hazard in authoritarian repression: In dictatorships that heavily rely on repression, their repressive agents – frequently their militaries – gain the muscle to resist political control. This is when the problem of authoritarian power-sharing emerges as an undesirable byproduct of the problem of authoritarian control: Soldiers metamorphize from obedient agents into political rivals. The latter is the political price of authoritarian repression. Whenever possible, therefore, dictatorships avoid paying that price by instead relying on the other principal tool for resolving the problem of authoritarian control: co-optation.

5.6 APPENDIX I: PROOFS

This appendix contains technical proofs from Section 5.3.

Comparative statics on α^* and β^*.

To see that α^* is decreasing in π and g, observe that

$$\frac{\partial \alpha^*}{\partial \pi} = -\frac{1 - [1 - \rho(r)]g}{\pi^2(g-1)} < 0 \quad \text{and} \quad \frac{\partial \alpha^*}{\partial g} = -\frac{(1-\pi)\rho(r)}{\pi(g-1)^2} < 0.$$

The numerator of $\partial \alpha^*/\partial \pi$ is positive because $\alpha^* > 0$ only as long as $[1 - \rho(r)]g < 1$ (which is assumed in the text). The remaining comparative statics can be confirmed by inspection of the relevant expressions for α^* and β^*.

The government's equilibrium choice of the military's resources r^*.

In equilibrium, r^* is weakly increasing in $\hat{R}$: When $\rho(r) \leq c/m$, the level of the military's resources r that maximizes (5.3) solves the first-order condition (5.4). Because $C'(r) > 0$ and $\phi'(\hat{R}, r) > 0$ by assumption, any increase in $\hat{R}$ must be optimally matched by a corresponding increase in r. An analogous argument applies to the case when $\rho(r) > (1 + c)/m$ after substituting 1 for g in (5.4). Finally, for $c/m < \rho(r) \leq (1 + c)/m$, we substitute G from (5.5) for g in (5.4). By envelope theorem, r^* is increasing in $\hat{R}$ as in the previous two cases since $\rho(r^*) > 0$.

5.7   APPENDIX II: MULTIPLE IMPUTATION

This appendix provides details of the multiple-imputation procedure in Section 5.4. I follow Honaker and King (2009) and use the Amelia II package for *R* (Honaker et al. 2009). This package allows for an imputation procedure that is appropriate for cross-sectional time-series data and leads to sensible imputed values.

I properly imputed the data as follows: I used countries and years to index the cross-section and time units. Furthermore, I used second-order polynomials as well as lags and leads on the inequality measures; these were interacted with the cross-section units. I transformed the inequality measures as well as ethnic fractionalization so imputations do not fall outside the sample extremes. The remaining covariates were transformed whenever appropriate. To minimize the extent to which missingness in the data depends on unobservables, I included in the imputation additional variables that are potential predictors of inequality but are not relevant for the estimation in the chapter. Finally, I used a 5 percent ridge prior to improve numerical stability of the imputations; instability may be caused by the high missingness in the inequality measures as well as the high correlation between the two measures.

The Theil statistic is available for at most 34 percent of the 5,393 country-years in the data. I used Rubin's (1987) concept of relative efficiency to determine the number of datasets to impute. Rubin (1987, 114) showed that the efficiency of an estimate based on m imputations relative to a fully efficient estimate based on an infinite number of imputations is approximately

$$\frac{1}{\sqrt{1 + \frac{\gamma}{m}}},$$

where γ is the rate of missingness.[41] Given the current rate of missingness of 66 percent, the relative efficiency of at least 99 percent is obtained with thirty-three or more imputations. That is, estimates based on thirty-three or more imputed datasets, on average, will have standard errors that are at most 1 percent larger than those based on an infinite number of imputations.

Finally, to avoid working with implausible imputations in the analysis, I use data only for countries that have at least one observation on inequality and do not use imputations that are further than ten years from the closest observed value. In turn, the analysis in this chapter is based on data with a rate of missingness of 44 percent rather than 66 percent. The forty imputations used in the analysis are thus very conservative.

---

[41] This expression measures relative efficiency on the scale of standard errors of the estimated quantity.

6

Why *Authoritarian* Parties? The Regime Party as an Instrument of Co-optation and Control

> While a party card is of course no guarantee of success, [the] lack of it is a guarantee that you will not have a career of any kind.
>
> Voslensky, *Nomenklatura* (1984, 98)

> What actually holds the present regime together is not a set of uncoordinated policies that pleases all sectors and paralyzes the government, but rather a system of mobility that attracts the personal allegiance of spokesmen for all the PRI sectors from the bottom to the top of the party hierarchy.
>
> Hansen, *The Politics of Mexican Development* (1971, 220)

A growing body of research finds that dictatorships with a single or a dominant political party represent an especially resilient form of authoritarian rule. In a seminal paper, Geddes (1999a) classified dictatorships into personalist, military, single-party, and their hybrids and showed that single-party dictatorships are less likely to break down and democratize than the remaining categories. Research on an institutionally related category of dictatorship – dominant or hegemonic party regimes – similarly concludes that these regimes are particularly robust, even in the face of economic crises and popular opposition (Slater 2003; Smith 2005; Magaloni 2006; Brownlee 2007a). In a complementary line of research, Gandhi and Przeworski (2007) report that leaders in single-party regimes survive longer in office, and Chapter 4 shows that leadership in dictatorships with parties is less likely to be deposed by noninstitutional means, such as coups and popular uprisings. Even when single- and dominant-party dictatorships democratize, former party elites frequently shape the transition process and, in many cases, continue to maintain economic and political influence (Grzymała-Busse 2002, 2007).

How does the *institution* of the party facilitate the survival of dictatorships? In spite this growing body of research and the emerging consensus that parties contribute to authoritarian resilience, we still lack a precise statement of the

The title of this chapter is inspired by the title of Aldrich's (1995) classic study of the American party system.

162

political mechanism by which particular organizational features of authoritarian parties account for the resilience of dictatorships with single or dominant parties.

Consider two prominent views of how authoritarian parties affect the survival of dictatorships. According to one view, parties are the vehicles through which the regime rewards its supporters (Geddes 1999b; Gandhi 2008). This political exchange is typically called co-optation and frequently takes the form of patronage (Magaloni 2006; Blaydes 2010). Yet dictatorships without parties also commonly appease popular discontent via policy concessions or material handouts, and patronage networks pervade many societies, operating both within and outside of authoritarian parties (see, e.g., Bratton and Van de Walle 1997; Van de Walle 2001; Kitschelt and Wilkinson 2007). What makes authoritarian parties such particularly apt vehicles for the co-optation of the masses?

According to another prominent view, authoritarian parties facilitate cooperation and prevent factionalism among a regime's elites (Geddes 1999b; Magaloni 2006; Brownlee 2007a). According to Geddes (1999b, 2003), for instance, in single-party regimes "everyone is better off if all factions remain united and in office." Arguably, however, incentives to "stick together or hang separately" – to paraphrase Benjamin Franklin – generically exist in most dictatorships. What is the mechanism by which authoritarian parties so effectively maintain elite cohesion?

This chapter addresses these questions by explaining (1) how and which specific *organizational features* of authoritarian parties contribute to authoritarian resilience, (2) why these beneficial functions cannot be carried out *without the institution of the party*, and (3) why *some* dictatorships establish and maintain a regime-sanctioned party whereas others do not.

I identify three organizational features of successful authoritarian parties that account for the effectiveness of parties as instruments of authoritarian co-optation, at both the mass and elite levels. These features are *hierarchical assignment of service and benefits*, *political control over appointments*, and *selective recruitment and repression*. Crucially, these features of internal party organization accomplish much more than simply distribute rewards in exchange for party members' support of the regime, as the existing literature often concludes. Rather than fora for political exchange, authoritarian parties are better thought of as incentive structures that encourage *sunk political investment* by their members. The three organizational features effectively exploit their members' opportunism and career aspirations to create a stake in the perpetuation of the regime among the most productive and ideologically agreeable segments of the population. In turn, authoritarian regimes that co-opt via a party with these organizational features survive under less favorable circumstances than dictatorships without a party, even if the latter expend the same resources on co-optation.

To examine the political logic that links internal party organization, career aspirations among the population, and survival of dictatorships, I develop a series of simple formal models of authoritarian co-optation. The analysis in Section 6.1 highlights that, jointly, the three institutional features of authoritarian parties that I identify contribute to the survival of dictatorships via two distinct political mechanisms.

The first of these may be called *party-based co-optation*. Co-optation via authoritarian parties differs from co-optation via transfers – which frequently takes the form of cash, price controls, subsidies, and redistribution – in a key political aspect: Co-optation via authoritarian parties breeds an enduring rather than momentary stake in the regime's survival. When the regime assigns costly party service to lower levels of the party hierarchy – and, hence, early in the party members' career – and the benefits of party membership to higher levels of the party hierarchy – and, hence, later in the party members' career – party members' costly service becomes sunk investment by the time they reap the benefits of party seniority. Therefore, what makes co-optation via a party so effective is not the distribution of benefits by itself – those could be easily distributed without a party. Rather, it is the conditioning of those benefits on prior costly service. Because the latter cannot be transferred across political coalitions and most likely will be lost if the regime or leadership changes, it becomes sunk investment. In turn, party members become political hostages of their own career success, with a vested interest in the perpetuation of the existing regime.

The three institutional features of successful authoritarian parties identified here additionally contribute to authoritarian resilience via another, conceptually separate mechanism, which we may call *direct political control*. This mechanism refers to those aspects of party activity that are aimed primarily at the general population, such as political communication, mobilization, intelligence gathering, and maintenance of political discipline (see, e.g., Friedrich and Brzezinski 1965; Huntington 1968). Smith (2005), for instance, identifies the ability of authoritarian parties to mobilize their constituencies in times of crisis as a key aspect of party "strength," Geddes (2008) argues that mass parties help dictators to counter threats from the military, Levitsky and Way (2010) claim that parties' "organizational power" helps authoritarian incumbents resist pressures for democratization after the end of the Cold War, and Magaloni (2008, 723) and Wintrobe (1998, 65) emphasize that long-lasting parties are essential for effective co-optation. The analysis here highlights how particular features of internal party organization – the party's recruitment, promotion, and retirement policies – ensure that sufficient incentives exist for key segments of the population to join the party and, in turn, provide the politically valuable service that results in the party's "lasting strength." By examining how optimal recruitment, promotion, and retirement policies depend on a regime's resources, ideology, and nonpartisan opportunities for career advancement, we gain a better understanding of the connection between organizational features of authoritarian parties and the potential and limits to their "lasting strength."

Results of the analysis in this chapter both corroborate and qualify existing explanations of how authoritarian parties contribute to the survival of dictatorships. Brownlee (2007a), Geddes (1999b, 2003), Gehlbach and Keefer (2008), and Magaloni (2006, 2008) argue that parties help to maintain elite cohesion. The analysis herein outlines the logic by which particular features of authoritarian parties' internal organization generate a stake in a regime's survival that grows with an individual's rank within the party hierarchy and goes beyond the immediate benefits that an individual receives. Yet in contrast to arguments that emphasize the contribution of parties to elite-level power-sharing, the analysis in this chapter underscores that party-based co-optation is most effective when the possibility of career advancement within an authoritarian party is available to select segments among the general population, not only to the elites.

In this regard, this chapter shares the focus on the co-optation of the masses with Blaydes (2010), Gandhi and Przeworski (2006, 2007), Gandhi (2008), and Malesky and Schuler (2010). However, in its emphasis on the softer, institutional aspects of authoritarian politics, the existing literature rarely considers co-optation alongside a quintessential instrument of authoritarian governance – that is, repression.[1] In fact, most dictatorships with single or dominant parties maintain a large repressive apparatus.[2]

The analysis in this chapter helps us understand the complementarity of repression and co-optation via regime-sanctioned political parties. To ensure that sufficient incentives exist for the population to join the party and provide the associated political service, party membership must be a consideration for a significant number of career appointments. In turn, the government must establish and maintain political control over not only political and administrative posts but also key economic and social posts. Thus effective co-optation via a regime-sanctioned party requires that the government command the repressive capacity to counter opposition to the exercise of widespread political control.

When I juxtapose co-optation via a regime-sanctioned political party and repression, I find that dictatorships co-opt most effectively when they aim at the ideologically most proximate segments of the population rather than actual opposition. Because the cost of co-optation is more sensitive than the cost of repression to the ideological distance between a member of the population and the regime, the regime expends scarce resources most effectively when it recruits those who are ideologically closest to it. This finding is consistent with historical and qualitative research on the selective nature of party recruitment and promotion policies, and it suggests a qualification to the frequent claim

---

[1] See Wintrobe (1998) and Gershenson and Gorossman (2001) for an exception; however, they do not examine whom a dictator will co-opt and whom he will repress.

[2] See, e.g., Waterbury (1983) on Egypt, Batatu (1981) on Syria, Gregory (2009) on the Soviet Union, Crouch (1978) on Indonesia, Stevens (1974) on Mexico, and Baum (1997) on China.

that parties serve to co-opt opposition.[3] The present analysis implies that the logic of party-based, selective co-optation is to enlist those segments of the population that will best help *marginalize* actual opposition rather than co-opt it.[4]

This chapter's findings about the contribution of regime-sanctioned parties to authoritarian resilience also suggest a qualification of Bueno de Mesquita et al.'s (2003) selectorate theory. At the heart of selectorate theory is the claim that potential defectors from an incumbent regime must weigh the certain benefits that they currently receive against the uncertain benefits that a challenger offers them. Bueno de Mesquita et al. (2003) assume that such uncertainty results in an incumbency advantage that decreases with the size of the incumbent's coalition. The present arguments imply that dictatorships that co-opt via a regime party with the organizational features examined here survive under less favorable circumstances and in the face of stronger challengers than those without such parties, even if the latter expends the same material resources on co-optation. In other words, the institutional architecture of a regime's ruling coalition critically conditions the loyalty of its members.

Although the questions that motivate this chapter are primarily theoretical, I also examine the empirical association between regime parties and the survival of dictatorships. Section 6.2 conducts a stronger test of this relationship than has been attempted in existing research. Specifically, I avoid confounding the effect of parties with the strength of individual leaders by measuring the survival of authoritarian ruling coalitions rather than individual leaders, and I use direct, institutional indicators of the partisan organization of dictatorships. I find that once we account for the legislative strength of regime-sanctioned political parties in dictatorships with multiple parties, dictatorships with parties that control a supermajority of seats in the legislature survive, on average, about as long as ruling coalitions with single parties. Thus in accordance with my theoretical arguments, what facilitates the survival of dictatorships is the presence of a strong party with the organizational features identified here, not necessarily a single one.

The empirical analysis in this chapter also shows that regime-sanctioned authoritarian parties effectively take one of three distinct forms. The first are regime parties in single-party regimes, which account for about 35 percent of all country-year observations. The remaining two groups exist in dictatorships that allow for multiple parties: The first group consists of hegemonic or dominant parties, which on average control roughly 76 percent of all legislative seats and account for 32 percent of all country-year observations; the second group consists of parties under a conceptual category of dictatorship frequently characterized as electoral or competitive authoritarianism (Levitsky and Way

---

[3] On party recruitment and promotion policies, see, e.g., Domínguez (1978, Chap. 8), Grzymała–Busse (2002), Shambaugh (2009), and Staar (1988).

[4] Cf. Geddes (1999b, 135) and Gandhi and Przeworski (2007).

2002; Schedler 2006).[5] Authoritarian parties in this last group typically control a bare majority or minority of legislative seats and account for about 11 percent of all country-year observations.[6] Existing literature so far has examined the categories of hegemonic or dominant parties and parties under competitive authoritarianism either by using qualitative data or by relying for their identification on a predefined criterion on their legislative strength or durability. The empirical analysis in this chapter identifies these distinct categories of authoritarian parties directly from the empirical distribution of comprehensive, large-N data on the legislative strength of authoritarian regime parties.

The core of this chapter addresses the first of the three questions asked at the outset: How and which organizational features of authoritarian parties contribute to authoritarian resilience? The chapter concludes by answering the two remaining questions: Why dictators need the actual institution of the party and why only some dictatorships establish a party. My analysis implies that two of the organizational features of authoritarian parties identified here – political control over appointments and selective recruitment and repression – act as catalysts for the third – hierarchical assignment of service and benefits. Hence dictatorships benefit from coordinating the three organizational features within a single institution – that is, a regime-sanctioned political party.

The analysis in this chapter contributes to our understanding of not only the potential but also the limits of party-based co-optation by suggesting why not all dictatorships establish a regime-sanctioned party. Because effective party-based co-optation requires that the regime control a significant number of appointments and channel significant resources through the party, dictatorships whose support base is limited to traditional elites – landed aristocracy or the owners of capital – will find co-optation and control via parties less advantageous than the alternatives of repression and co-optation via direct transfers.

6.1 THE LOGIC OF PARTY-BASED AUTHORITARIAN CO-OPTATION

Which organizational features of authoritarian parties facilitate the survival of dictatorships and how do they do it? Historical and case-based research on single and dominant parties reveals a striking degree of similarity in the internal makeup of long-lasting regime-sanctioned parties across a wide range of dictatorships. This section builds on this research and examines the political logic by which three common organizational features of single and dominant parties – that is, hierarchical assignment of service and benefits, political control

---

[5] On hegemonic or dominant parties, see Magaloni (2006), Greene (2007), Magaloni and Kricheli (2010), Blaydes (2010), and Reuter and Gandhi (2010).

[6] A fourth, smallest group of authoritarian parties is composed of those that control only a fraction of legislative seats and typically exist in transitioning regimes; 18 percent of all dictatorships ban political parties. See Section 6.2 for details.

over appointments, and selective recruitment and repression – contribute to the survival of dictatorships.

6.1.1 Hierarchical Assignment of Service and Benefits

Most authoritarian parties entail a hierarchical apparatus that spans several levels of membership.[7] As a representative example, consider the Syrian Baath Party. In the 1980s, according to Hinnebusch (2002, Chap. 4), the internal structure of the Party consisted of 11,163 cells grouped into 1,395 basic units at the level of villages, factories, neighborhoods, and public institutions; in turn, these formed 154 sub-branches at the district or town level; which then constituted 18 branches in the provinces, cities, and major institutions. The leadership of the Party consisted of regional and national commands, with the general secretary at the very top (Hinnebusch 2002, 75–9).

Realistically, the administration of any large organization requires a vertical command structure, which may account for the hierarchical aspects of the party apparatus. Yet a notable feature of such party hierarchies is the differentiated allocation of the benefits and service associated with party membership across the levels of the party hierarchy. Simply stated, lower ranks within the party provide most of the service, while higher ranks of party membership reap most of the benefits. In fact, most political-party service – frequently in the form of ideological work, intelligence gathering, and popular mobilization – occurs at the lowest level of the party hierarchy. Accordingly, many single and dominant parties have entry-level membership ranks, such as candidate member, apprentice, and "friend of the party." Party statutes commonly condition the advancement to full membership on grassroots party service and sometimes even stipulate a minimum time that a prospective member must spend in such probationary status before acquiring full membership.[8] To take one example, probationary membership in the Iraqi Baath Party took a minimum of seven years and entailed a progression through the ranks of sympathizer, supporter, candidate, and trainee (Sissons 2008).

Some aspects of party service understandably differ between dictatorships with single and dominant parties because the latter have multiparty elections, even if highly manipulated. Whereas party service in single-party regimes may involve activities whose purpose is to maintain political discipline, social stability, and turnout at regime-sanctioned events, party service in dictatorships with

---

[7] Of course, hierarchical assignment of service and benefits is not unique to authoritarian parties or even to parties as organizations. Parties in democracies as well as other organizations – such as militaries – routinely assign service and benefits hierarchically. However, most of the tools available to authoritarian parties, including political control over appointments and repression, are simply illegal in most democracies. Meanwhile, the unique functional demands on militaries – especially proficiency in warfare – limit their capacity to serve as a general institution of authoritarian co-operation.

[8] On Communist parties, see, e.g., Simons and White (1984) and Staar (1988); on Baath parties, see Perthes (1995, Chap. 4) and Batatu (1978, Chap. 58).

dominant parties additionally involves voter mobilization and campaigning in multiparty elections.[9] According to Chan (1976), for instance, candidates for the People's Action Party in Singapore were chosen based on their potential to play one or more of four basic roles: technocrat, mobilizer, Malay vote-getter, and Chinese-educated intellectual. Evidence from other dictatorships with dominant parties indicates that voter mobilization and the delivery of set vote quotas – possibly by engaging in electoral fraud and voter intimidation – are a key part of rank-and-file–level party service.[10]

On the other hand, benefits of party membership range from employment for full-time party functionaries to better promotion prospects within the government bureaucracy and government-controlled enterprises and privileged access to educational opportunities and social services, such as child care and public housing (see, e.g., Voslensky 1984; Walder 1995). Those benefits typically increase with one's rank within the party and many positions of economic or social significance may be accessible only to those with established partisan credentials.

Nevertheless, the complete scope of benefits to party membership is rarely recognized officially. Consider the *nomenklatura* system adopted by the Communist regimes of Eastern Europe and China and emulated by the Baathist regimes in Syria and Iraq. The system was – and, in the case of China, still is – based on a list (or several lists) of lucrative positions for which a history of service within the party and a demonstrated loyalty to the regime is an essential precondition. In the Soviet Union and China, the *nomenklatura* lists have been administered by the Organization Department of the Party's Central Committee and contain positions within the party, government, military, state-controlled enterprises, and other politically sensitive entities (e.g., universities and professional and civic associations). Although the *nomenklatura* system probably represents the most systematic form of administrative formalization of benefits to party membership and service, the precise content of *nomenklatura* lists and criteria for promotion to a position on the lists are rarely publicly stated.[11]

What are the political consequences of such hierarchical assignment of service and benefits within authoritarian parties? Before examining in detail the role of recruitment, promotion, and retirement policies that shape this feature of authoritarian parties, consider a simple illustration of how the hierarchical assignment of service and benefits contributes to the survival of dictatorships.

---

[9] See Edin (2003) on social stability as a criterion for local cadre promotion in China; see Staar (1988) on Communist parties in Eastern Europe.

[10] See Magaloni (2006), Greene (2007), and Langston and Morgenstern (2009) on the PRI in Mexico; Brownlee (2007a) and Blaydes (2010) on the National Democratic Party in Egypt; Elson (2001) and Smith (2005) on Golkar in Indonesia; and Abrami et al. (2008) and Malesky and Schuler (2010) on Vietnam.

[11] On the Soviet Union and Eastern Europe, see Grzymała-Busse (2002), Rigby (1988), and Voslensky (1984); on China, see Landry (2008) and Shambaugh (2009); on Cuba, see Domínguez (1978).

To keep this illustration as simple as possible, suppose that a *dictator* needs the active support of only two citizens to stay in power. Consider first co-optation within the institutional structure of a regime party. To stay with the most rudimentary concept of a hierarchical party structure, suppose that the party apparatus consists of only two ranks of membership: *junior* and *senior* members. Juniors provide costly service for the regime at the individual *cost* $c > 0$, whereas seniors enjoy the individual *benefit* b, $b > c$. For now, assume that citizens live for two periods only; a junior automatically becomes a senior after one period of service and all seniors retire after one period. Then, in any period and after accounting for the costly service that juniors provide, the dictator's total net expenditures on the party are $b - c$.

I refer to co-optation without an authoritarian party as co-optation via *transfers*. Such transfers frequently take the form of cash, subsidies, price regulation, land reform, and programmatic redistribution.[12] All such policies, in effect, are transfers of income from the government to a targeted segment of the population. For instance, in attempts to appease the masses during the wave of protests that swept through the Middle East and North Africa at the beginning of 2011 – now known as the Arab Spring – Bahrain's King Hamad ibn Isa al-Khalifa gave each Bahraini family the equivalent of US \$2,650; the Syrian Government of Bashar al-Asad froze electricity prices and announced a 72 percent rise in heating-oil benefits for public workers; and the Saudi Government announced an increase in subsidies for new marriages, homeowners, and businesses.[13]

In order to explicitly contrast co-optation with and without a regime party, suppose that the dictator distributes via transfers an amount equivalent to his total net expenditures on partisan co-optation, $b - c$. That is, in any period, the dictator compensates each of the two citizen's loyalty to the regime by a *transfer* in the amount of $(b - c)/2$.

How much does a *challenger* have to offer to each citizen in order to attract both citizens' support? Suppose that the challenger does not have a party and simply offers a period-by-period transfer to each of the two citizens. In the case of co-optation via transfers, the two citizens will be willing to join him if he offers each an equivalent transfer – that is, at least $(b - c)/2$. Hence a challenger must have a budget of at least $b - c$ to replace an incumbent who co-opts via transfers.

By contrast, a challenger who would like to attract defectors from a dictator who co-opts via a party must consider not only their current costs and benefits but also the effect of the party hierarchy on their incentives to defect. As in the setting without a party, the junior expects to receive $b - c$ over the two stages of her career in the party and therefore must be offered an average payoff of at

---

[12] Magaloni (2008) refers to these as "transfers on the spot."
[13] "Bahrain's King Gives out Cash Ahead of Protests," *Reuters*, 12 February 2011; "Hard Choices for the Government," *The Economist*, 20 January 2011; and "Bahrain King in Saudi Arabia to discuss Unrest," *The New York Times*, 23 February 2011.

TABLE 6.1. *Comparison of Co-optation Via Transfers and Co-optation Via a Regime Party*

Party Rank	Transfers	Regime Party		
	Per-period Payoff	Current Rank Payoff	Expected Lifetime Payoff	Average Per-period Payoff
Senior	$\frac{b-c}{2}$	b	b	b
Junior	$\frac{b-c}{2}$	$-c$	$b-c$	$\frac{b-c}{2}$

least $(b-c)/2$ in each period to defect to the challenger. However, that would not be enough for the senior: She must be offered at least b to defect to the challenger, corresponding to the benefit she will obtain from the incumbent in the current period. Thus when facing an incumbent with a party, the challenger must command greater resources to replace him: $b + (b-c)/2 > b - c$. Or equivalently, the incumbent must command fewer resources to deter the same challenger when he co-opts via a regime party.

Table 6.1 contrasts the costs of co-opting the two citizens with and without a regime party. By assigning costly service to the early stages of party members' career and delaying the benefits of membership to the latter stages, the hierarchical structure of the party renders the incumbent dictator more resilient to potential challengers. Because they have already expended the costly service at the junior stage and only expect to reap the benefits, senior party members have a stake in the incumbent dictator's survival that is absent in a regime that co-opts without the institution of the party, even if the latter spends the same resources on co-optation.

This logic is frequently articulated in studies of party dictatorships. In their analysis of patrimonial politics in Africa, Bratton and Van de Walle (1997, 86) identify "plebiscitary" and "competitive" one-party regimes as an important subset of African dictatorships. Insiders within these regimes have strong incentives to remain loyal because:

[they] have typically risen through the ranks of political service and ... derive livelihood principally from state or party offices. Because they face the prospect of losing all visible means of support in a political transition, they have little option but to cling to the regime, to sink or swim with it.

In a similar spirit, Hough (1980, 33) explained that prospects for regime change in the Soviet Union under Brezhnev were grim because:

... the Soviet government has thus far been skillful in the way it has tied the fate of many individuals in the country to the fate of the regime. By admitting such a broad range of the educated public into the party, it has provided full opportunities for upward social mobility for those who avoid dissidence, while giving everyone in the managerial class reason to wonder what the impact of an anti-Communist revolution would be on him or her personally.

The Party Hierarchy and Incentives for Party Membership. As these examples illustrate, the key political advantage of allocating party service and benefits hierarchically is the stake in the regime's survival that arises endogenously among the senior ranks of the party. A key challenge for authoritarian parties that structure party service and benefits hierarchically therefore is to create sufficient incentives for juniors to join the party and provide costly service at a manageable cost to the regime. When the demands on service and the entitlement to benefits vary across the ranks of the party, the provision of too-large benefits may strain the regime's resources; the demand of too much service may discourage prospective members.

To better understand the implications of hierarchical assignment of service and benefits for incentives to join the party, we may extend our rudimentary model as follows. Suppose that each citizen now lives indefinitely over time periods $t = 1, 2, \ldots$. In any period, a citizen who is not a party member earns a wage w. As before, if a citizen joins the regime party, she starts at the junior rank and provides party service that entails a per-period cost c; once promoted to the senior rank, she obtains the per-period benefit $b > w > 0$.

A citizen's payoff from a career within the party depends on the regime's promotion and retirement policies. In any period, a junior member is promoted to a senior rank with the probability $p \in [0, 1]$. Meanwhile, a senior member is retired with the probability $r \in [0, 1]$ and receives the wage w after retiring.[14] Thus senior party member i's expected discounted career payoff is

$$u_i^S = b + \delta[r u_i^N + (1 - r)u_i^S], \tag{6.1}$$

where $u_i^N = w/(1 - \delta)$ is the discounted career payoff of nonmembers and $\delta \in (0, 1)$ is a discount factor.[15] Solving (6.1) for u_i^S, we obtain

$$u_i^S = \frac{b + \delta r u_i^N}{1 - \delta(1 - r)}. \tag{6.2}$$

Then citizen i's expected payoff from party membership, which begins at the junior level, is

$$u_i^J = -c + \delta[p u_i^S + (1 - p)u_i^J]. \tag{6.3}$$

Solving (6.3) for u_i^J, we obtain

$$u_i^J = \frac{-c + \delta p u_i^S}{1 - \delta(1 - p)}.$$

[14] Lazarev (2005, 2007) develops a related model of a single party with two levels of membership and examines the optimal structure of promotion and retirement rules. The present model differs from Lazarev's by explicitly comparing the resilience of dictatorships with and without a regime party to potential challengers.

[15] Because the citizens here (unrealistically) are infinitely lived, the discount factor δ may be interpreted as a natural mortality rate. That is, in each period, a citizen expects to die with the probability δ.

Thus citizen i has an incentive to join the party as long as

$$u_i^J \geq u_i^N \quad \text{or, equivalently,} \quad p \geq \frac{1 - \delta(1-r)}{\delta} \frac{c+w}{b-w}. \tag{6.4}$$

We may call inequality (6.4) the *party-service constraint*. The party service constraint implies that to maintain party membership, the regime must (1) maintain a minimal rate of promotions and (2) balance its promotion and retirement policies. More precisely, the minimal rate of promotions implied by the party-service constraint is positive and, intuitively, increasing in the cost of party of service c and nonparty wage w; it is decreasing in the benefit from seniority b.

At the same time, the total resources available to the regime will limit the generosity of the benefits to senior party members and, hence, the party's promotion and retirement policies. Assuming that the regime intends to maintain constant party membership over time, the rate of retirement implies an upper bound on the rate of promotions. That is, in any period, junior members can only be promoted into vacancies created by retired seniors,

$$r N^S = p N^J, \tag{6.5}$$

where N^S and N^J are the number of seniors and juniors in the party. Thus equation (6.5) is an assumption about *constant party size*.[16] When B are the total resources that the regime can spend on the party, the party's retirement policy must respect the *budget constraint,*

$$B \geq N^S b. \tag{6.6}$$

Combining the assumption about constant party size and the budget constraint, we see that the retirement rate must be at least

$$r \geq \frac{pbN^J}{B},$$

or, equivalently, the promotion rate can be at most

$$p \leq \frac{rB}{bN^J}.$$

Intuitively, when the regime has fewer resources, it must retire senior ranks at a higher rate and promote junior ranks at a lower rate.

Suppose that the regime's benefit $s(c)$ from a junior party member's service is increasing and concave in c, $s'(c) > 0$ and $s''(c) < 0$ and that $s(0) = 0$. If the regime did not need to consider incentives for party membership, it would

---

[16] This assumption can be relaxed easily: the evolution party membership at the senior rank is described by the equation $N_t^S = (1-r)N_{t-1}^S + pN_{t-1}^J$. The analysis here assumes that $N_t^S = N_{t-1}^S$; therefore, strategies p and r are stationary. Also note that the balance on the probabilities p and q implied by constant party size is a "long-run" balance. That is, across individual periods, the realizations of p and q may actually reduce or exceed the previous period's party size, but party size will be constant in the long run.

never promote ($p = 0$) and retire immediately ($r = 1$). By contrast, a resource-constrained regime will adopt promotion and retirement policies that respect the budget constraint and hold the party-service constraint at equality. Jointly, the resource and party-service constraints imply a set of limits on the feasible structure of career incentives within the party hierarchy: For the promise of seniority to attract new members, the rate of promotions p must be positive; to be fiscally sustainable, the retirement rate r must be above a certain minimum level; and, within these boundaries, a resource-constrained regime will balance the two policies – a higher rate of promotions p will be compensated by a higher retirement rate r and vice versa.

More precisely, the regime chooses promotion and retirement policies that maximize its discounted net payoff subject to binding party service and budget constraints,

$$\max_{p,r} \left[\frac{s(c)}{1 - \delta(1 - p)} - \frac{b}{1 - \delta(1 - r)} \right]$$

subject to $\qquad p = \frac{1 - \delta(1 - r)}{\delta} \frac{c + w}{b - w} \quad$ and $\quad r \geq \frac{b - (1 - \delta)\bar{B}}{\delta \bar{B}}.$

Intuitively, the optimal promotion rate p^* is decreasing in the benefit from party service s and the compensation to seniors b; p^* is increasing in the wage earned by nonparty members w and the costs of party service c. The party-service constraint implies that any increase or decrease in p^* will be compensated by a corresponding change in r^*. The optimal trade-off between the promotion and retirement policies therefore reflects the relative political relevance of the parameters b, w, and c.

This analysis illuminates several organizational dilemmas that we frequently observe in single- and dominant-party regimes. The party-service constraint implies that – to attract new members who provide politically valuable service – the regime must maintain a minimal rate of promotions and, in turn, a positive rate of retirement. The Chinese Communist Party, for instance, has strived to maintain an appropriate balance between these two policies at various levels of the Party hierarchy. In the 1980s, Deng Xiaoping initiated efforts at rejuvenating the Party's leadership by promoting age limits for Politburo members (Manion 1992, 1993) and, in 2002, Jiang Zemin instituted term limits and rotation for leading local cadres in the Party and government (Bo 2007; Nathan 2003).

Understandably, we may expect senior ranks within the Party to resist such political retirement. The implementation of an appropriate balance in promotion and retirement policies may present a political challenge for the Party leadership. Consider Nikita Khrushchev's proposal at the twenty-two Party Congress in 1961 to revise CPSU's statutes and implement a "systematic renewal of cadres" that would consist of term limits for individuals in elected Party posts and rules for turnover in other Party bodies (Burlatsky 1991, 129–30). According to Thompson, for instance, Khrushchev worried that "a gradual freezing of personnel policy would block up the system, and stagnation would occur" (Tompson 1995, 242–4). In terms of the present model, Khrushchev was concerned about the increasing costs of the existing retirement policy (i.e., a too low r and a too high b in the present model) and the diminishing incentives to provide Party service among the junior ranks within the Party. On the other hand, membership of the Party opposed the proposed changes because "older officials were faced with the constant threat of replacement by younger men, while younger officials believed that the rules would prevent them from enjoying long careers at the top" (Tompson 1995, 244). In fact, some attribute Khrushchev's fall to the Party elite's hostility to these policies (Tompson 2003, 22). Hence both Khrushchev's putative motives as well as the Party membership's negative reaction to this policy change accords with the implications of the present model.

The present model clarifies the political risk that reforms that reduce benefits to senior ranks within the Party entail. By curtailing the benefits to Party seniority, Khrushchev was threatening those ranks within the Party who would otherwise have the largest stake in his survival – as long as their benefits were preserved. As in the previous, simpler model, a challenger who would like to attract defectors from the leader's ruling coalition must offer a per-period benefit of at least $(1 - \delta)u_i^J$ and $(1 - \delta)u_i^S$ to any junior and senior Party member, respectively. Because the seniors' cost of Party service is sunk, they must be offered more than juniors to be willing to defect, $u_i^S > u_i^J$.

But note that Party-based co-optation only protects the incumbent dictator against those challengers who might dismantle the Party hierarchy after they come into office, as is typically the case after a regime change or the arrival of a different ruling coalition. Party-based co-optation does not safeguard against challengers from within the Party who propose to maintain or even increase benefits to the senior ranks. Thus after he removed Khrushchev from power in 1964, Brezhnev reversed Khrushchev's cadre policies and instead emphasized the "stability of cadres." This earned him the loyalty of the Party's senior membership but at the long-term cost of an ossified Party structure, the emergence of local fiefdoms, and lack of incentives for a younger generation of Party members to provide political service (Mawdsley and White 2000; Tompson 2003).[17] Geddes (1999b, 122) prominently observed that single-party regimes "tend to be brought down by exogenous events rather than internal splits." The present analysis helps us understand why single-party regimes remain resilient to elite defections *in spite of* frequent internal factionalism.

The maintenance of an appropriate balance in promotion and retirement policies poses a distinct challenge in dominant-party systems. Because these regimes have multiparty elections, disgruntled juniors who were passed up for a promotion and seniors who are being pressured into retirement may challenge the party as independents or opposition candidates. When, in attempts at party "renewal," Lee Kuan Yew pressured senior party members into political retirement, he reluctantly kept the former government minister Toh Chin Chye

---

[17] A major internal policy theme in Gorbachev's tenure as General Secretary was a correction to this trend (Rush 1991; Bunce 1999; Mawdsley and White 2000).

as member of parliament for the People's Action Party because Toh could easily win his district as an independent. Only when the boundaries of his district had been redrawn could Toh be retired and even then he became one of Lee's most powerful critics (Mauzy and Milne 2002).

A related concern shaped the process by which presidential candidates for Mexico's ruling Institutional Revolutionary Party used to be unveiled: The incumbent president tactically delayed the announcement of the next PRI nominee as long as possible so all influential cabinet members believed they stood a chance. Otherwise, they might have attempted to defect from the Party with enough time to promote an independent candidacy, as Cuauhtémoc Cárdenas did in 1988 after he unsuccessfully tried to win the presidential nomination within the PRI (Castañeda 2000). Although the official nomination to the presidential candidacy guaranteed the chosen candidate the presidency – and was therefore technically a promotion – it implied political retirement for most of the unsuccessful hopefuls.

In fact, Mexico under the PRI provides an example of uniquely intertwined promotion *and* retirement policies within a dominant-party regime. Due to a constitutionally mandated one-term limit for all elected posts, a change in the administration every six and, at the municipal level, three years implied the reassignment or retirement for not only elected politicians but also for thousands of government employees who held a position due to their political or clientelistic association with a politician in an elected post. Thus in the 1960s, according to Brandenburg (1964, 157), every six-year administration witnessed "a turnover of approximately 18,000 elective offices and 25,000 appointive posts." The coupling of the fixed, term-based time horizon with the PRI's political dominance in Mexico resulted in a system of upward and downward political mobility that was distinctively interlocked.

The expectation of such mobility is consistent with the present model's emphasis on an appropriate balance in the provision of incentives for political party service between the promise of promotion and a positive rate of political retirement.[18] In the case of Mexico, the nature of this incentive-preserving balance was eloquently summarized by Grindle (1977, 42):

The six-year procession often resembles a national game of musical chairs in which the same actors may reappear in different positions; new players are freely admitted, however, and the number of chairs may be enlarged to accommodate some of them.

---

[18] In fact, the 1961 revision of CPSU's statutes under Khrushchev also implied a high degree of mobility. According to Tatu (1970, 182), the proposed "systematic renewal of cadres" entailed two elements. "First, a fixed proportion of all the leading Party organs, from the Central Committee Presidium down to the cell committees, was to be replaced at each election. The proportions were: one-quarter for the Presidium and the Central Committee, one-third for the same bodies at the republic and regional levels, and one-half at the lowest level. Secondly ... no one could be elected more than a certain number of times to membership in the principal organs of the Party. The number was: three times for Presidium members, three times at the regional level and twice for a cell Secretary." These reforms were abandoned after Khrushchev's removal from office, before they could come into effect at the next Party Congress.

Those who fail to find a chair and must leave the game do so knowingly they have the possibility of reentering it at a later date.

Note, however, that this analysis does not require that the regime's *leadership* retire on a regular basis or even with a positive probability, as was the case in Mexico under the PRI. This was a unique feature of the Mexican dictatorship, which I address in the book's conclusion and for which the present model does not account.

Nevertheless, the regular reassignment or dismissal of thousands of senior elected and administrative posts raises an important question about the credibility of retirement rules: Why don't the senior party ranks simply attempt to stay?

A quick but inadequate answer is that the senior ranks retire because the regime's leadership tells them to go. Gorbachev initiated a large-scale retirement of senior Party cadres in the Communist Party's Central Committee and throughout the Soviet administration after years of "stagnation" under Brezhnev (Mawdsley and White 2000, Chap. 6), and Lee Kuan Yew steadily pressured for "leadership renewal" throughout the People's Action Party's existence (Hong and Huang 2008, 101–7). Stalin's Great Purges and Mao's Cultural Revolution may be interpreted in part as an exceedingly ruthless way of replacing old by new party cadres (Rigby 1968; MacFarquhar and Schoenhals 2006).

However, an answer that stops with the regime's leadership is incomplete because it only begs the question of why a leader would feel compelled to retire senior party cadres. The present model shows that incentives for party service among the junior ranks are inextricably tied to the promise of a promotion, which in turn depends on an appropriate rate of retirement among the senior ranks. At the same time, however, the benefits that senior party members enjoy depend on the continuing survival of the regime and, in turn, on the junior ranks' party service. Hence the credibility of the leadership's promise to retire the senior ranks rests on the indispensability of party service for the survival of the regime. If the senior ranks retire at a lower rate or refuse to retire, the motivation to provide costly party service among aspiring and junior party members will diminish or disappear. That is, they may join a challenger who promises better prospects within the regime or opposition that aims to overthrow the regime and establish democracy. Therefore, the regime's promise to maintain an appropriate balance in its promotion and retirement policies is credible only as far as the regime's survival depends on the juniors' party service.[19]

---

[19] This intuition could be formalized easily: The interaction between junior and senior party members can be seen as a two-period snapshot of an infinitely repeated overlapping generations game. Co-operation in such a game can then be enforced by a grim trigger threat according to which junior party members withdraw their service if the senior ranks do not retire at a promised rate. In the case of Mexico, for instance, the prohibition on the reelection for all elected offices may have been interpreted by the party's rank-and-file membership as a focal

The present analysis also highlights that to launch the co-optation mechanism, the regime needs to signal its strength and, hence, durability at the time of the party's founding. This initial, exogenous impetus is needed so prospective party members anticipate that the party will last long enough for their costly investment to come to fruition in the form of party seniority. Hence the establishment of a single- or dominant-party regime should witness more repression and, in the case of dominant-party regimes, more restrictions on competition than later periods. According with Huntington's (1970) and Smith's (2005) observations that the strength of single and dominant parties depends on the intensity of the struggle that brought them to power, this logic suggests that dictatorships that came to power by revolutionary means may be in a better position to initiate a party-based co-optation mechanism. Yet departing from Huntington and Smith, the present analysis suggests that these initial demands on credibility abate once the overlapping, intergenerational co-optation mechanism self-perpetuates and independently contributes to the expectation of the regime's continuing survival. Hence party dictatorships should become less repressive over time.

Finally, we have been working with a highly simplified model of hierarchical assignment of service and benefits within authoritarian parties. The assumption of only two party ranks is probably the starkest departure from real-world partisan hierarchies. This is a simplification whose sole purpose is to facilitate our examination of the incentives that emerge within party hierarchies by keeping our analysis tractable. This assumption can easily be relaxed: We can view the present setting as a partial model of career incentives across any two levels of a multilevel party hierarchy. For instance, our partial analysis implies that to provide sufficient incentives for party membership and costly service by the junior ranks, the chances of promotion must be only positive, not necessarily certain. When applied across several levels of the party hierarchy, this result explains the pyramid-shaped structure of party apparatuses that we typically observe in authoritarian parties.[20] Similarly, we saw that after a junior party member provides costly service, she acquires an interest in the regime's perpetuation. When applied across any two levels of the party hierarchy, this insight implies that a stake in the regime's survival compounds with a member's rank.

6.1.2 Political Control over Appointments

Many single-party dictatorships appear to have aspired for total political and social control of their society. As articulated by Benito Mussolini's "everything in the State, nothing outside the State, nothing against the State" (Mussolini

---

indicator of the elite's commitment to upward mobility. On Folk Theorems for repeated games with overlapping generations, see Smith (1992).

[20] See, e.g., Brownlee (2007a, Chap. 2), Hinnebusch (2002, Chap. 4), Landry (2008), and Staar (1988).

1935, 30), the presumed political ambition of these regimes was a complete fusion of the state, the party, and the society. Classic works on totalitarianism attribute this tendency to the social atomization of modern mass societies (Arendt 1951, 308–17) and the emergence of all-encompassing ideologies whose ultimate goal was to transform human nature (Friedrich and Brzezinski 1965, 130–2). Thus according to Arendt, the aim of totalitarianism is "the permanent domination of each single individual in each and every sphere of life" (Arendt 1951, 326). Yet even by admission of its theorists, this totalitarian ideal was rarely approximated outside a few emblematic cases, especially those of Adolf Hitler's Germany and Joseph Stalin's Soviet Union.

The present framework suggests a different interpretation of the tightly knit nexus of the party, government, and key economic and social positions that we observe across single- and dominant-party dictatorships. Rather than an end in itself – as classic theorists of totalitarianism may view it – single- and dominant-party regimes aim for political control of their economy and society because such control is key to effective party-based co-optation. Individual incentives to provide the costly party service that the regime values are inversely related to the ease with which significant career advances can occur outside the framework of the party. Only if sufficiently many desirable careers depend on partisan credentials will the party be able to co-opt a politically consequential fraction of the society while accomplishing the direct objective of political control.

To examine this intuition, we may extend our model of party-based co-optation by assuming that in any period, a citizen who is not a party member is promoted to a position that pays a wage that equals the benefit to party seniority b with probability q. In turn, the expected discounted payoff to a career outside the party is now

$$u_i^{NJ} = w + \delta[qu_i^{NS} + (1-q)u_i^{NJ}], \tag{6.7}$$

where u_i^{NJ} is the expected discounted payoff to a party nonmember i before a promotion and $u_i^{NS} = b/(1-\delta)$ is her payoff after a promotion. The modified party-service constraint (6.7) asks that $u_i^J \geq u_i^{NJ}$. Intuitively, incentives for party membership and the provision of the associated costly service are stronger when the likelihood q of obtaining benefits equivalent to party seniority outside the party is minimal.

The present explanation also suggests that – even though dictatorships with single parties may maintain deeper and more extensive political control over their society than dictatorships with dominant parties – the underlying political logic is identical. Thus one extreme may be exemplified by the Soviet *nomenklatura* system whose essence, according to Rigby (1988, 523), was to "consciously manage every area of socially relevant activity, outside a closely circumscribed private sphere, through an array of hierarchically structured formal organizations, all coordinated and directed at the center and at successively lower levels by the apparatus of the Communist Party." When Deng Xiaoping's economic reforms compromised the Chinese Communist Party's ability to maintain such control in the emerging private sector, Jiang Zemin recommended that private entrepreneurs be allowed to join the CCP and encouraged the formation of grassroots party organizations within private corporations (Dickson 2003).

On the other hand, party control over key economic and social appointments in dictatorships with dominant and hegemonic parties is typically less formalized and pervasive than in those with single parties. These regimes rely primarily on a bloated public sector for the distribution of politically administered patronage (Blaydes 2010; Magaloni 2006; Van de Walle 2001) as well as the regulation and co-ownership of the private sector. In Singapore, for example, the sole legal trade union since 1968 is the progovernment National Trade Union Congress, and the government maintains political influence throughout the city-state's economy through "government-linked companies," as they are known, whose corporate boards fuse government, party, and business elites (Mauzy and Milne 2002, 28–35).

Nevertheless, in most dictatorships with dominant and hegemonic parties, the government and the party may frequently be "perceived as a single structure in terms of the pursuit of regime goals" as Grindle (1977, 47) observed about Mexico under the PRI. After Suharto's government in Indonesia decided to hold its first postcoup election in 1971, it put in force a policy of "monoloyalty" according to which a "civil servant was obliged to serve unstintingly the government that employed him, and to renounce other competing ties"(Ward 1974, 33). In practice, all civil servants were required to sever their ties with any other party and encouraged to join the government-sanctioned Golkar (Elson 2001, 186–91).

Because dictatorships with dominant and hegemonic parties have multiparty elections, political control over the public sector serves the dual role of providing incentives for party service as well as ensuring electoral hegemony. Magaloni (2006, 8) shows how in the case of Mexico "a public image of invincibility" discouraged both defections from within the ruling party and helped maintain dominance at the polls. The present model highlights the importance of a large and politically administered public sector, which, in combination with the expectation of a continued control of the government, strengthens the incentives for service within the governing party. As an Egyptian member of parliament for the ruling National Democratic Party explained:

The NDP is good. But I am not talking about ideology or anything like that. This is not important. I do not think any of us [NDP deputies] care about that. What I mean is that it provides access to the services needed by the people. This is because it is the President's Party. I or anybody else in the NDP would join any party that is in the NDP's position. This is because it would be able to provide the necessary services to the constituents. (Kassem 1999, 81)

The party's control over a large public sector also facilitates continued electoral dominance by allowing it to condition the distribution of public funds on the manifestation of political loyalty at the polls.[21] When the ruling People's Action Party (PAP) in Singapore faced the risk of receiving less than 60 percent of the popular vote in 1997, Prime Minister Goh Chok Tong exploited the government's widespread control over public housing – as of 2000, 86 percent of Singaporeans lived in public housing (Mauzy and Milne 2002, 90) – by threatening to turn into "a slum" any district that would not vote for the ruling party. The prime minister considered this strategy "the single most important" factor in preserving the PAP's dominance at the polls.[22]

The modified party-service constraint (6.7) also suggests that the regime can strengthen incentives for party service in two different but related ways. First, it can provide more attractive terms of party membership. More specifically, the former alternative implies that better outside opportunities w must be matched by a larger promotion rate p. Consistently with this prediction, one observer of Cuba notes that admission standards for Cuba's Communist Party membership rose and fell depending on the state of the economy: Standards rose in the 1970s and 1990s, when the economy was doing poorly; standards declined in the 1980s, when the economy improved (Corbett 2002, 178). Similarly, Schnytzer and Sustersic (1998) reported that membership in the League of Communists of Yugoslavia was positively correlated with unemployment and negatively with real wages across the federal republics. Because nonpartisan opportunities for upward mobility may vary across the population, recruitment and promotion policies must be targeted accordingly. Guo (2005) documents the downward trend in interest in Party membership among the college-educated in China during the economic rise of the 1980s and the ensuing targeting of the college-educated by the Party in the 1990s via a screening process that favors those with a higher education.

The second way in which the regime can strengthen incentives for party service is to extend the number of career appointments for which party membership is a consideration. More precisely, the modified party-service constraint (6.7) implies that the regime can accomplish this by both requiring partisan credentials for a larger number of positions (i.e., a decrease in q) and by focusing on lucrative careers (i.e., a decrease in w). The intuition behind the latter is illustrated by Grzymała-Busse's (2002, 31) observation about the differing incentives for membership in the Communist Party of Czechoslovakia between white- and blue-collar employees:

White-collar workers had considerable incentives to join the party – employment in the state sector was made exclusively the provenance of the party, as was advancement within its ranks. The [party] had wanted to recruit blue-collar workers but had fewer

---

[21] See, e.g., Blaydes (2010) on Egypt under the National Democratic Party and Magaloni (2006) on Mexico under the PRI.

[22] Eventually, the PAP won 65 percent the popular vote and eighty-one of eighty-three legislative seats. See "Upgrading Link Swung Vote in GE," *The Straits Times*, 12 January 1998; and "Singapore's Voters Get a Choice: Slums or the Ruling Party," *The Wall Street Journal Asia*, 31 December 1996.

incentives for blue-collar workers to join, and far fewer sanctions to keep them from leaving. For example, while white-collar workers were demoted to menial jobs if they were expelled from the party, blue-collar workers faced no such punishments.

To summarize, widespread partisan control over political, administrative, and economic appointments enhances incentives for costly and valuable party service. Hence this organizational feature of authoritarian parties complements the feature examined previously – that is, hierarchical assignment of service and benefits – and thus facilitates party-based co-optation. Although such incentives would be strongest when partisan credentials are required for essentially any career, the exercise of such widespread political control would encounter significant opposition, thereby requiring a corresponding level of repression. As the example of the Communist Party of Czechoslovakia illustrates, rather than maintaining a monopoly over all types of careers, party-based co-optation may be most effective if political control over appointments is selective.

6.1.3   Selective Recruitment, Promotion, and Repression

I now turn to a closer examination of the complementarity between party-based co-optation and repression suggested by the above discussion. Co-optation must be accompanied by repression because policies that establish state control over a wide range of careers – ranging from outright expropriation of key industries to heavy regulation – encounter opposition from society. Although the discussion highlighted the benefits to partisan control over lucrative careers, a dictatorship may also benefit from being selective about the type of individuals it chooses to co-opt.

Whom should the regime co-opt and whom repress? The following analysis focuses on selective co-optation along a single dimension – the ideological affinity for the regime. To examine the relationship between ideological affinity and co-optation, suppose that, in addition to the material benefits from co-optation via the party, each citizen considers the incumbent dictator's and the challenger's ideology when deciding whether to defect to the challenger. I use the term *ideology* in a broad sense, incorporating any nonmaterial factors that may affect a citizen's preference for the incumbent dictator vis-à-vis the challenger, including religious, ethnic, and charismatic attributes of the dictator and the challenger.

Suppose that the population's *ideology* g is distributed on the real line according to the probability distribution function $F(g) = Pr(g_i < g)$, and $g_i \in \mathbb{R}$ is citizen i's ideology. To keep the exposition simple, assume that ideological concerns enter each citizen's preferences additively, in the form of a quadratic loss function $-(g_i - g_j)^2$, where $g_j \in \{g_I, g_C\}$ is the incumbent's and the challenger's ideological position, respectively. Thus when deciding between supporting the incumbent dictator and defecting to the challenger, each citizen is comparing her material and ideological payoffs under the two regimes, $u_I = \hat{b}_I - (g_i - g_I)^2$ and $u_C = \hat{b}_C - (g_i - g_C)^2$, where $\hat{b}_I$ and $\hat{b}_C$ denote the expected per-period payoff under the incumbent dictator and the challenger, respectively. When the incumbent co-opts via a regime-sanctioned party, $\hat{b}_I$ will correspond to the average per-period payoffs $(1 - \delta)u_i^J$ or $(1 - \delta)u_i^S$, depending on citizen i's party rank.

In addition to co-opting, the incumbent can also *repress*. In any period, the cost of repressing a single citizen is r. I adopt a rudimentary notion of repression: Repressing a citizen prevents her from defecting to the challenger and the cost of repression is constant in a citizen's ideology.[23]

Whom should the incumbent dictator co-opt and whom should the incumbent dictator repress? Without a loss of generality, suppose that the incumbent dictator's ideology is to the left of the challenger's ideology, $g_I < g_C$. To keep the analysis interesting, also assume that the benefit from co-optation under the incumbent $\hat{b}_I$ is large enough so the citizen whose ideological positions is identical to that of the incumbent would prefer to support the incumbent rather than defect to the challenger, $\hat{b}_I \geq \hat{b}_C - (g_i - g_C)^2$. In turn, any citizen whose ideology is to the left of the incumbent will prefer the incumbent dictator to the challenger. Thus, the dictator's decision of whom to co-opt and whom to repress amounts to finding a citizen with the threshold ideological position $g_i^* > g_I$, such that the marginal cost $\hat{b}_I$ of co-opting this citizen equals the cost r of repressing her. In other words, the threshold ideological position g_i^* solves the quadratic equation:

$$r - (g_i - g_I)^2 = \hat{b}_C - (g_i - g_C)^2.$$

Because the marginal cost of co-optation is increasing in the ideological distance from the incumbent dictator, the dictator optimally co-opts all citizens to the left of g_i^* and represses all citizens to the right of g_i^*.

A key insight that follows from this simple analysis is that the incumbent regime will co-opt those who are ideologically close to it and repress those who are more distant.[24] This result is consistent with evidence on the targets of repression as well as recruitment policies and the social structure of membership across dictatorships with single and dominant parties.[25] But note that those who are co-opted are not being "useful idiots" – party-based co-optation

---

[23] The latter reflects the idea that once an individual decides to defect to the challenger, the cost of imprisoning her does not vary with that individual's ideology. A more realistic model of an opposition resistance might assume that the cost of repression is increasing in a citizen's ideological distance from the incumbent. The argument below follows as long as the marginal cost of repression is increasing in a citizen's ideological distance from the incumbent at a lower rate that the marginal cost of co-optation.

[24] Many single and dominant parties also aim at the most productive and educated among their population (e.g., China, Singapore, and Mexico.) As argued previously, this may be because there are political benefits to the control of economically desirable appointments. However, such a co-optation strategy may also have an additional deterrent effect: Any challenger will have to convince his followers that he can deliver better results than a regime that already co-opts the most productive and educated.

[25] On repression, see Gregory (2009); on recruitment policies, see Domínguez (1978, Chap. 8), Grzymała–Busse (2002), Perthes (1995, Chap. 4), Shambaugh (2009), and Staar (1988).

exploits natural career aspirations within the general population to marginalize actual, ideological opposition.

To summarize, this chapter's theoretical argument is that three organizational features of authoritarian parties – hierarchical assignment of service and benefits, political control over appointments, and selective recruitment and repression – contribute to the survival of dictatorships. These features have been well known at the descriptive level, but the precise mechanisms by which they may account for authoritarian resilience is frequently left underspecified. A key empirical implication of this theoretical analysis is that authoritarian regimes that co-opt via a party with these organizational features – not necessarily a single one – survive under less favorable circumstances and in the face of stronger challengers than dictatorships without a party. The next section empirically assesses this prediction.

6.2 REGIME PARTIES AND AUTHORITARIAN RESILIENCE

Does the establishment and maintenance of a regime-sanctioned political party contribute to the survival of a dictatorship, as the previous theoretical analysis suggests? Existing empirical research takes two approaches to this question. The first was initiated by Geddes (1999a), who classified dictatorships into personalist, military, single-party, and their hybrids and studied the differences in the survival of these regime categories.[26] The second is exemplified by Gandhi and Przeworski (2007), who studied the association between the number of parties under dictatorship and the survival of dictators.[27]

While both approaches find that authoritarian parties are associated with the survival of regimes or leaders, they face two limitations: Because Geddes's classification of dictatorships is not based on formal and exclusively party-based institutional criteria, inferences based on these data raise questions about whether the longer survival of single-party regimes can indeed be attributed to the institution of the authoritarian party. On the other hand, studies that examine the association between the number of parties and the survival of dictators may be confounding the effect of parties with the strength of individual leaders.

Consider first the approaches based on Geddes's classification. Geddes's discussion of the rationale for her classification indicates that she devised it in order to describe the distinct patterns of leadership origin, political interests, and exercise of power across dictatorships; it is not a classification based on formal institutional characteristics.[28] As a result, some personalist and military dictatorships in fact have either multiple political parties (e.g., Brazil during the military dictatorship from 1965 to 1979) or maintain a single party (e.g., the Cameroon People's Democratic Movement under Paul Biya between 1985

---

[26] See also Brownlee (2007a, Chap. 2), Geddes (2003, Chap. 2), Hadenius and Teorell (2007), Magaloni (2008), and Smith (2005).
[27] See also Gandhi and Przeworski (2006) and Gandhi (2008).
[28] See Geddes (1999a, 17–22), Geddes (1999b, 123–5), and Geddes (2003, 69–78).

and 1990). On the other hand, some single-party regimes allow for a nontrivial participation of more than one party (e.g., PAN, and later PRD, in Mexico). That is, because Geddes's classification is based on a set of criteria that attempt to reflect the functioning of a dictatorship broadly rather than specific institutional characteristics, the distinction among the categories of personalist, military, and single-party provides only a limited measure of the restrictions on and the presence of political parties across these categories.

More importantly, if we are interested in whether political parties contribute to the survival of dictatorships, the contrast between personalist, military, and single-party dictatorships is not the conceptually appropriate one. Rather, the relevant conceptual distinction should reflect differences in the partisan organization across dictatorships. Some regimes ban political parties entirely, some sanction the existence of a single party, and others allow multiple parties to operate. Hence the proper conceptual baseline to which single-party regimes should be compared are not military or personalist dictatorships but instead those that ban parties entirely and those that allow for multiple political parties. Crucially, single-party regimes may compare differently to either of these categories than to the categories of military and personalist dictatorships. Therefore, the latter two may not be the appropriate comparison groups when we are interested in the effect of political parties on the survival of dictatorships.

Meanwhile, approaches that use the length of leader tenures to assess whether authoritarian parties contribute to authoritarian survival potentially confound the effect of parties with the strength of individual leaders. Consider, for instance, the Popular Movement of the Revolution, which was founded and maintained as the sole party in the Congo by Mobutu, between 1967 and 1997. In spite of Mobutu's long tenure in office, the Popular Movement of the Revolution did not survive his fall from power and appears to have merely been his propaganda tool, lacking any substantive institutional structure (Callaghy 1984, 10, 320). By contrast, Mexican presidents left office every six years, yet the same party ruled Mexico for more than seventy years and, according to most accounts, was a key factor behind the regime's stability (Magaloni 2006).

Hence the duration of leader tenures is an imperfect metric of the potential contribution of authoritarian parties to regime survival. First, this approach risks confounding the effect of the party with the strength of the leader, as illustrated by those cases in which the latter uses his power to establish a weak single party that collapses when the leader is removed from power or dies. Second, this approach potentially underestimates the contribution of the party to authoritarian survival when the same political coalition remains in power in spite of frequent leadership changes within the governing party, as was the case in Mexico.

I address these limitations of the existing approaches in two ways: (1) I use the survival of authoritarian ruling coalition spells as a measure of authoritarian stability and (2) direct, institutional indicators of the partisan organization of dictatorships. Recall from Chapter 2 that a ruling coalition spell consists of an

TABLE 6.2. *Restrictions on Political Parties and Survival of Authoritarian Ruling Coalitions, 1946–2008*

Restrictions on Party Organization	At the Beginning of a Ruling Coalition			At the End of a Ruling Coalition		
	Median	Mean	N	Median	Mean	N
Parties banned	9	16.56	81	3	13.85	57
	(3, 15)	(12.33, 20.78)		(2, 8)	(8.63, 19.08)	
Single party	27	29.87	51	22	25.08	49
	(20, 35)	(24.51, 34.24)		(15, 30)	(20.00, 30.17)	
Multiple parties	8	15.91	195	10	17.90	223
	(7, 10)	(13.10, 18.53)		(8, 13)	(15.26, 20.54)	

Note: The unit of observation is an authoritarian ruling coalition; 95% confidence intervals are in parentheses. Longest ruling coalition durations are right-censored; means are therefore underestimated.

uninterrupted succession in office of politically affiliated authoritarian leaders. It therefore provides a more appropriate measure of authoritarian stability than either the length of individual dictators' tenures or the survival of dictatorship as a regime type.

To study the effect of authoritarian parties on the survival of authoritarian ruling coalitions, I directly measure two features of the partisan organization of dictatorships: *restrictions on political parties* and maintenance of a *regime party*. I outlined my measurement of restrictions on political parties in detail in Chapter 2, where I distinguished among authoritarian regimes that *ban political parties*, sanction the existence of only a *single* party, or allow *multiple* parties to operate.

In addition to restrictions on political parties, I record whether a dictatorship maintained a regime party. We may say that a dictatorship has a *regime party* when the head of the executive is a member of a party or endorses a particular political party (or a party front). This was trivially the case in single-party regimes. However, dictatorships that allowed for multiple parties did not have a regime party in about one-fourth of the country-years in the data. Many of these cases are military dictatorships and monarchies that do not ban all parties but at the same time do not openly endorse a particular party, as has been the case in Morocco since its independence.

Do parties contribute to the survival of authoritarian ruling coalitions? Table 6.2 presents the estimated mean and median survival times of ruling coalitions by the type of restriction on political parties. The 95 percent confidence is listed interval below each estimated quantity.[29] Because restrictions on political parties may vary throughout the duration of a ruling coalition,

---

[29] These confidence intervals are calculated using the Kaplan–Meier estimator, which accounts for the presence of right-censored data in the sample; see Klein and Moeschberger (2003, Chap. 4).

TABLE 6.3. *Do Survival Functions of Authoritarian Ruling Coalitions Differ Depending on Their Restrictions on Political Parties?*

Restrictions on Party Organization	At the Beginning of a Ruling Coalition		At the End of a Ruling Coalition	
	Log-rank	Wilcoxon	Log-rank	Wilcoxon
Single party vs. parties banned	11.77***	19.56***	7.78***	20.28***
Single party vs. multiple parties	16.83***	25.64***	4.94**	11.53***
Multiple parties vs. parties banned	0.01	0.47	4.36**	14.43***

Note: The unit of observation is an authoritarian ruling coalition. Significance levels *10%, **5%, ***1% are for the χ_1^2 statistic.

I present estimates based on the type of restrictions on political parties in place both at the beginning and at the end of a ruling coalition's existence.[30]

Table 6.2 indicates that ruling coalitions with single parties indeed survive from two to three times longer than either those without parties or those ruling coalitions that allow for the existence of multiple parties. We see that this difference is statistically significant as there is almost no overlap between the 95 percent confidence intervals for the mean or the median of ruling coalitions with single parties and those of the other two categories. However, there is substantial overlap between the confidence intervals for either the mean or the median of ruling coalitions without parties and those with multiple parties. Hence, only single parties appear to contribute to the survival of authoritarian ruling coalitions; ruling coalitions that allow for the existence of multiple parties have a much shorter lifespan and do not differ significantly from ruling coalitions that ban parties.

This conclusion is partially corroborated by tests for the overall equality of survivor functions. Table 6.3 reports the χ^2 statistics based on the log-rank and Wilcoxon tests, which compare overall survivor functions – rather than particular summary statistics – across the three forms of restrictions on political parties in dictatorships. Both tests indicate that the survival dynamics of ruling coalitions in dictatorships with single parties differs significantly from the remaining two categories. However, the tests do not lead to an unambiguous conclusion about the differences in the survival dynamics of ruling coalitions without parties and those with multiple parties; the two categories differ significantly when we compare restrictions on political parties at the end of a ruling coalition's tenure but not at the beginning.

Do regime parties in dictatorships that allow for multiple parties contribute to their survival at all? If – as this analysis indicates – single parties significantly

---

[30] We may directly account for the variation in restrictions on political parties by including this information as a covariate in a survival model. Estimates based on both the Cox proportional hazard model and parametric accelerated failure-time models lead to conclusions identical to those discussed here.

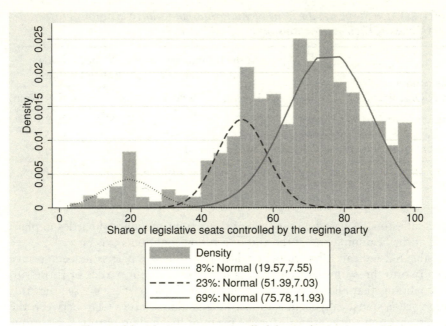

FIGURE 6.1. Share of legislative seats controlled by authoritarian regime parties in dictatorships with multiple parties, 1946–2008.

contribute to the survival of authoritarian ruling coalitions, then we may wonder whether, even in those dictatorships that allow for multiple parties, strong parties still contribute to regime survival, even if they do not control all legislative seats. To investigate this hypothesis, we need to differentiate among authoritarian regime parties based on their legislative strength. The histogram in Figure 6.1 summarizes the distribution of the share of legislative seats controlled by authoritarian regime parties across all dictatorships with multiple parties.

A notable feature of the distribution in Figure 6.1 is that it appears to contain three qualitatively distinct groups of observations. From left to right, there first appears to be a small subset of regime parties that control only a minority of legislative seats; next there is a larger group of parties that, on average, control a bare majority of legislative seats; and, finally, there is a large group of regime parties that command a supermajority of legislative seats.

To better understand and quantify the differences among these three groups, I fit to these data a mixture of three Normal densities.[31] As Table 6.4 summarizes and the density plots in Figure 6.1 illustrate, the three groups are reasonably well represented by Normal densities with mean seat shares of

---

[31] Because the share of legislative seats is bounded between 0 and 1, the Normal distribution is not the most appropriate probability model for this setting; I adopt it primarily because its parameters are easily interpreted. On the estimation of finite-mixture models, see McLachlan and Peel (2000).

TABLE 6.4. *Three Subgroups of Authoritarian Regime Parties by Legislative Seat Share*

Subgroup	Fraction	Legislative Seat Share		
		Mean	Variance	95% Confidence Intervals
Dominant/hegemonic parties	69.35%	75.78	11.93	(73.41, 78.15)
Parties under competitive authoritarianism	22.88%	51.39	7.04	(48.90, 53.88)
Transitional cases	7.78%	19.57	7.55	(17.21, 21.94)

Note: The unit of observation is a country-year. Maximum-likelihood estimates are of a three-component mixture of Normal densities.

19.57, 51.39, and 75.78. The estimates in Table 6.4 also indicate that the three groups are distinct: The 95 percent confidence intervals for the three means do not overlap.

The largest of these subgroups contains roughly 69 percent of all observations and describes parties that, on average, control about three-fourths of all legislative seats. Two examples of well-known observations in this subgroup are the PRI in Mexico during the period 1946–1987 and Golkar in Indonesia under Suharto (1971–1998). The observations in this subgroup thus correspond to a conceptual category that has been alternately referred to as dominant parties (Greene 2007; Magaloni and Kricheli 2010; Reuter and Gandhi 2010) or hegemonic parties (Magaloni 2006; Blaydes 2010).

The second largest of these three groups has a mean legislative seat share of 51.39 percent and accounts for roughly one-fifth of all observations. In this group, the regime party has close to a bare majority or minority in the legislature. One prominent observation in this subgroup is the Kenya African National Union (KANU) after Daniel Arap Moi restored multiparty elections in 1992; KANU controlled 53 and 51 percent of legislative seats in the two terms between 1992 and 2002. Another example is the PRI, which controlled only 52 and 48 percent of legislative seats in the Mexican Chamber of Deputies for parts of Carlos Salinas's and Ernesto Zedillo's presidencies.[32] As these cases illustrate, significant legislative opposition exists in this subgroup of regimes, even if it is divided. Hence the political setting under which regime parties in this subgroup operate may be conceptually characterized as "electoral authoritarianism" (Schedler 2006) or "competitive authoritarianism" (Levitsky and Way 2002).

The last of these three groups may seem somewhat perplexing: With the mean legislative seat share of only 19.57 percent, the authoritarian leader's party is hardly in charge of the legislature. However, once we examine the observations corresponding to this group, we see that they primarily reflect temporary transitional scenarios, in which either a democracy has recently

---

[32] These are the legislative terms of 1988–1990 and 1998–2000, respectively.

TABLE 6.5. *Effect of a Regime Party's Legislative Seat Share on Survival of Authoritarian Ruling Coalitions*

	(1)	(2)	(3)
Legislative seat share	0.982***	0.983***	0.976***
	(0.005)	(0.005)	(0.009)
Log of GDP per capita		0.975	1.367
		(0.153)	(0.453)
GDP growth		0.983	0.953
		(0.015)	(0.031)
Fuel exports (% of total exports)			0.977**
			(0.011)
Ore exports (% of total exports)			1.010
			(0.010)
Civilian (vs. military)			0.823
			(0.319)
Cold War			1.382
			(0.591)
Democratic neighbors			1.301
			(0.861)
Log-likelihood	−377.402	−299.732	−101.849
Ruling coalitions	126	108	65
Country-years	1,224	1,035	534

Note: In a Cox survival model, coefficients are expressed as hazard ratios. Breslow method is used for ties. Significance levels *10%, **5%, ***1%. Robust standard errors are in parentheses.

transitioned to dictatorship or a dictatorship is about to democratize. Alberto Fujimori is an example of the former: Before he subverted democracy in Peru, he established Cambio 90, a party whose primary purpose was to promote his presidential candidacy in 1990. Although it strengthened its standing in the legislature in 1992 and 1995, Cambio 90 initially won only 17 percent of the seats (see, e.g., Klaren 1999). Empirically, these temporary transitional scenarios are rare and account for only 8 percent of all observations.

Does the legislative strength of regime parties in dictatorships that allow for multiple parties parallel the contribution of single parties to the survival of authoritarian ruling coalitions? Table 6.5 presents an estimate of the association between a regime party's legislative seat share and the survival of authoritarian ruling coalitions based on the Cox survival model. The estimated coefficients are presented in the form of a hazard ratio: A coefficient smaller than 1 implies that the associated covariate reduces the relative risk that an authoritarian ruling coalition loses power.

Model 1 preserves the largest number of observations; Models 2 and 3 control for economic and institutional covariates typically employed in the research on authoritarian survival. The covariate data on GDP per capita and GDP growth are from Maddison (2008), the data on fuel and ore exports

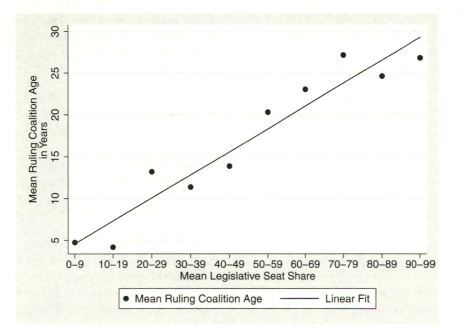

FIGURE 6.2. Association between legislative seat share and age of authoritarian ruling coalitions, 1946–2008.

are from World Bank (2008), and the data on democratic neighbors were constructed by combining the contiguity data from the Correlates of War Project (2006) and the regime data described in Chapter 2.

We see that there is a strong association between legislative seat share and the survival of authoritarian ruling coalitions: Each percentage-point increase in the regime party's seat share lowers the risk of a ruling coalition's demise by about 2 percent. For instance, an increase in a regime party's legislative seat share from 55 to 75 percent corresponds to a 30 percent reduction in the annual risk of a ruling coalition's demise. This association survives even after controlling for economic and institutional covariates typically used in the research on authoritarian survival. The only other covariate that is significantly associated with the survival of authoritarian ruling coalitions is the percentage of fuel exports. In fact, each point increase in fuel exports as a percentage of a dictatorship's total exports has roughly the same effect on regime survival as does a corresponding increase in the regime party's legislative seat shares.

To illustrate this association, Figure 6.2 plots the mean age of authoritarian ruling coalitions against the mean share of legislative seats that the coalition's regime party controlled. To simplify the presentation, the latter quantity is grouped into ten equally spaced intervals. We see that dictatorships with regime parties that control a supermajority of legislative seats survive, on average, almost as long as those with single parties.

To summarize, the findings of this empirical analysis are consistent with the implications of the theoretical analysis in Section 6.1. We see that the empirical association between dictatorships with single parties and the survival of the regimes that maintain them is robust. I attempted a stronger test of this association than has been carried out in existing research. Specifically, I avoid confounding the effect of parties with the strength of individual leaders by measuring the survival of authoritarian ruling coalitions rather than individual leaders and I use direct, institutional indicators of the partisan organization of dictatorships.

We also arrive at several new insights into the relationship between authoritarian regime parties and the survival of dictatorships. What appears to be key to the survival of authoritarian ruling coalitions is the presence of a strong party, not necessarily a single one. Once we control for the regime party's legislative strength in dictatorships with multiple parties, we see that ruling coalitions with parties that control a supermajority of seats in the legislature survive, on average, about as long as ruling coalitions with single parties. Consistent with the theoretical analysis in this chapter, this finding suggests that – to better understand the institutional origins of this resilience – we should focus on those institutional features of regime parties that are common to both single and hegemonic or dominant parties, as I attempt in the theoretical part of this chapter.

Finally, this chapter's analysis of the data on the legislative seat share of authoritarian regime parties shows that these parties come in three distinct forms: hegemonic or dominant parties, parties under competitive authoritarianism, and parties in transitioning regimes. Since the first two groups account for more than 90 percent of all observations, the present analysis suggests that regime parties in multiple-party dictatorships effectively take one of these two forms. Importantly, the same party may take each of these forms, depending on the regime's evolving strength, as the example of the PRI illustrates. When I empirically identify these categories of authoritarian regime parties, I do not rely on a predefined criterion on their legislative strength or durability, as is common in the extant literature. Especially the latter criterion precludes the valid use of such data in the study of authoritarian durability since survival in power past a fixed time threshold is assumed in the definition of a dominant or hegemonic party.[33] By contrast, I infer the presence of these categories directly from the empirical distribution of their legislative seat share.

6.3   CONCLUSION: WHY AUTHORITARIAN REGIME PARTIES?

This chapter examines the internal make-up of regime-sanctioned authoritarian parties and identifies the organizational features by which parties

---

[33] For instance, Magaloni (2006, 36–7) and Greene (2007, 12) ask that a dominant party controls the executive and the legislature for at least twenty years; Geddes (1999b, 125) calls an authoritarian regime single-party if the "dominant party has never lost control of the executive since coming to power and usually wins more than two thirds of the seats in the legislature."

contribute to authoritarian resilience. While extant literature frequently concludes that single- and dominant-party dictatorships co-opt opposition and
maintain elite cohesion, the precise mechanism by which the *institution* of the
party accounts for these functions frequently remains elusive. Geddes (1999b,
135), for instance, influentially observed that single-party regimes survive
longer than personalist and military dictatorships "because their institutional
structures make it relatively easy for them to allow greater participation and
popular influence on policy without giving up their dominant role in the political system." In this chapter, I attempt to advance this research by identifying
the specific institutional structures and the underlying political mechanisms by
which the institution of the single or dominant party accounts for Geddes's
observation.

Three organizational features of authoritarian parties – hierarchical assignment of service and benefits, political control over appointments, and selective
recruitment and repression – take advantage of natural career aspirations to
create an enduring stake in the regime's survival among the most productive
and ideologically agreeable segments of the population. This analysis highlights the need to analytically distinguish between co-optation via policies or
transfers and co-optation via the institution of the party. The advantages and
operation of the latter are intimately linked to specific organizational features
of authoritarian parties.

I further suggest that we may differentiate between two distinct political
functions that these three institutional features of authoritarian parties enable:
direct political control and party-based co-optation. Direct political control
refers to the immediate outcomes of party members' service. It may range from
intelligence gathering, maintenance of social stability, and monitoring of political discipline in single-party regimes to electoral mobilization, intimidation,
fraud, and campaigning in dictatorships with dominant and hegemonic parties.
These activities contribute to authoritarian survival directly and primarily aim
outward at nonparty members in state institutions and the general population.
As Saddam Hussein boasted in 1971, commenting of the three-year process
of establishing the Baath Party's control over all major organized sectors of
the Iraqi state and society, "with our party methods, there is no chance for
anyone who disagrees with us to jump on a couple of tanks and overthrow the
government."[34]

On the other hand, party-based co-optation is directed mainly inward,
at existing or prospective party members. Party-based co-optation strives to
exploit party members' career aspirations to create among them a stake in the
perpetuation of the regime. Extant research often characterizes authoritarian
co-optation as the exchange of political support for the regime in return for
material benefits.[35] The arguments in this section highlight that the analogy

---

[34] Cited in Karsh (2002, 49–50); originally from "The Terror from Takrit," *The Guardian*, 26
November 1971.

[35] See, e.g., Gandhi and Przeworski (2006, 25).

of "political exchange" is only partially valid and inadequate if we want to explain why co-optation takes place within the organizational framework of an authoritarian party. A contrast of co-optation via transfers and partisan co-optation suggests that the latter is better thought of as a "sunk investment" on the part of party members. The implications of the present analysis are therefore closer to Magaloni (2008, 717), who argues that dominant parties encourage elites to "invest in the existing institutions rather than in subversive coalitions." In a similar spirit, I attempt to identify the specific organizational features of authoritarian parties that encourage such investment and emphasize that one of their political functions is to ensure that such investment becomes sunk, making it nontransferable across political coalitions, thereby giving party members a vested interest in the perpetuation of the incumbent regime.

Parallelling the conceptual arguments in Chapter 4, these models help us understand not only the potential of party-based co-optation but also its limits. We saw that co-optation via the institution of the party must be initiated by a signal of the regime's strength; it requires the maintenance of a politically sensitive balance among recruitment, promotion, and retirement policies within the party; and contributes to the regime's resilience to challengers from the outside but not from the inside.

Nonetheless, the theoretical analysis in this chapter has focused primarily on the first of the three questions asked at the outset: How and which organizational features of authoritarian parties contribute to authoritarian resilience? An explicit focus on both the potential of but also the limits to party-based co-optation allows us to address the two remaining, affiliated questions.

Why cannot dictators obtain the political benefits of party-based co-optation and control without the actual institution of the party? According to the arguments outlined in this chapter, the institution of the party provides the organizational skeleton through which the regime jointly manages the hierarchical assignment of service and benefits, and selective recruitment and repression, and maintains political control over appointments. The primary role of the latter two organizational features is to enhance the effectiveness with which hierarchical assignment of service and benefits generates incentives for party members to remain loyal and provide costly political service. Although the three organizational features, in principle, could be administered in isolation, within separate institutions, their complementarity creates benefits to their coordination and management within a single institution – that is, the regime party.

Why do not all dictatorships establish and maintain a regime-sanctioned party? By examining the political logic that underlies the functioning of authoritarian parties, we also gain insight into the limits of party-based co-optation and control. The analysis in this chapter implies that the effective operation of the three organizational features requires that the regime provide partisan access to numerous political, economic, and social appointments and thus channel significant resources through the party. We therefore may expect that dictatorships whose support base is limited to traditional elites – landed aristocracy or the owners of capital – will not be willing to give up the resources necessary for the party to effectively perform its co-optation and control functions. These regimes will find co-optation and control via parties less advantageous than the alternatives of repression and co-optation via direct transfers. The analysis in this chapter thus helps us understand why dictatorships in particular structural conditions do not establish regime-sanctioned parties or maintain parties without the organizational features examined here, which in turn remain politically inconsequential.

7

Conclusion

Incentives and Institutions in Authoritarian Politics

All absolute governments must very much depend on the administration; and this is one of the great inconveniences of that form of government.

David Hume, *That Politics May Be Reduced to a Science*

Mexicans avoid personal dictatorship by retiring their dictators every six years.

Brandenburg, *The Making of Modern Mexico* (1964, 141)

The army, the people, one hand!

A chant on Cairo's Tahrir Square during the Arab Spring[1]

If we were to ask a political scientist, "What drives politics in democracies?," the most likely consensual answer would be "The goal of winning elections." In democracies, candidates' platforms, government policies, party organization, and the composition of governing coalitions all reflect the decisive role that elections play in allocating political power.

In this book, I answer an analogous, fundamental question about authoritarian regimes: "What drives politics in dictatorships?" I argue that all dictatorships must respond to the political imperatives of two overriding political conflicts: the problems of authoritarian power-sharing and control. But whether and how dictators resolve them is shaped by the distinctively dismal environment in which authoritarian politics takes place: Dictatorships inherently lack an independent authority with the power to enforce agreements among key political actors, and violence is never off the table. The two substantive political conflicts along with the two environmental constraints offer a general analytical heuristic for thinking about authoritarian politics.

Here, I highlight several implications of my arguments for three prominent policy questions. First, I explain why so many dictators preside over policy disasters. I next clarify why so few dictatorships depersonalize political authority,

---

[1] See "Mubarak's Backers Storm Protesters as U.S. Condemns Egypt's Violent Turn," *The New York Times*, 3 February 2011.

solve succession crises, and maintain viable institutions of collective leadership. I conclude with a discussion of why the Middle East's authoritarian past casts a long shadow over its prospects for democracy after the popular uprisings of 2011, now commonly known as the Arab Spring.

7.1 WHY DICTATORS PRESIDE OVER POLICY DISASTERS

In 1966, Nicolae Ceaușescu decided that the best way to increase Romania's national wealth was by expanding the size of its labor force. Ceaușescu banned contraception and abortion, restricted divorce, imposed taxes on childless couples, and instituted government honors for mothers of more than five children. The result was a debacle and the opposite of what the dictator had intended: A short-lived increase in the birth rate was followed by years of increasing poverty rates and a crisis of the welfare system.[2]

The arguments developed in Chapter 3 offer a framework for thinking about the origins of such policy disasters in dictatorships. Recall that the two power-sharing regimes of contested and established autocracy entail sharply different constraints on the dictator by the rest of the authoritarian elite. Under contested autocracy, the dictator's allies can credibly threaten him with removal; under established autocracy, dictator has effectively monopolized power. In this sense, contested autocrats are responsive, if not accountable, to at least their inner circle. By contrast, established autocrats face no checks, in terms of both their drive for more power and their capacity to unilaterally set policies.

Dictatorships are naturally thought of as being less accountable than democracies.[3] Because the population has only limited means of punishing a leader's poor performance, dictators are expected to adopt policies that favor the few in power at the expense of the many excluded from power.[4] However, the virtual absence of political constraints on established dictators goes further than that. It explains why established autocracies adopt disastrous policies that clearly serve no one's interest: Under an established autocracy, even the dictator's inner circle entirely lacks the capacity to oppose the dictator's misguided policies or utopian experiments. As David Hume observed, "all absolute governments must very much depend on the administration, and this is one of the great inconveniences of that form of government."[5]

This logic helps us understand the calamitous policies adopted by some iconic established dictators: Joseph Stalin's strategic blunders during World War II, especially his obdurate refusal to believe that the Soviet Union had

---

[2] On Ceaușescu's demographic policies, see Kligman (1998).

[3] Dictatorship has not always been the inferior political system that it is considered today. Most classical political thinkers associated democracy with instability and mob rule; see, for example, Hanson (1989).

[4] On authoritarian accountability and economic policy in dictatorships, see also Acemoglu et al. (2003), Besley and Kudamatsu (2007), Cox (2011), Guriev and Sonin (2009), Haber et al. (2003), Haber (2007), and Malesky and Schuler (2010).

[5] "That politics may be reduced to a science" in Hume (1748).

been attacked by Germany in the summer of 1941; Saddam Hussein's successive rejections of diplomatic attempts to resolve the crisis preceding the Gulf War of 1990–1991; and Mao's attempt to lift rural China out of backwardness by shifting from agriculture to backyard iron foundries during the Great Leap Forward.[6] Under established autocracy, no one dares to point out that the emperor has no clothes.

7.2 WHY SO FEW DICTATORSHIPS SOLVE SUCCESSION CRISES AND DEPERSONALIZE POLITICAL AUTHORITY

The gradual adoption of term limits and mandatory retirement-age provisions in China, discussed in Chapter 4, exemplifies how institutions alleviate commitment and monitoring problems in authoritarian power-sharing. As argued in Chapter 3, time in office alone provides authoritarian leaders with not only the temptation to consolidate power but also the opportunity to conceal it. A term limit on a leader's tenure therefore amounts to a line in the sand: Compliance is easily and publicly observable. Term limits thus both embody a compromise about the limited authority of any single leader and provide an unambiguous signal of commitment to such a constraint.

Such formal, temporal limits on a dictator's tenure further illuminate how dictatorships may overcome a perennial source of authoritarian instability – leadership succession – and why so few are able to accomplish it.[7] Term limits do not merely place a sharp limit on a leader's political trajectory. A new leadership implies the departure of an entire generation of officials. Thus once in place, term limits coordinate the political horizons of multiple generations of authoritarian elites: They encourage ambitious political clients to invest their career in their own generation of leaders rather than the current political leadership. A dictator who is intent on overstaying an established term limit thus anticipates opposition from not only his heir apparent but also from the multitude of clients who have invested their career in patrons belonging to a different generation of leadership. It is this intertemporal coordination of political loyalties that allowed PRI–era Mexicans to retire their dictators every six years, as Brandenburg (1964, 141) eloquently put it, and have facilitated leadership succession in post–Deng Xiaoping China.

Yet however beneficial term limits may be for any dictatorship, they do not eliminate the two aspects of authoritarian politics that account for its gruesome character: the lack of an independent authority that would enforce mutual agreements and the ever-possible recourse to violence. Term limits only alleviate the monitoring problems that arise from these circumstances. The dictator's commitment to formal, institutional constraints on his power – such

---

[6] For the history and analysis of these cases, see Bialer (1969), Atkinson (1993), and Dikötter (2010), respectively.

[7] On the problem of succession, see, e.g., Herz (1952), Jackson and Rosberg (1982, 67–73), and Tullock (1987, 82–106). On hereditary succession in dictatorships, see Brownlee (2007b).

as term limits – ultimately rests on his allies' ability to punish him for their violation.

This contingency of formal institutions on the credibility of nonformal, violent threats helps us understand why only few dictatorships adopt effectively constraining term limits, as in PRI–era Mexico, post–Deng China, and the Brazilian military junta of 1964–1985, and why so many more have them on paper but find blatant ways to circumvent them, as Rafael Trujillo did when he appointed his brother to the presidency of the Dominican Republic and as Vladimir Putin does when he moves between the posts of Russian president and prime minister.

The key role played by the credibility of the allies' threat to replace the dictator also accounts for why political authority formally vested in authoritarian leadership posts can only rarely be separated from the person holding the post, even if term limits or mandatory retirement-age provisions encourage such separation.[8] Depersonalization of authority succeeds only when a significant fraction of the authoritarian elite find the threat to replace the dictator credible and therefore automatically shift their loyalty to the new leadership once a leader steps down. This is why in China, Mao and Deng continued to wield enormous influence even after they stepped down from their official posts (Li 2010, 184) but also why Jiang Zemin's clout eroded rapidly after he stepped down (Huang 2008, 81).

Depersonalization of political authority has an additional benefit: Once it is in place, those who step down no longer have to fear annihilation because they no longer wield the power to hurt their successors.[9] Thus Lázaro Cárdenas may have been thinking about his own retirement when he ordered one of his predecessors and the last Mexican caudillo Plutarco Elías Calles into exile instead of killing him.

7.3 A DEMOCRATIC FUTURE FOR THE ARAB SPRING?

The popular uprisings of 2011, now commonly known as the Arab Spring, brought down some of the most entrenched and repressive authoritarian regimes in the Middle East. A key actor in the uprisings were those regimes' own militaries. In Tunisia and Egypt, their refusal to quell the uprisings quickly sealed their leader's fate; in Libya and Syria, their initial loyalty to the leadership resulted in protracted, violent confrontations between the rebels and the regimes; and in Bahrain, 1,200 troops from neighboring Saudi Arabia saved a crumbling monarchy.

Why did soldiers stick with some dictators and break with others? My arguments in Chapter 5 suggest that the political position that militaries take during mass, prodemocratic uprisings is critically shaped by their role in authoritarian

---

[8] On the role of focal coordination in bestowing political authority, see also Myerson (2004).
[9] See Debs (2009) and Egorov and Sonin (2005) on the role of expectations about the elimination of departing leadership in succession struggles.

repression. Although everyday repression in Middle Eastern dictatorships – as in most dictatorships – has been handled not by soldiers but instead by the police and specialized internal-security agencies, these repressive agents simply do not have enough personnel, equipment, or training to suppress an uprising of several tens of thousands of protesters. During the Arab Spring, therefore, soldiers were the Middle Eastern dictators' repressive agent of last resort.

Chapter 5 explains why dictators are wary about relying on their military for repression. They understand that involving their military in the repression of internal opposition entails a fundamental moral hazard: The very resources and privileges that enable soldiers to suppress the regime's opposition also empower them to act against the regime itself.

The ousted Tunisian President Zine El Abidine Ben Ali, therefore, deliberately kept the Tunisian military small and underequipped, fearing that it might turn against him (Nelson 1986, Chap. 5). In Egypt and Syria, by contrast, Hosni Mubarak and Bashar al-Asad inherited politically entrenched militaries from their predecessors. The Egyptian military has been the repressive pillar of the regime since the Free Officers brought down the monarchy in 1952 (Waterbury 1983, Chap. 14), and the military's role in repression was formalized by an Emergency Law that has been in effect with minor suspensions since 1967 (Cook 2007, 26–7). Meanwhile, the Syrian military came to dominate internal politics after a 1970 intraparty coup d'état that pitted the military wing of the Baath Party against the civilian wing. After the then-Minister of Defense Hafez al-Asad prevailed, he purged the defeated faction and jailed its leaders for life.[10] This is precisely the kind of praetorianism that most dictators fear.

As outlined in Chapter 5, three regimes of interaction between dictators and their military emerge as the military's political indispensability grows. I call the first perfect political control: It obtains when dictators either do not need to use their military for internal repression or when they are consciously accepting some vulnerability to threats from the masses in exchange for maintaining political control over their military. This is a trade-off that Tunisian presidents Bourguiba and Ben Ali appear to have found acceptable. At the other extreme, when dictators face mass threats of unusual magnitude, they have no choice but to endow their military with expansive resources and concede to any of the military's institutional or policy demands – they are effectively under military tutelage. And when mass threats to the regime or the military's inherited capacity to intervene are between these extremes, genuine bargaining over the military's institutional privileges and the government's policies takes place. Because this bargaining entails the conscious manipulation of the risk of an actual military intervention, I call it brinkmanship bargaining.

These findings suggest that differences in dictators' reliance on their military for repression have far-reaching consequences for the political role that militaries take during prodemocracy uprisings and in the politics of democracies

---

[10] Van Dam (1979, Chap. 5); see also Seale (1990) and Zisser (2001).

that may emerge from them. When their position under dictatorship approximates the theoretical case of perfect political control, militaries do not have the material capacity, legal immunities, or vested political interest in taking an active role during prodemocratic uprisings. Hence it may not be surprising that after seeing the magnitude of the protests, the Tunisian Army Chief of Staff General Rachid Ammar defied Ben Ali's orders to assist the overwhelmed police and internal-security services, thereby sealing his fate.[11]

By contrast, politically pivotal militaries have a vested institutional interest in picking the right side during a prodemocracy uprising. If they side with the regime, they certainly will preserve or even expand their privileges, but they also risk losing everything if the uprising succeeds. The incentives to stay with the regime may be compounded by the institutional measures that dictators take in order to overcome the moral hazard in authoritarian repression. These measures frequently exploit sectarian and ethnic loyalties: In Baathist Iraq, internal-security services were overwhelmingly staffed by individuals from Tikrit (Karsh 2002) – Saddam Hussein's (as well as his predecessor, Ahmed Hassan al-Bakr's) place of origin; in Jordan, Transjordanians (as opposed to Palestinians) receive preferential treatment in military recruitment (Brooks 1998, 49); and in Libya, Muammar Qaddafi appointed his family and tribal relatives to the most sensitive security posts (Martínez 2007, 94).

In Syria, Alawis – a minority Shia sect to which the al-Asads belong – have been favored in key security positions as well as the bureaucracy and the governing Baath Party since Hafez al-Asad's ascent to the presidency in 1971 (Van Dam 1979, Chap. 9). Because differences between the regime and the rest of the country have been drawn along these sectarian lines for decades, the officers within the Syrian military may fear that if the regime falls, all Alawis will fall with it. They therefore have an incentive to fight "tooth and nail" for the regime's survival.

If, on the other hand, authoritarian militaries side with the masses, they may preserve their privileges in the short run but risk losing them over time as the need for their services in the fight against internal opposition naturally declines under democracy. This seems to be the calculated risk taken by the Egyptian military. During the negotiations over Egypt's future constitution, the Supreme Council of the Armed Forces – Egypt's interim governing military body – proposed a set of drafting principles according to which the Council alone handles "all the affairs of the armed forces," including its budget; approves "any legislation relating to the armed forces"; and protects the country's "constitutional legitimacy."[12] The Egyptian military hopes to entice the prodemocratic, liberal Egyptian elite into a Faustian deal similar to the one it used to offer to their authoritarian predecessors: We will protect your vision of democracy against

---

[11] See, e.g., "Tunisia's Upheaval: No One Is Really in Charge," *The Economist*, 27 January 2011.

[12] Constitutional principles according to the text issued by the SCAF–appointed Deputy Prime Minister Ali al-Selmi on November 1, 2011.

mass threats from the country's poor, Islamist majority in exchange for the perpetuation of our political privileges and institutional autonomy.[13]

Hence any future potentially democratic Egyptian leadership will govern in the shadow of the country's military-dominated authoritarian past. However, unlike dictators, most elected governments can take advantage of their popular support to discourage their military from intervening. In Egypt, therefore, future elected governments may face even more pronounced incentives to engage in brinkmanship with their military than most dictators – they will want to exploit their popular support to assert their democratic authority. Egypt's post–Arab Spring politics therefore may be overshadowed by the specter of a looming military intervention.[14] The moral hazard in authoritarian repression examined in Chapter 5 thus helps us understand not only the repressive choices but also the resulting vulnerabilities of dictatorships. It also sheds light on the fate of prodemocratic uprisings and the challenges to democracies that emerge from them. A country's authoritarian past thus casts a long shadow over its democratic future.

---

[13] "Egypt's Military Expands Power, Raising Alarms," *The New York Times*, 15 October 2011.
[14] These implications are also consistent with large-N studies of democratic survival. Cheibub (2007), in the most comprehensive examination to date, finds that the reason why presidential democracies frequently revert to authoritarianism is not in the deficiencies of presidentialism but rather because they overwhelmingly used to be governed by the military before their transition to democracy.

Bibliography

Cited Works

Abrami, Regina, Edmund Malesky, and Yu Zheng. 2008. "Accountability and Inequality in Single-Party Regimes: A Comparative Analysis of Vietnam and China." Working Paper.

Acemoglu, Daron, and James A. Robinson. 2001. "A Theory of Political Transitions." *American Economic Review* 91(4): 938–63.

Acemoglu, Daron, James A. Robinson, and Thierry Verdier. 2003. "Kleptocracy and Divide-and-Rule: A Model of Personal Rule." NBER Working Paper.

Acemoglu, Daron, and James A. Robinson. 2005. *Economic Origins of Dictatorship and Democracy*. New York: Cambridge University Press.

Acemoglu, Daron, Georgy Egorov, and Konstantin Sonin. 2008a. "Coalition Formation in Non-Democracies." *Review of Economic Studies* 75(4): 987–1009.

Acemoglu, Daron, Davide Ticchi, and Andrea Vindigni. 2008b. "A Theory of Military Dictatorships." Working Paper.

Albertus, Michael, and Victor A. Menaldo. Forthcoming. "If You're Against Them You're with Us: The Effect of Expropriation on Autocratic Survival." *Comparative Political Studies*.

Aldrich, John H. 1995. *Why Parties? The Origin and Transformation of Party Politics in America*. Chicago, IL: University of Chicago Press.

Ali Khan, M. S., A. Khalique, and A. M. Abouammoh. 1989. "On Estimating Parameters in a Discrete Weibull Distribution." *IEEE Transactions on Reliability* 38(3): 348–50.

Alvarez, Michael, José Antonio Cheibub, Fernando Limongi, and Adam Przeworski. 1996. "Classifying Political Regimes." *Studies in Comparative International Development* 31(2): 3–36.

Arendt, Hannah. 1951. *The Origins of Totalitarianism*. New York: Harvest Books.

Aristotle. 1988. *The Politics*. Cambridge: Cambridge University Press.

Arriagada, Genaro. 1988. *Pinochet: The Politics of Power*. Boston, MA: Allen & Unwin.

Atkinson, Rick. 1993. *Crusade: The Untold Story of the Persian Gulf War*. Boston, MA: Houghton Mifflin.

Aumann, Robert J. 1985. "What Is Game Theory Trying to Accomplish?" In Kenneth J. Arrow and Seppo Honkapohja (Eds.), *Frontiers of Economics*. London: Basil Blackwell, pp. 27–76.

Babones, Salvatore J. 2008. "Standardized Income Inequality Data for Use in Cross-National Research." *Sociological Inquiry* 77(1): 3–22.

Banks, Arthur S. 2001. "Cross National Time-Series Data Archive." Dataset.

Barros, Robert. 2002. *Constitutionalism and Dictatorship: Pinochet, the Junta, and the 1980 Constitution*. New York: Cambridge University Press.

Batatu, Hanna. 1978. *The Old Social Classes and the Revolutionary Movements in Iraq*. Princeton, NJ: Princeton University Press.

Batatu, Hanna. 1981. "Some Observations on the Social Roots of Syria's Ruling, Military Group and the Causes for Its Dominance." *Middle East Journal* 35(3): 331–44.

Bates, Robert H. 2008. *When Things Fell Apart: State Failure in Late-Century Africa*. New York: Cambridge University Press.

Bates, Robert H., Avner Greif, Margaret Levi, and Jean-Laurent Rosenthal. 1998. *Analytic Narratives*. Princeton, NJ: Princeton University Press.

Baum, Richard. 1997. "The Road to Tiananmen: Chinese Politics in the 1980s." In Roderick MacFarquhar (Ed.), *The Politics of China: The Eras of Mao and Deng*. New York: Cambridge University Press, pp. 340–71.

Beck, Nathaniel, and Jonathan N. Katz. 2001. "Throwing out the Baby with the Bath Water: A Comment on Green, Kim, and Yoon." *International Organization* 55(2): 487–95.

Beck, Thorsten, George Clarke, Alberto Groff, Philip Keefer, and Patrick Walsh. 2001. "New Tools in Comparative Political Economy: The Database of Political Institutions." *World Bank Economic Review* 15(1): 165–76.

Belkin, Aaron, and Evan Schofer. 2003. "Toward a Structural Understanding of Coup Risk." *Journal of Conflict Resolution* 47(5): 594–620.

Benvenuti, Francesco. 1988. *The Bolsheviks and the Red Army, 1918–1922*. Cambridge: Cambridge University Press.

Besley, Timothy, and Masayuki Kudamatsu. 2007. "Making Autocracy Work." STICERD Development Economics Discussion Paper No. 48.

Bethell, Leslie. 1985. *The Cambridge History of Latin America, Volume 3: From Independence to c. 1870*. New York: Cambridge University Press.

Bialer, Seweryn (Ed.). 1969. *Stalin and His Generals: Soviet Military Memoirs of World War II*. New York: Pegasus.

Blaydes, Lisa. 2007. "Electoral Budget Cycles under Authoritarianism: Economic Opportunism in Mubarak's Egypt." Unpublished manuscript, Stanford University.

Blaydes, Lisa. 2010. *Elections and Distributive Politics in Mubarak's Egypt*. New York: Cambridge University Press.

Bo, Zhiyue. 2007. *China's Elite Politics: Political Transition and Power Balancing*. New Jersey: World Scientific.

Bobbio, Norberto. 1989. *Democracy and Dictatorship*. Minneapolis: University of Minnesota Press.

Boix, Carles, 2003. *Democracy and Redistribution*. Cambridge: Cambridge University Press.

Boix, Carles, and Milan Svolik. 2011. "The Foundations of Limited Authoritarian Government: Institutions and Power-Sharing in Dictatorships." Unpublished manuscript, Princeton University.

Bowman, Kirk. 2002. *Militarization, Democracy, and Development: The Perils of Praetorianism in Latin America*. University Park: Pennsylvania State University Press.

Box-Steffensmeier, Janet M., and Bradford S. Jones. 2004. *Event History Modeling*. New York: Cambridge University Press.

Box-Steffensmeier, Janet M., Peter M. Radcliffe, and Brandon L. Bartels. 2005. "The Incidence and Timing of PAC Contributions to Incumbent U.S. House Members, 1993–94." *Legislative Studies Quarterly* 30(4): 549–79.

Brandenburg, Frank. 1964. *The Making of Modern Mexico*. Englewood Cliffs, NJ: Prentice-Hall.

Bratton, Michael, and Nicolas Van de Walle. 1997. *Democratic Experiments in Africa: Regime Transitions in Comparative Perspective*. New York: Cambridge University Press.

Breslauer, George W. 1982. *Khrushchev and Brezhnev as Leaders: Building Authority in Soviet Politics*. London: Allen & Unwin.

Brooker, Paul. 2000. *Non-Democratic Regimes: Theory, Government, and Politics*. New York: St. Martin's Press.

Brooks, Risa. 1998. *Political–Military Relations and the Stability of Arab Regimes*. London: Oxford University Press (Adelphi Paper, International Institute for Strategic Studies).

Brown, Archie. 2009. *The Rise and Fall of Communism*. London: Bodley Head.

Brownlee, Jason. 2002. "And Yet They Persist: Explaining Survival and Transition in Neopatrimonial Regimes." *Studies in Comparative International Development* 37(3): 35–63.

Brownlee, Jason. 2007a. *Authoritarianism in an Age of Democratization*. New York: Cambridge University Press.

Brownlee, Jason. 2007b. "Hereditary Succession in Modern Autocracies." *World Politics* 59(4): 595–628.

Brownlee, Jason. 2009. "Portents of Pluralism: How Hybrid Regimes Affect Democratic Transitions." *American Journal of Political Science* 53(3): 515–32.

Buchta, Wilfried. 2000. *Who Rules Iran? The Structure of Power in the Islamic Republic*. Washington, DC: Washington Institute for Near East Policy.

Bueno de Mesquita, Bruce, Alastair Smith, Randolph M. Siverson, and James D. Morrow. 2003. *The Logic of Political Survival*. Cambridge, MA: MIT Press.

Bunce, Valerie. 1999. *Subversive Institutions: The Design and the Destruction of Socialism and the State*. Cambridge: Cambridge University Press.

Burlatsky, Fedor. 1991. *Khrushchev and the First Russian Spring*. London: Weidenfeld & Nicolson.

Callaghy, Thomas M. 1984. *The State–Society Struggle: Zaire in Comparative Perspective*. New York: Columbia University Press.

Cameron, A. Colin, and Pravin K. Trivedi. 2005. *Microeconometrics: Methods and Applications*. New York: Cambridge University Press.

Campbell, J. B. 1994. *The Roman Army, 31 BC–AD 337: A Sourcebook*. London: Routledge.

Carlsson, Hans, and Eric van Damme. 1993. "Global Games and Equilibrium Selection." *Econometrica* 61(5): 989–1018.

Castañeda, Jorge G. 2000. *Perpetuating Power: How Mexican Presidents Were Chosen*. New York: New Press.

Chan, Heng Chee. 1976. "The Role of Parliamentary Politicians in Singapore." *Legislative Studies Quarterly* 1(3): 423–41.

Cheibub, José Antonio. 2007. *Presidentialism, Parliamentarism, and Democracy*. New York: Cambridge University Press.

Cheibub, José Antonio, and Jennifer Gandhi. 2005. "Classifying Political Regimes: A Six-Fold Measure of Democracies and Dictatorships." Dataset.

Cheibub, José A., Jennifer Gandhi, and James R. Vreeland. 2010. "Democracy and Dictatorship Revisited." *Public Choice* 143(1): 67–101.

Chwe, Michael. 2001. *Rational Ritual: Culture, Coordination, and Common Knowledge*. Princeton, NJ: Princeton University Press.

Collier, David, and Steven Levitsky. 1997. "Democracy with Adjectives: Conceptual Innovation in Comparative Research." *World Politics* 49(3): 430–51.

Collier, Paul, and Anke Hoeffler. 1998. "On Economic Causes of Civil War." *Oxford Economic Papers* 50(14): 563–73.

Colton, Timothy J. 1979. *Commissars, Commanders, and Civilian Authority: The Structure of Soviet Military Politics*. Boston: Harvard University Press.

Communist Party of China. 1981. *Resolution on CPC History (1949–1981)*. Beijing: Foreign Languages Press.

Conquest, Robert. 1967. *Power and Policy in the USSR: The Struggle for Stalin's Succession, 1945–1960*. New York: Harper & Row.

Constable, Pamela, and Arturo Valenzuela. 1993. *A Nation of Enemies: Chile under Pinochet*. New York: W. W. Norton & Company.

Cook, Steven A. 2007. *Ruling but Not Governing*. Baltimore, MD: Johns Hopkins University Press.

Corbett, Ben. 2002. *This Is Cuba: An Outlaw Culture Survives*. Cambridge, MA: Westview Press.

Correlates of War Project. 2006. *Direct Contiguity Data, 1816–2006*. Version 3.1.

Cox, Gary. 2011. "War, Moral Hazard, and Ministerial Responsibility: England after the Glorious Revolution." *The Journal of Economic History* 71(1): 133–61.

Cox, Gary W. 1997. *Making Votes Count: Strategic Coordination in the World's Electoral Systems*. New York: Cambridge University Press.

Crankshaw, Edward. 1966. *Khrushchev: A Career*. New York: Viking Press.

Crouch, Harold. 1978. *The Army and Politics in Indonesia*. Ithaca, NY: Cornell University Press.

Crowder, Martin J. 2001. *Classical Competing Risks*. Boca Raton, FL: Chapman & Hall.

Dahl, Robert A. 1971. *Polyarchy: Participation and Opposition*. New Haven, CT: Yale University Press.

Davenport, Christian. 2007. "State Repression and the Tyrannical Peace." *Journal of Peace Research* 44(4): 485–504.

Debs, Alexandre. 2007. "The Wheel of Fortune: Agency Problems in Dictatorship." Unpublished manuscript, Yale University.

Debs, Alexandre. 2009. "Living by the Sword and Dying by the Sword? Leadership Transitions in and out of Dictatorships." Working Paper.

Decalo, Samuel. 1990. *Coups and Army Rule in Africa: Motivations and Constraints*. New Haven, CT: Yale University Press.

Deininger, Klaus, and Lyn Squire. 1996. "A New Data Set Measuring Income Inequality." *World Bank Economis Review* 10(3): 565–91.

Demick, Barbara. 2009. *Nothing to Envy: Ordinary Lives in North Korea*. New York: Spiegel & Grau.

Desch, Michael C. 1999. *Soldiers, States, and Structure: Civilian Control of the Military in a Changing Security Environment*. Baltimore, MD: Johns Hopkins University Press.

Diamond, Larry. 2002. "Thinking about Hybrid Regimes." *Journal of Democracy* 13(2): 21–35.

Diamond, Larry. 2008. "The Democratic Rollback: The Resurgence of the Predatory State." *Foreign Affairs* 87(2): 36–48.

Dickson, Bruce J. 2003. *Red Capitalists in China: The Party, Private Entrepreneurs, and Prospects for Political Change.* New York: Cambridge University Press.

Dikötter, Frank. 2010. *Mao's Great Famine: The History of China's Most Devastating Catastrophe, 1958–1962.* New York: Walker & Co.

Dittmer, Lowell. 2002. "Chinese Factional Politics under Jiang." In Gang Lin and Susan Shirk (Eds.), *The 16th CCP Congress and Leadership Transition in China.* Washington, DC: The Woodrow Wilson Center Asia Program, pp. 20–7.

Djilas, Milovan. 1962. *Conversations with Stalin.* New York: Harcourt.

Domínguez, Jorge I. 1978. *Cuba: Order and Revolution.* Cambridge, MA: Belknap Press.

Drake, Paul W. 1996. *Labor Movements and Dictatorships: The Southern Cone in Comparative Perspective.* Baltimore, MD: Johns Hopkins University Press.

Droz-Vincent, Philippe. 2007. "From Political to Economic Actors: The Changing Role of Middle Eastern Armies." In Oliver Schlumberger (Ed.), *Debating Arab Authoritarianism: Dynamics and Durability in Nondemocratic Regimes.* Stanford, CA: Stanford University Press, pp. 195–214.

Edin, Maria. 2003. "State Capacity and Local Agent Control in China: CCP Cadre Management from a Township Perspective." *The China Quarterly* 173: 35–52.

Edmond, Chris. 2007. "Information Manipulation, Coordination, and Regime Change." Unpublished manuscript, New York University.

Egorov, Georgy, Sergei M. Guriev, and Konstantin Sonin. 2009. "Why Resource-Poor Dictators Allow Freer Media: A Theory and Evidence from Panel Data." *American Political Science Review* 103(4): 645–68.

Egorov, Georgy, and Konstantin Sonin. 2005. "The Killing Game: Reputation and Knowledge in Politics of Succession." Unpublished manuscript, Northwestern University.

Egorov, Georgy, and Konstantin Sonin. Forthcoming. "Dictators and Their Viziers: Endogenizing the Loyalty–Competence Trade-Off." *Journal of the European Economic Association.*

Eichengreen, Barry, and David Leblang. 2008. "Democracy and Globalization." *Economics and Politics* 20(3): 289–334.

Elkins, Zachary. 2000. "Gradations of Democracy? Empirical Tests of Alternative Conceptualizations." *American Journal of Political Science* 44(2): 293–300.

Elson, R. E. 2001. *Suharto: A Political Biography.* Cambridge: Cambridge University Press.

Escribà-Folch, Abel, and Joseph Wright. 2008. "Dealing with Tyranny: International Sanctions and Autocrats' Duration." Working Paper.

Farcau, Bruce W. 1994. *The Coup: Tactics in the Seizure of Power.* Westport, CT: Praeger.

Farouk-Sluglett, Marion, and Peter Sluglett. 1987. *Iraq Since 1958: From Revolution to Dictatorship.* London: I. B. Tauris.

Fearon, James D. 2005. "Primary Commodity Exports and Civil War." *Journal of Conflict Resolution* 49(4): 483–507.

Fearon, James D. 2008. "Self-Enforcing Democracy." Unpublished manuscript, Stanford University.

Feaver, Peter D. 1999. "Civil–Military Relations." *Annual Review of Political Science* 2: 211–41.

Finer, S. E. 1999. *The History of Government from the Earliest Times: The Intermediate Ages.* New York: Oxford University Press.

Finer, Samuel E. 1962. *The Man on Horseback.* London: Pall Mall.

Fontana, Andres Miguel. 1987. *Political Decision Making by a Military Corporation: Argentina 1976–1983.* The University of Texas at Austin: Ph.D. Dissertation.

Frantz, Erica. 2007. "Tying the Dictator's Hands: Leadership Survival in Authoritarian Regimes." Unpublished manuscript, Bridgewater State University.

Frantz, Erica, and Natasha Ezrow. 2009. "'Yes Men' and the Likelihood of Foreign Policy Mistakes Across Dictatorships." Paper presented at the 2009 Annual Meeting of the American Political Science Association.

Frantz, Erica, and Natasha M. Ezrow. 2011. *The Politics of Dictatorship: Institutions and Outcomes in Authoritarian Regimes.* Boulder, CO: Lynne Rienner Publishers.

Friedrich, Karl, and Zbigniew Brzezinski. 1965. *Totalitarian Dictatorship and Autocracy.* Cambridge, MA: Harvard University Press.

Galetovic, Alexander, and Ricardo Sanhueza. 2000. "Citizens, Autocrats, and Plotters: A Model and New Evidence on Coups D'État." *Economics and Politics* 12(2): 183–204.

Gandhi, Jennifer, 2008. *Political Institutions under Dictatorship.* New York: Cambridge University Press.

Gandhi, Jennifer, and Adam Przeworski. 2006. "Cooperation, Cooptation, and Rebellion Under Dictatorships." *Economics & Politics* 18(1): 1–26.

Gandhi, Jennifer, and Adam Przeworski. 2007. "Authoritarian Institutions and the Survival of Autocrats." *Comparative Political Studies* 40(11): 1279–1301.

Geddes, Barbara. 1999a. "Authoritarian Breakdown: Empirical Test of a Game Theoretic Argument." Working Paper.

Geddes, Barbara. 1999b. "What Do We Know about Democratization after Twenty Years?" *Annual Review of Political Science* 2: 115–44.

Geddes, Barbara. 2003. *Paradigms and Sand Castles: Theory Building and Research Design in Comparative Politics.* Ann Arbor, MI: University of Michigan Press.

Geddes, Barbara. 2005. "Authoritarian Breakdown." Working Paper.

Geddes, Barbara. 2008. "Party Creation as an Autocratic Survival Strategy." Unpublished manuscript, UCLA.

Geddes, Barbara. 2009. "How Autocrats Defend Themselves against Armed Rivals." Working Paper.

Gehlbach, Scott G., and Philip Keefer. 2008. "Investment without Democracy: Ruling-Party Institutionalization and Credible Commitment in Autocracies." Unpublished manuscript, University of Wisconsin-Madison.

Gelman, Andrew, and Jennifer Hill. 2006. *Data Analysis Using Regression and Multi-level/Hierarchical Models.* Cambridge: Cambridge University Press.

George, Alan. 2003. *Syria: Neither Bread nor Freedom.* New York: Zed Books.

Gerber, Hans U. 1991. "From the Generalized Gamma to the Generalized Negative Binomial Distribution." *Insurance: Mathematics and Economics* 10(4): 303–9.

Gerolymatos, Andre. 2009. "The Road to Authoritarianism: The Greek Army in Politics, 1935–49." *Journal of the Hellenic Diaspora* 35(1): 7–26.

Gershenson, Dmitriy, and Hershel I. Gorossman. 2001. "Co-option and Repression in the Soviet Union." *Economics and Politics* 13(1): 31–47.

Ghazvinian, John. 2008. *Untapped: The Scramble for Africa's Oil.* Orlando, FL: Houghton Mifflin Harcourt.

Gillespie, Charles. 1991. *Negotiating Democracy: Politicians and Generals in Uruguay.* New York: Cambridge University Press.

Gleditsch, Nils Petter, Peter Wallensteen, Mikael Eriksson, Margareta Sollenberg, and Håvard Strand. 2002. "Armed Conflict 1946–2001: A New Dataset." *Journal of Peace Research* 39(5): 615–37.

Goemans, Hein E. 2008. "Which Way Out? The Manner and Consequences of Losing Office." *Journal of Conflict Resolution* 52(6): 771–94.

Goemans, Hein, Kristian Skrede Gleditsch, and Giacomo Chiozza. 2009. "Introducing Archigos: A Data Set of Political Leaders." *Journal of Peace Research* 46(2): 269–83.

Goodwin, Jeff. 2001. *No Other Way Out: States and Revolutionary Movements, 1945–1991.* New York: Cambridge University Press.

Gorlizki, Yoram, and Oleg Khlevniuk. 2004. *Cold Peace: Stalin and the Soviet Ruling Circle, 1945–1953.* Oxford: Oxford University Press.

Gorlizki, Yoram, and Oleg Khlevniuk. 2006. "Stalin and His Circle." In Ronald G. Suny (Ed.), *The Cambridge History of Russia, Volume 3.* New York: Cambridge University Press, pp. 243–67.

Green, Donald P., and Alan S. Gerber. 2004. *Get Out The Vote! How to Increase Voter Turnout.* Washington, DC: Brookings Institution Press.

Greene, Kenneth F. 2007. *Why Dominant Parties Lose: Mexico's Democratization in Comparative Perspective.* New York: Cambridge University Press.

Gregory, Paul R. 2009. *Terror by Quota: State Security from Lenin to Stalin.* New Haven, CT: Yale University Press.

Gregory, Paul R., Philipp J. H. Schroder, and Konstantin Sonin. 2006. "Dictators, Repression and the Median Citizen: An 'Eliminations Model' of Stalin's Terror." Working Paper.

Grindle, Merilee Serrill. 1977. *Bureaucrats, Politicians, and Peasants in Mexico: A Case Study in Public Policy.* Berkeley, CA: University of California Press.

Grzymała-Busse, Anna. 2002. *Redeeming the Communist Past: The Regeneration of Communist Parties in East Central Europe.* Cambridge: Cambridge University Press.

Grzymała-Busse, Anna. 2007. *Rebuilding Leviathan: Party Competition and State Exploitation in Post-Communist Democracies.* New York: Cambridge University Press.

Guriev, Sergei, and Konstantin Sonin. 2009. "Dictators and oligarchs: A dynamic theory of contested property rights." *Journal of Public Economics* 93(1–2): 1–13.

Guo, Gang. 2005. "Party Recruitment of College Students in China." *Journal of Contemporary China* 14(43): 371–93.

Haber, Stephen H. 2007. "Authoritarian Regimes." In Barry R. Weingast and Donald Wittman (Eds.), *The Oxford Handbook of Political Economy.* New York: Oxford University Press, pp. 693–707.

Haber, Stephen H., Noel Maurer, and Armando Razo. 2003. *The Politics of Property Rights: Political Instability, Credible Commitments, and Economic Growth in Mexico, 1876–1929.* New York: Cambridge University Press.

Hadenius, Axel, and Jan Teorell. 2007. "Pathways from Authoritarianism." *Journal of Democracy* 18(1): 143–57.

Hale, William M. 1994. *Turkish Politics and the Military.* London: Routledge.

Hanson, Russell L. 1989. "Democracy." In Terrence Ball, James Farr, and Russell L. Hanson (Eds.), *Political Innovation and Conceptual Change.* Cambridge: Cambridge University Press.

Hanson, Stephen. 2006. "The Brezhnev Era." In Ronald G. Suny (Ed.), *The Cambridge History of Russia, Volume 3*. New York: Cambridge University Press, pp. 292–315.

Harding, Harry. 1997. "The Chinese State in Crisis, 1966–9." In Roderick MacFarquhar (Ed.), *Politics of China 1949–1989: Eras of Mao and Deng*. New York: Cambridge University Press, pp. 148–247.

Herb, Michael. 1999. *All in the Family*. Albany, NY: State University of New York Press.

Herz, John H. 1952. "The Problem of Successorship in Dictatorial Regimes: A Study in Comparative Law and Institutions." *The Journal of Politics* 14(1): 19–40.

Hinnebusch, Raymond. 2002. *Syria: Revolution from Above*. London: Routledge.

Hinnebusch, Raymond A. 1990. *Authoritarian Power and State Formation in Ba'thist Syria: Army, Party, and Peasant*. Boulder, CO: Westview Press.

Hirshleifer, Jack. 1989. "Conflict and Rent-Seeking Success Functions: Ration vs. Difference Models of Relative Success." *Public Choice* 63(2): 101–12.

Hobbes, Thomas. 1996 [1651]. *Leviathan*. Cambridge: Cambridge University Press.

Holmes, Stephen. 2003. "Lineages of the Rule of Law." In Jose Maria Maravall and Adam Przeworski (Eds.), *Democracy and the Rule of Law*. New York: Cambridge University Press, pp. 19–61.

Honaker, James, and Gary King. 2009. "What to Do About Missing Values in Time-Series Cross-Section Data." Working Paper.

Honaker, James, Gary King, and Matthew Blackwell. 2009. *AMELIA II: A Program for Missing Data*. Version 1.2–14.

Hong, Lysa, and Jianli Huang. 2008. *The Scripting of a National History: Singapore and its Past*. Hong Kong: Hong Kong University Press.

Horowitz, Donald L. 1985. *Ethnic Groups in Conflict*. Berkeley, CA: University of California Press.

Hough, Jerry F. 1980. *Soviet Leadership in Transition*. Washington, DC: The Brookings Institution.

Huang, Jing. 2008. "Institutionalization of Political Succession in China: Progress and Implications." In Cheng Li (Ed.), *China's Changing Political Landscape*. Washington, DC: The Brookings Institution Press, pp. 80–97.

Hume, David. 1748. "Of the First Principles of Government." In *Essays, Moral and Political*, London: Cadell.

Humphreys, Macartan. 2005. "Natural Resources, Conflict, and Conflict Resolution: Uncovering the Mechanisms." *Journal of Conflict Resolution* 49(4): 508–37.

Huntington, Samuel P. 1957. *The Soldier and the State*. Cambridge, MA: Harvard University Press.

Huntington, Samuel P. 1968. *Political Order in Changing Societies*. New Haven, CT: Yale University Press.

Huntington, Samuel P. 1970. "Social and Institutional Dynamics of One-Party Systems." In Samuel P. Huntington and Clement H. Moore (Eds.), *Authoritarian Politics in Modern Society: The Dynamics of Established One-Party Systems*. New York: Basic Books, pp. 3–45.

Huntington, Samuel P. 1993. *The Third Wave: Demoratization in the Late Twentieth Century*. Norman, OK: University of Oklahoma Press.

Jackson, Robert H., and Carl G. Rosberg. 1982. *Personal Rule in Black Africa: Prince, Autocrat, Prophet, Tyrant*. Berkeley, CA: University of California Press.

Janowitz, Morris. 1964. *The Military in the Political Development of New Nations: An Essay in Comparative Analysis*. Chicago, IL: University of Chicago Press.

Johnson, John J. 1958. *Political Change in Latin America: The Emergence of the Middle Sectors*. Stanford, CA: Stanford University Press.

Karl, Terry Lynn. 1997. *The Paradox of Plenty: Oil Booms and Petro-States*. Berkeley, CA: University of California Press.

Karsh, Efraim. 2002. *Saddam Hussein: A Political Biography*. New York: Grove Press.

Kassem, May. 1999. *In the Guise of Democracy: Governance in Contemporary Egypt*. Reading, NY: Ithaca Press.

Kechichian, Joseph A. 2008. *Power and Succession in Arab Monarchies*. Boulder, CO: Lynne Rienner Publishers.

Khlevniuk, Oleg V. 2009. *Master of the House: Stalin and His Inner Circle*. New Haven, CT: Yale University Press.

Khrushchev, Nikita Sergeevich. 1970. *Khrushchev Remembers*. Boston: Little, Brown.

King, Gary, James Honaker, Anne Joseph, and Kenneth Scheve. 2001. "Analyzing Incomplete Political Science Data: An Alternative Algorithm for Multiple Imputation." *The American Political Science Review* 95(1): 49–69.

Kitschelt, Herbert, and Steven Wilkinson. Eds. 2007. *Patrons, Clients, and Policies: Patterns of Democratic Accountability and Political Competition*. New York: Cambridge University Press.

Klaren, Peter F. 1999. *Peru: Society and Nationhood in the Andes*. New York: Oxford University Press.

Klein, John P., and Melvin L. Moeschberger. 2003. *Survival Analysis Techniques for Censored and Truncated Data*. New York: Springer.

Klieman, Aaron S. 1980. "Confined to Barracks: Emergencies and the Military in Developing Societies." *Comparative Politics* 12(2): 143–63.

Kligman, Gail. 1998. *The Politics of Duplicity: Controlling Reproduction in Ceausescu's Romania*. Berkeley, CA: University of California Press.

Knight, Amy. 1995. *Beria*. Princeton, NJ: Princeton University Press.

Krauze, Enrique. 1997. *Biography of Power: A History of Modern Mexico, 1810–1996*. New York: Harper Collins.

Kreps, David M. 1990. *Game Theory and Economic Modelling*. New York: Oxford University Press.

Kuran, Timur. 1991. "Now Out of Never: The Element of Surprise in the East European Revolution of 1989." *World Politics* 44: 7–48.

La Porta, Rafael, Florencio Lopez de Silanes, Andrei Shleifer, and Robert Vishny. 1999. "The Quality of Government." *Journal of Law, Economics and Organization* 15(April): 222–79.

Lai, Brian, and Dan Slater. 2006. "Institutions of the Offensive: Domestic Sources of Dispute Initiation in Authoritarian Regimes, 1950–1992." *American Journal of Political Science* 50(1): 113–26.

Lamb, David. 1984. *The Africans*. New York: Vintage Books.

Landry, Pierre F. 2008. *Decentralized Authoritarianism in China: The Communist Party's Control of Local Elites in the Post-Mao Era*. New York: Cambridge University Press.

Langston, Joy, and Scott Morgenstern. 2009. "Campaigning in an Electoral Authoritarian Regime: The Case of Mexico." *Comparative Politics* 41(2): 165–81.

Laver, Michael, and Norman Schofield. 1990. *Multiparty Government: The Politics of Coalition in Europe*. Oxford: Oxford University Press.

Lazarev, Valery. 2005. "Economics of One-Party State: Promotion Incentives and Support for the Soviet Regime." *Comparative Economic Studies* 47(2): 346–363.

Lazarev, Valery. 2007. "Political Labor Market, Government Policy, and Stability of a Nondemocratic Regime." *Journal of Comparative Economics* 35(3): 546–63.

Leverett, Flynt. 2005. *Inheriting Syria: Bashar's Trial by Fire*. Washington, DC: The Brookings Institution Press.

Levitsky, Steven, and Lucan A. Way. 2002. "The Rise of Competitive Authoritarianism." *Journal of Democracy* 13(2): 51–65.

Levitsky, Steven, and Lucan A. Way. 2010. *Competitive Authoritarianism: Hybrid Regimes after the Cold War*. New York: Cambridge University Press.

Lewis, Paul H. 1978. "Salazar's Ministerial Elite, 1932–1968." *Journal of Politics* 40(3): 622–47.

Lewis, Paul H. 2002. *Latin Fascist Elites: The Mussolini, Franco, and Salazar Regimes*. Westport, CT: Praeger.

Li, Cheng. 2010. "China's Communist Party-State: The Structure and Dynamics of Power." In William A. Joseph (Ed.), "Politics in China: An Introduction," New York: Oxford University Press, pp. 165–91.

Li, Kim-Hung, Xiao-Li Meng, T. E. Raghunathan, and Donald B. Rubin. 1991. "Significance Levels from Repeated p-Values with Multiply-Imputed Data." *Statistica Sinica* 1: 65–92.

Lingle, Christopher. 1996. *Singapore's Authoritarian Capitalism: Asian Values, Free Market Illusions, and Political Dependency*. Barcelona, Spain: Edicions Sirocco.

Linz, Juan. 1975. "Totalitarian and Authoritarian Regimes." In Fred Greenstein and Nelson Polsby (Eds.), *Handbook of Political Science*, Vol. 3. Reading, MA: Addison Wesley Publishing Company, pp. 191–357.

Linz, Juan J., and H. E. Chehabi. 1998. *Sultanistic Regimes*. Baltimore, MD: Johns Hopkins University Press.

Londregan, John B., and Keith T. Poole. 1990. "Poverty, the Coup Trap, and the Seizure of Executive Power." *World Politics* 42: 151–83.

López-Calvo, Ignacio. 2005. *God and Trujillo: Literary and Cultural Representations of the Dominican Dictator*. Gainesville: University Press of Florida.

Lorentzen, Peter L. 2008. "The Value of Incomplete Censorship for an Authoritarian State." Working Paper presented at the 2008 Annual Meeting of the American Political Science Association.

Lorentzen, Peter L. 2009. "Regularizing Rioting: Permitting Public Protest in an Authoritarian Regime." Working Paper.

Loveman, Brian. 1993. *The Constitution of Tyranny: Regimes of Exception in Spanish America*. Pittsburgh, PA: University of Pittsburgh Press.

Lust-Okar, Ellen, and Amaney Ahmad Jamal. 2002. "Rulers and Rules: Reassessing the Influence of Regime Type on Electoral Law Formation." *Comparative Political Studies* 35(3): 337–67.

Luttwak, Edward. 1968. *Coup D'état: A Practical Handbook*. New York: Knopf.

MacCulloch, Robert. 2005. "Income Inequality and the Taste for Revolution." *Journal of Law and Economics* 48(1): 93–123.

MacFarquhar, Roderick. 1974–1997. *The Origins of the Cultural Revolution*. New York: Columbia University Press.

MacFarquhar, Roderick. 1997a. *The Politics of China: The Eras of Mao and Deng*. New York: Cambridge University Press.

MacFarquhar, Roderick. 1997b. "The Succession to Mao and the End of Maoism, 1969–82." In Roderick MacFarquhar (Ed.), *Politics of China 1949–1989: Eras of Mao and Deng*. New York: Cambridge University Press, pp. 248–339.

MacFarquhar, Roderick, and Michael Schoenhals. 2006. *Mao's Last Revolution*. Cambridge, MA: Harvard University Press.

Machiavelli, Niccolò. 2005[1513]. *The Prince*. Oxford: Oxford University Publication. Translated by Peter Bondanella.

Maddison, Angus. 2008. "Statistics on World Population, GDP and Per Capita GDP, 1–2006 AD." Dataset.

Magaloni, Beatriz. 2006. *Voting for Autocracy: Hegemonic Party Survival and Its Demise in Mexico*. New York: Cambridge University Press.

Magaloni, Beatriz. 2008. "Credible Power-Sharing and the Longevity of Authoritarian Rule." *Comparative Political Studies* 41(4/5): 715–41.

Magaloni, Beatriz, and Ruth Kricheli. 2010. "Political Order and One-Party Rule." *Annual Review of Political Science* 13: 123–43.

Makiya, Kanan. 1998. *Republic of Fear: The Politics of Modern Iraq*. Berkeley, CA: University of California Press.

Malesky, Edmund. 2009. "Gerrymandering Vietnam Style: Escaping the Partial Reform Equilibrium in a Non-Democratic Regime." *Journal of Politics* 71(1): 132–59.

Malesky, Edmund, and Paul Schuler. 2010. "Nodding or Needling: Analyzing Delegate Responsiveness in an Authoritarian Parliament." *American Political Science Review* 104(3): 482–502.

Manin, Bernard. 1997. *The Principles of Representative Government*. New York: Cambridge University Press.

Manion, Melanie. 1992. "Politics and Policy in Post-Mao Cadre Retirement." *The China Quarterly* 129: 1–25.

Manion, Melanie. 1993. *Retirement of Revolutionaries in China: Public Policies, Social Norms, Private Interests*. Princeton, NJ: Princeton University Press.

Mao, Zedong. 1954. *Problems of War and Strategy*. Beijing: Foreign Languages Press.

Marr, Phebe A. 1975. "The Political Elite in Iraq." In George Lenczowski (Ed.), *Political Elites in the Middle East*. Washington, DC: American Enterprise Institute for Public Policy Research.

Marshall, Monty G., and Keith Jaggers. 2008. "Polity IV: Political Regime Characteristics and Transitions, 1800–2008." Dataset.

Martínez, Luis. 2007. *The Libyan Paradox*. New York: Columbia University Press.

Mattes, Hanspeter. 2008. "Formal and Informal Authority in Libya since 1969." In Dirk J. Vandewalle (Ed.), *Libya since 1969: Qadhafi's Revolution Revisited*. New York: Palgrave Macmillan.

Mauzy, Diane K., and R. S. Milne. 2002. *Singapore Politics under the People's Action Party*. London: Routledge.

Mawdsley, Evan, and Stephen White. 2000. *The Soviet Elite from Lenin to Gorbachev: The Central Committee and Its Members, 1917–1991*. New York: Oxford University Press.

McCarty, Nolan, and Adam Meirowitz. 2007. *Political Game Theory*. New York: Cambridge University Press.

McLachlan, Geoffrey, and David Peel. 2000. *Finite Mixture Models*. New York: Wiley.

Medina, Luis Fernando. 2007. *A Unified Theory of Collective Action and Social Change*. Ann Arbor: University of Michigan Press.

Merkel, Wolfgang. 2010. "Are Dictatorships Returning? Revisiting the 'Democratic Rollback' Hypothesis." *Contemporary Politics* 16(1): 17–31.

Mićunović, Veljko. 1980. *Moscow Diary*. Garden City, NY: Doubleday.

Migdal, Joel S. 1988. *Strong Societies and Weak States: State-Society Relations and State Capabilities in the Third World.* Princeton, NJ: Princeton University Press.

Miller, Alice L. 2004. "Hi Jintao and the Party Politburo." *China Leadership Monitor* (9).

Miller, Alice L. 2008. "Institutionalization and the Changing Dynamics of Chinese Leadership Politics." In Cheng Li (Ed.), *China's Changing Political Landscape.* Washington, DC: The Brookings Institution Press, pp. 61–79.

Miller, Alice L. 2011. "The Politburo Standing Committee under Hu Jintao." *China Leadership Monitor* 35: 1–9.

Miranda, Carlos R. 1990. *The Stroessner Era: Authoritarian Rule in Paraguay.* Boulder, CO: Westview Press.

Montesquieu, Charles de Secondat. 1989 [1748]. *The Spirit of the Laws.* Cambridge: Cambridge University Press.

Morris, Stephen, and Hyun Song Shin. 2003. "Global Games: Theory and Applications." In Mathias Dewatripont, Lars Peter Hansen, and Stephen J. Turnovsky (Eds.), *Advances in Economics and Econometrics.* New York: Cambridge University Press, pp. 56–114.

Morrison, Kevin. 2009. "Oil, Non-Tax Revenue, and the Redistributional Foundations of Regime Stability." *International Organization* 63(1): 107–38.

Morrow, James D. 1994. *Game Theory for Political Scientists.* Princeton, NJ: Princeton University Press.

Morton, Rebecca B. 1999. *Methods and Models: A Guide to the Empirical Analysis of Formal Models in Political Science.* New York: Cambridge University Press.

Muller, Edward N., and Mitchell A. Seligson. 1987. "Inequality and Insurgency." *American Political Science Review,* 81(2): 425–51.

Mulvenon, James. 2003a. "The Crucible of Tragedy: SARS, the Ming 361 Accident, and Chinese Party-Army Relations." *China Leadership Monitor* (8): 1–12.

Mulvenon, James. 2003b. "The PLA and the 16th Party Congress: Jiang Controls the Gun?" *China Leadership Monitor* (5): 20–29.

Mulvenon, James. 2003c. "Reduced Budgets, the 'Two Centers,' and Other Mysteries of the 2003 National People's Congress." *China Leadership Monitor* (7): 1–8.

Mulvenon, James. 2005. "The King Is Dead! Long Live the King! The CMC Leadership Transition from Jiang to Hu." *China Leadership Monitor* (13): 1–8.

Mussolini, Benito. 1935. *Fascism: Doctrine and Institutions.* Rome: Ardita.

Mutibwa, Phares Mukasa. 1992. *Uganda since Independence: A Story of Unfulfilled Hopes.* Kampala, Uganda: Fountain Publishers.

Myerson, Roger. 2004. "Justice, Institutions, and Multiple Equilibria." *Chicago Journal of International Law* 5(1): 91–107.

Myerson, Roger B. 1991. *Game Theory: Analysis of Conflict.* Cambridge, MA: Harvard University Press.

Myerson, Roger B. 1992. "On the Value of Game Theory in Social Science." *Rationality and Society* 4(1): 62–73.

Myerson, Roger B. 1999. "Nash Equilibrium and the History of Economic Theory." *Journal of Economic Literature* 37(3): 1067–82.

Myerson, Roger B. 2008. "The Autocrat's Credibility Problem and Foundations of the Constitutional State." *American Political Science Review* 102(1): 125–39.

Nathan, Andrew J. 2003. "Authoritarian Resilience." *Journal of Democracy* 14(1): 6–17.

Nawaz, Shuja. 2008. *Crossed Swords: Pakistan, Its Army, and the Wars Within*. Karachi: Oxford University Press.

Nelson, Harold D. (Ed.). 1986. *Tunisia: A Country Study*. Washington, DC: American University Foreign Area Studies.

Nordlinger, Eric A. 1977. *Soldiers in Politics: Military Coups and Governments*. Englewood Cliffs, NJ: Prentice-Hall.

North, Douglass C., and Barry R. Weingast. 1989. "Constitutions and Commitment: The Evolution of Institutions Governing Public Choice in Seventeenth-Century England." *Journal of Economic History* 49(4): 803–32.

O'Donnell, Guillermo A. 1973. *Modernization and Bureaucratic-Authoritarianism*. Berkeley: Institute of International Studies, University of California.

O'Donnell, Guillermo, and Philippe C. Schmitter. 1986. *Transitions from Authoritarian Rule: Comparative Perspective*, vol. 4. Baltimore: Johns Hopkins University Press.

Oh, Kong Dan, and Ralph C. Hassig. 2000. *North Korea through the Looking Glass*. Washington, DC: The Brookings Institution Press.

O'Kane, Rosemary H. T. 1981. "A Probabilistic Approach to the Causes of Coups D'etat." *British Journal of Political Science* 11: 287–308.

Osborne, Martin J. 2004. *An Introduction to Game Theory*. Oxford: Oxford University Press.

Ottaway, Marina. 2003. *Democracy Challenged: The Rise of Semi-Authoritarianism*. Washington, DC: Carnegie Endowment for International Peace.

Paige, Jeffery M. 1997. *Coffee and Power: Revolution and the Rise of Democracy in Central America*. Cambridge, MA: Harvard University Press.

Payne, Stanley G. 1987. *The Franco Regime, 1936–1975*. Madison, WI: University of Wisconsin Press.

Pepinsky, Thomas B. 2009. *Economic Crises and the Breakdown of Authoritarian Regimes: Indonesia and Malaysia in Comparative Perspective*. New York: Cambridge University Press.

Pérez, Louis A. 1976. *Army Politics in Cuba, 1898–1958*. Pittsburgh, PA: University of Pittsburg Press.

Pérez, Louis A., Jr. 1995. *Cuba: Between Reform and Revolution*. New York: Oxford University Press.

Perlmutter, Amos. 1977. *Military and Politics in Modern Times: Professionals, Praetorians and Revolutionary Soldiers*. New Haven, CT: Yale University Press.

Persson, Torsten, and Guido Tabellini. 2009. "Democratic Capital: The Nexus of Political and Economic Change." *American Economic Journal: Macroeconomics* 1(2): 88–126.

Perthes, Volker. 1995. *The Political Economy of Syria under Asad*. London: I. B. Tauris.

Perthes, Volker. 2006. *Syria under Bashar al-Asad: Modernisation and the Limits of Change*. London: Routledge.

Pion-Berlin, David. 1992. "Military Autonomy and Emerging Democracies in South America." *Comparative Politics* 25(1): 83–102.

Powell, Robert. 1999. *In the Shadow of Power: States and Strategies in International Politics*. Princeton, NJ: Princeton University Press.

Przeworski, Adam. 1991. *Democracy and the Market: Political and Economic Reforms in Eastern Europe and Latin America*. Cambridge: Cambridge University Press.

Przeworski, Adam. 2005. "Democracy as an Equilibrium." *Public Choice* 123(2): 253–73.

Przeworski, Adam. 2007. "Capitalism, Democracy and Science." In Geraldo L. Munck and Richard Snyder (Eds.), *Passion, Craft, and Method in Comparative Politics*. Baltimore, MD: Johns Hopkins University Press, pp. 456–503.

Przeworski, Adam. 2011. "Force and Elections." Unpublished manuscript, New York University.

Przeworski, Adam, Michael E. Alvarez, Jose Antonio Cheibub, and Fernando Limongi. 2000. *Democracy and Development: Political Institutions and Well-Being in the World, 1950–1990*. New York: Cambridge University Press.

Puddington, Arch. 2008. "Freedom in Retreat: Is the Tide Turning? Findings of Freedom in the World 2008." Freedom House Report.

Quinlivan, James T. 1999. "Coup-Proofing: Its Practice and Consequences in the Middle East." *International Security* 24(2): 131–65.

Rabe-Hesketh, Sophia, and Anders Skrondal. 2008. *Multilevel and Longitudinal Modeling Using Stata, Second Edition*. Stata Press, 2nd ed.

Ramseyer, J. Mark, and Frances M. Rosenbluth. 1995. *The Politics of Oligarchy: Institutional Choice in Imperial Japan*. New York: Cambridge University Press.

Rees, E. A. (Ed.). 2004. *The Nature of Stalin's Dictatorship: The Politburo, 1924–1953*. New York: Palgrave Macmillan.

Reich, Bernard. 1990. *Political Leaders of the Contemporary Middle East and North Africa: A Biographical Dictionary*. New York: Greenwood Press.

Remmer, Karen L. 1989. *Military Rule in Latin America*. Boston: Unwin Hyman.

Reuter, Ora John, and Jennifer Gandhi. 2010. "Economic Performance and Elite Defection from Hegemonic Parties." *Brit* 41: 83–110.

Rigby, T. H. 1968. *Communist Party Membership in the U.S.S.R., 1917–1967*. Princeton, NJ: Princeton University Press.

Rigby, T. H. 1988. "Staffing USSR Incorporated: The Origins of the Nomenklatura System." *Soviet Studies* 40(4): 523–37.

Rivero, Gonzalo. 2011. "Oligopoly of Violence." Working Paper.

Robertson, Graeme B. 2011. *The Politics of Protest in Hybrid Regimes: Managing Dissent in Post-communist Russia*. New York: Cambridge University Press.

Rock, David. 1987. *Argentina, 1516–1987: From Spanish Colonization to Alfonsin*. Berkeley, CA: University of California Press.

Ross, Michael. 2004. "How Does Natural Resource Wealth Influence Civil War? Evidence from Thirteen Cases." *International Organization* 58(1): 35–68.

Roth, Guenther. 1968. "Personal Rulership, Patrimonialism, and Empire-Building in the New States." *World Politics* 20(2): 194–206.

Rouquié, Alain. 1987. *The Military and the State in Latin America*. Berkeley: University of California Press.

Rubin, Barry M. 2008. *The Truth about Syria*. New York: Palgrave Macmillan.

Rubin, Donald B. 1987. *Multiple Imputation for Nonresponse in Surveys*. New York: Wiley.

Rubinstein, Ariel. 1991. "Comments on the Interpretation of Game Theory." *Econometrica* 59: 909–24.

Rush, Myron. 1991. *The Fate of the Party Apparatus under Gorbachev*. RAND Corporation.

Safford, Frank. 1985. "Politics, Ideology and Society in Post-Independence Spanish America." In Leslie Bethell (Ed.), *The Cambridge History of Latin America, Volume 3: From Independence to c. 1870*. New York: Cambridge University Press, pp. 347–421.

Sarkees, Meredith Reid. 2000. "The Correlates of War Data on War: An Update to 1997." *Conflict Management and Peace Science* 18(1): 123–44.

Schedler, Andreas. 2006. *Electoral Authoritarianism: The Dynamics of Unfree Competition*. Boulder, CO: Lynne Rienner Publishers.

Schelling, Thomas C. 1960. *The Strategy of Conflict*. Cambridge, MA: Harvard University Press.

Schmitter, Philippe, and Terry Lynn Karl. 1991. "What Democracy Is . . . and Is Not." *Journal of Democracy* 2(5): 75–88.

Schnytzer, Adi, and Janez Sustersic. 1998. "Why Join the Party in a One-Party System? Popularity versus Political Exchange." *Public Choice* 94(1): 117–34.

Schumacher, Edward. 1986/1987. "The United States and Libya." *Foreign Affairs* 65: 329–34.

Schumpeter, Joseph. 1950. *Capitalism, Socialism, and Democracy*. New York: Harper.

Seale, Patrick. 1990. *Asad: The Struggle for the Middle East*. Berkeley: University of California Press.

Shadmehr, Mehdi. 2011. "The Repression Puzzle: Grievances, Opportunities, and Rationality." Working Paper.

Shambaugh, David. 2009. *China's Communist Party: Atrophy and Adaptation*. Berkeley: University of California Press.

Shih, Victor. 2010. "The Autocratic Difference: Information Paucity." Working Paper.

Shirk, Susan. 2002. "The Succession Game." In Gang Lin and Susan Shirk (Eds.), *The 16th CCP Congress and Leadership Transition in China*, Washington, DC: The Woodrow Wilson Center Asia Program, pp. 5–9.

Siani-Davies, Peter. 2007. *The Romanian Revolution of December 1989*. Ithaca, NY: Cornell University Press.

Simons, William B., and Stephen White. 1984. *The Party Statutes of the Communist World*. Boston, MA: Kluwer.

Sissons, Miranda. 2008. "Iraq's New Accountability and Justice Law." International Center for Transitional Justice Briefing Paper.

Skaperdas, Stergios. 1996. "Contest Success Functions." *Economic Theory* 7(2): 283–90.

Skidmore, Thomas E. 1990. *The Politics of Military Rule in Brazil, 1964–1985*. New York: Oxford University Press.

Slater, Dan. 2003. "Iron Cage in an Iron Fist: Authoritarian Institutions and the Personalization of Power in Malaysia." *Comparative Politics* 36(1): 81–101.

Smith, Benjamin. 2005. "Life of the Party: The Origins of Regime Breakdown and Persistence Under Single-Party Rule." *World Politics* 57(3): 421–51.

Smith, Lones. 1992. "Folk Theorems in Overlapping Generations Games." *Games and Economic Behavior* 4(3): 426–49.

Snyder, Richard. 1992. "Explaining Transitions from Neopatrimonial Dictatorships." *Comparative Politics* 24(October): 379–99.

Snyder, Richard, and Ravi Bhavnani. 2005. "Diamonds, Blood, and Taxes: A Revenue-Centered Framework for Explaining Political Order." *Journal of Conflict Resolution* 49(4): 563–97.

Snyder, Timothy. 2010. *Bloodlands: Europe between Hitler and Stalin*. New York: Basic Books.

Spooner, Mary Helen. 1999. *Soldiers in a Narrow Land: The Pinochet Regime in Chile*. Berkeley, CA: University of California Press.

Staar, Richard F. 1988. *Communist Regimes in Eastern Europe*. Stanford, CA: Hoover Institution Press.

Stanley, William. 1996. *The Protection Racket State: Elite Politics, Military Extortion, and Civil War in El Salvador*. Philadelphia, PA: Temple University Press.

Stepan, Alfred. 1974. *The Military in Politics: Changing Patterns in Brazi*. Princeton, NJ: Princeton University Press.

Stepan, Alfred. 1988. *Rethinking Military Politics: Brazil and the Southern Cone*. Princeton, NJ: Princeton University Press.

Stevens, Evelyn P. 1974. *Protest and Response in Mexico*. Cambridge, MA: MIT Press.

Suny, Ronald Grigor. 1997. "Stalin and His Stalinism: Power and Authority in the Soviet Union, 1930–53." In Ian Kershaw and Moshe Lewin (Eds.), *Stalinism and Nazism: Dictatorships in Comparison*. Cambridge: Cambridge University Press, pp. 26–52.

Suny, Ronald Grigor. 1998. *The Soviet Experiment: Russia, the USSR, and the Successor States*. New York: Oxford University Press.

Svolik, Milan. 2008. "Authoritarian Reversals and Democratic Consolidation." *American Political Science Review* 102(2): 153–68.

Svolik, Milan. 2009. "Power-Sharing and Leadership Dynamics in Authoritarian Regimes." *American Journal of Political Science* 53(2): 477–94.

Tatu, Michel. 1970. *Power in the Kremlin: From Krushchev to Kosygin*. New York: Viking Press.

Taubman, William. 2004. *Khrushchev: The Man and His Era*. New York: W.W. Norton.

Teiwes, Frederick. 2010. "Mao Zedong in Power (1949–1976)." In William A. Joseph (Ed.), *Politics in China: An Introduction*. New York: Oxford University Press, pp. 165–91.

Teiwes, Frederick C. 1987. "Establishment and Consolidation of the New Regime." In Roderick MacFarquhar and John K. Fairbank (Eds.), *The People's Republic, Part 1: The Emergence of Revolutionary China 1949–1965*. New York: Cambridge University Press.

Teiwes, Frederick C. 2001. "Normal Politics with Chinese Characteristics." *The China Journal* 45(January): 69–82.

Themnér, Lotta, and Peter Wallensteen. 2011. "Armed Conflict, 1946–2010." *Journal of Peace Research* 48(4): 525–36.

Tolstoy, Leo. 1961 [1873–1877]. *Anna Karenina*. New York: New American Library.

Tompson, William. 2003. *The Soviet Union under Brezhnev*. Harlow, England: Pearson.

Tompson, William J. 1995. *Khrushchev: A Political Life*. New York: Macmillan.

Treharne, R. F. 1986. *Simon de Montfort and Baronial Reform: Thirteenth-Century Essays*. London: Hambledon Press.

Tripp, Charles. 2000. *A History of Iraq*. New York: Cambridge University Press.

Trivedi, Kishor S. 2002. *Probability and Statistics with Reliability, Queuing, and Computer Science Applications*. New York: Wiley.

Tsebelis, George. 1990. *Nested Games: Rational Choice in Comparative Politics*. Berkeley: University of California Press.

Tullock, Gordon. 1987. *Autocracy*. Boston, MA: Kluwer Academic Publishers.

Ulfelder, Jay. 2005. "Contentious Collective Action and the Breakdown of Authoritarian Regimes." *International Political Science Review* 26(3): 311–34.

UNU-WIDER. 2008. *World Income Inequality Database*. Helsinki, Finland: UNU-WIDER.

U.S. Department of Justice. 2009. "Interview Session Number 5." In Joyce Battle (Ed.), "Saddam Hussein Talks to the FBI: Twenty Interviews and Five Conversations with 'High Value Detainee No. 1' in 2004." Washington, DC: National Security Archive.

UTIP-UNIDO. 2008. *Estimated Household Income Inequality Data Set*. Austin, TX: UTIP-UNIDO.

Van Dam, Nikolaos. 1979. *The Struggle for Power in Syria*. New York: St. Martin's Press.

Van de Walle, Nicolas. 2001. *African Economies and the Politics of Permanent Crisis, 1979–1999*. New York: Cambridge University Press.

Van de Walle, Nicolas. 2007. "Meet the New Boss, Same As the Old Boss? The Evolution of Political Clientelism in Africa." In Herbert Kitschelt and Steven I. Wilkinson (Eds.), *Patrons, Clients and Policies: Patterns of Democratic Accountability and Political Competition*. New York: Cambridge University Press, pp. 50–67.

Vargas Llosa, Mario. 2001. *The Feast of the Goat*. New York: Farrar, Straus, and Giroux.

Vogel, Ezra F. 2011. *Deng Xiaoping and the Transformation of China*. Cambridge, MA: Harvard University Press.

Von Hagen, Mark. 1990. *Soldiers in the Proletarian Dictatorship: The Red Army and the Soviet Socialist State, 1917–1930*. Ithaca, NY: Cornell University Press.

Voslensky, Michael. 1984. *Nomenklatura: The Soviet Ruling Class*. Gorden City, NY: Doubleday.

Walder, Andrew G. 1995. "Career Mobility and the Communist Political Order." *American Sociological Review* 60(3): 309–28.

Ward, Ken. 1974. *The 1971 Elections in Indonesia: An East Java Case Study*. Monash University: Center of Southeast Asian Studies.

Ware, L. B. 1985. "The Role of the Tunisian Military in the Post-Bourgiba Era." *Middle East Journal* 39(1): 27–47.

Ware, L. B. 1988. "Ben Ali's Constitutional Coup in Tunisia." *Middle East Journal* 42(4): 587–601.

Waterbury, John. 1983. *The Egypt of Nasser and Sadat: The Political Economy of Two Regimes*. Princeton, NJ: Princeton University Press.

Weber, Max. 1964. *The Theory of Social and Economic Organization*. New York: The Free Press.

Wedeen, Lisa. 1999. *Ambiguities of Domination: Politics, Rhetoric, and Symbols in Contemporary Syria*. Chicago: University of Chicago Press.

Weeks, Jessica L. 2008. "Autocratic Audience Costs: Regime Type and Signaling Resolve." *International Organization* 62(Winter): 35–64.

Weinstein, Martin. 1975. *Uruguay: The Politics of Failure*. Westport, CT: Greenwood Press.

Wintrobe, Ronald. 1998. *The Political Economy of Dictatorship*. Cambridge: Cambridge University Press.

World Bank. 2008. *World Development Indicators*. Dataset.

Wright, Joseph. 2008a. "Do Authoritarian Institutions Constrain? How Legislatures Impact Economic Growth and Foreign Aid Effectiveness." *American Journal of Political Science* 52(2): 322–342.

Wright, Joseph. 2008b. "To Invest or Insure? How Authoritarian Time Horizons Impact Foreign Aid Effectiveness." *Comparative Political Studies* 41(7): 971–1000.

Wright, Thomas C. 2001. *Latin America in the Era of the Cuban Revolution*. Westport, CT: Praeger.

Young, Crawford. 1985. *The Rise and Decline of the Zairian State*. Madison, WI: University of Wisconsin Press.

Zakaria, Fareed. 1997. "The Rise of Illiberal Democracy." *Foreign Affairs* 76(6): 22–43.

Zemtsov, Ilya. 1991. *Encyclopedia of Soviet Life*. New Brunswick: Transaction Publishers.

Zisser, Eyal. 2001. *Asad's Legacy: Syria in Transition*. New York: New York University Press.

Zolberg, Aristide R. 1966. *Creating Political Order: The Party-States of West Africa*. Chicago: Rand McNally.

Zürcher, Erik Jan. 2004. *Turkey: A Modern History*. London: I. B. Tauris.

News Sources

Amsterdam, Robert. "The Real Power Struggle." *The New York Times*. 2 December 2008, Online Edition.

Bakri, Nada, and Steven Erlanger. "E.U. Bans Syrian Oil as Protests Continue." *The New York Times*, 3 September 2011, p. A-8.

Barry, Ellen. "Putin Once More Moves to Assume Russia's Top Job." *The New York Times*, 24 September 2011, p. A-1.

Bush, George W. "Remarks by the President-Elect Following a Meeting with Congressional Leaders," *The American Presidency Project*, December 18, 2000, online at http://www.presidency.ucsb.edu/ws/?pid=84891.

Crossette, Barbara. "A Soldier's Soldier, Not a Political General." *The New York Times*, 13 October 1998, p. A-12.

Cullison, Alan. "Russia Releases Official From Jail in Fraud Case." *The Wall Street Journal*, 22 October 2008, p. A-12.

Dugger, Celia W. "Pakistani Premier Prevails in Clash With General." *The New York Times*, 20 October 1998, p. A-4.

Eckholm, Erik. "China's Leader Won't Hold On, Anonymous Author Says." *The New York Times*, 5 September 2002, p. A-3.

Eckholm, Erik. "Chinese Leader Gives Up a Job But Not Power." *The New York Times*, 16 November 2002, p. A-1.

The Economist. "Whose Cash Is It?" 31 August 1996, p. 39.

The Economist. "The Fog and Dogs of War." 20 March 2004, p. 45.

The Economist. "Toughs at the Top." 18 December 2004, pp. 70–2.

The Economist. "Oil Makes Friends of Us All." 18 July 2009, pp. 70–2.

The Economist. "Intrigue in Equatorial Guinea." 24 February 2009, p. 68.

The Economist. "A Coup Against the Constitution." 1 January 2011, p. 31.

The Economist. "A Dictator Deposed." 15 January 2011. Online.

The Economist. "Ali Baba Gone, But What About the 40 Thieves?" 22 January 2011, pp. 31–3.

The Economist. "Hard Choices for the Government." 22 January 2011, p. 56.

The Economist. "Tunisia's Upheaval: No One Is Really in Charge." 29 January 2011, pp. 44–5.

The Economist. "A Cycle of Violence May Take Hold." 9 April 2011, pp. 52–3.

Fahim, Kareem and David D. Kirkpatrick. "Mubarak's Backers Storm Protesters as U.S. Condemns Egypt's Violent Turn." *The New York Times*, 3 February 2011, p. A-1.

Harden, Blaine. "Zaire's President Mobutu Sese Seko: Political Craftsman Worth Billions," *The Washington Post*, 10 November 1987, p. A-1.

Hirst, David. "The Terror from Takrit." *The Guardian*, 26 November 1971, p. 15.

Kahn, Joseph. "China's 2 Top Leaders Square Off in Contest to Run Policy." *The New York Times*, 2 September 2002, p. A-3.

Kahn, Joseph. "China Ex-President May Be Set to Yield Last Powerful Post." *The New York Times*, 7 September 2002, p. A-1.

Kahn, Joseph. "Officially, Jiang Is History; In News, He's Still on Top." *The New York Times*, 17 November 2002, p. A-18.

Kahn, Joseph. "Analysts See Tension in China Within the Top Leadership." *The New York Times*, 1 July 2003, p. A-1.

Kahn, Joseph. "Former Leader Is Still a Power In China's Life." *The New York Times*, 16 July 2004, p. A-1.

Kahn, Joseph. "Hu Takes Full Power in China As He Gains Control of Military." *The New York Times*, 20 September 2004, p. A-1.

Kirkpatrick, David D. "Egypt's Military Expands Power, Raising Alarms." *The New York Times*, 15 October 2011, p. A-1.

Lipman, Masha. "Putin's 'Sovereign Democracy.'" *The Washington Post*, 15 July 2006.

Mason, John. "Qatar to Pursue Case Against Ex-emir." *Financial Times*, 24 September 1996, p. 3.

McDermott, Darren. "Singapore's Voters Get a Choice: Slums or the Ruling Party." *The Wall Street Journal Asia*, 31 December 1996, p. 1.

Nakvi, M. B. "Pak Army Chief Tells Sharif to Create a Security Council." *The Times of India*, 8 October 1998, p. 1.

Page, Jeremy. "China Anoints Its Next Leader." *The Wall Street Journal*, 19 October 2010, p. A-1.

Pang, Gek Choo. "Upgrading Link Swung Vote in GE." *The Straits Times*, 12 January 1998, p. 3.

Reuters. "Bahrain's King Gives out Cash Ahead of Protests." 12 February 2011.

Slackman, Michael and Nadim Audi. "Bahrain King in Saudi Arabia to Discuss Unrest." *The New York Times*, 24 February 2011, Online.

Swirtz, Michael. "Belarus Leader Blames Excess of Democracy for Bombing." *The New York Times*, 22 April 2011, p. A-9.

The Times of India. "Backdoor Junta," 8 October 1998, p. 10.

Weiner, Tim, "C.I.A. Spent Millions to Support Japanese Right in 50's and 60's." *The New York Times*, 9 October 1994, p. A-1.

Weiner, Tim, "Countdown to Pakistan's Coup: A Duel of Nerves in the Air." *The New York Times*, 17 October 1999, p. A-10.

Index